D0769083

DISCARDED
3 4444 00039 9717

JOURNAL FOR THE STUDY OF THE NEW TESTAMENT SUPPLEMENT SERIES

123

Sheffield Academic Press

Household Conversion Narratives in Acts

Pattern and Interpretation

David Lertis Matson

Journal for the Study of the New Testament
Supplement Series 123

In memory of my grandfather, Lertis Ross Ellett,
whose name I bear and whose legacy
I gladly embrace.

Published by Sheffield Academic Press Ltd
Mansion House
19 Kingfield Road
Sheffield, S11 9AS
England

Printed on acid-free paper in Great Britain
by Bookcraft Ltd
Midsomer Norton, Bath

British Library Cataloguing in Publication Data

A catalogue record for this book is available
from the British Library

ISBN 1-85075-586-8

CONTENTS

Part II
THE PATTERN IMPLEMENTED:
HOUSEHOLD CONVERSIONS IN THE ACTS OF THE APOSTLES

PREFACE

This study is an exercise in biblical interpretation; more narrowly defined, it is a literary investigation of a noteworthy phenomenon in Luke's story of the early church: the conversion of entire households to the Christian faith. Using features of the narrative-critical method, this book interprets the household conversion stories of Acts (Cornelius, Lydia, the Roman jailer and Crispus) against a pre-established pattern of household evangelistic activity in Luke. The primary value of this approach lies in the way that it permits literary insight into a subject that, up until now, has been understood chiefly in doctrinal or sociological terms, opening up new vistas of interpretation for Acts as well as uncovering new levels of 'unity' and 'disunity' between the Lukan writings.

I wish to thank the members of my doctoral dissertation committee at Baylor University who guided the process and oversaw the completion of this work: Mikeal C. Parsons, my primary reader and mentor, for his unwavering confidence in my abilities and his expert interpretation in Acts; Naymond H. Keathley, for his remarkable knowledge of grammar, both English and Greek; and Robert L. Reid, Master Teacher and Professor Emeritus of History, for his contributions from the sphere of Greco-Roman thought. Thanks must also go to R. Alan Culpepper, whose special interest in my ideas resulted in his offering many timely and valuable suggestions along the way, and James M. Kennedy, who ably critiqued portions of my work.

Most of all, I must thank my dear and precious family for their years of sacrifice and toil, especially my wife Mary who graciously absorbed the good moments and the bad. Like the forgiven women in the house of Simon the Pharisee, I owe you a debt of thanks that simply exceeds the capacity of words to express. I truly thank God for our 'household'.

ABBREVIATIONS

AB	Anchor Bible
ACNT	Augsburg Commentary on the New Testament
AnBib	Analecta biblica
AUSS	*Andrews University Seminary Studies*
BA	*Biblical Archaeologist*
BAGD	W. Bauer, W.F. Arndt, F.W. Gingrich and F.W. Danker, *Greek–English Lexicon of the New Testament*
Bib	*Biblica*
BSac	*Bibliotheca Sacra*
BTB	*Biblical Theology Bulletin*
BZ	*Biblische Zeitschrift*
CBQ	*Catholic Biblical Quarterly*
CH	*Church History*
EKKNT	Evangelisch-Katholischer Kommentar zum Neuen Testament
ExpTim	*Expository Times*
IB	*Interpreter's Bible*
IBC	Interpretation: A Bible Commentary for Preaching and Teaching
IDB	G.A. Buttrick (ed.), *Interpreter's Dictionary of the Bible*
Int	*Interpretation*
JBL	*Journal of Biblical Literature*
JETS	*Journal of the Evangelical Theological Society*
JRH	*Journal of Religious History*
JRS	*Journal of Roman Studies*
JSNT	*Journal for the Study of the New Testament*
KPG	Knox Preaching Guides
LCL	Loeb Classical Library
LSJ	Liddell–Scott–Jones, *Greek–English Lexicon*
NAC	New American Commentary
NBD	New Bible Dictionary
NCB	New Century Bible
NCV	New Century Version
NIB	New Interpreter's Bible
NIBC	New International Biblical Commentary
NICNT	New International Commentary on the New Testament

NIDNTT	C. Brown (ed.), *The New International Dictionary of New Testament Theology*
NIGTC	The New International Greek Testament Commentary
NovT	*Novum Testamentum*
NTS	*New Testament Studies*
RevExp	*Review and Expositor*
SBLSP	*SBL Seminar Papers*
SJT	*Scottish Journal of Theology*
TDNT	G. Kittel and G. Friedrich (eds.), *Theological Dictionary of the New Testament*
TNTC	Tyndale New Testament Commentaries
TPINTC	Trinity Press International New Testament Commentaries
WBC	Word Biblical Commentary
WTJ	*Westminster Theological Journal*

Chapter 1

INTRODUCTION

Next to the speeches, the conversion stories may represent the most important formal grouping in Acts, comprising just over one-fourth of its narrative material.[1] Among these stories, however, is a group with a form and function all its own—those accounts aptly termed 'household conversions'. Cornelius (10.1–11.18), Lydia (16.11-15), the Roman jailer (16.25-34), and Crispus (18.1-11) are four householders in Acts who receive salvation with their entire households, creating a certain 'type of response' to the gospel of the early church.[2] To this collection one may add the story of Zacchaeus, who also receives salvation with his entire household (Lk. 19.1-10). The preponderance of these stories in the Lukan writings suggests that they hold special interest for the author apart from his other accounts of religious conversion.[3]

The importance of household conversions for the growth and spread of early messianic communities cannot be underestimated. In Acts, the church of the Diaspora grows quite literally from 'house to house' (κατ' οἴκους, 20.20).[4] Similarly, the disciples in Jerusalem find the

1. So Robert Allen Black, 'The Conversion Stories in the Acts of the Apostles: A Study of Their Forms and Functions' (PhD dissertation, Emory University, 1985), p. 213.

2. In a literary study of the Gospel of John, R. Alan Culpepper observes: 'When several characters who are colorfully different from one another respond to Jesus in a similar manner, it creates a type of response' (*Anatomy of the Fourth Gospel: A Study in Literary Design* [Philadelphia: Fortress Press, 1983], p. 146). While these four householders share certain common traits, they also represent a wide spectrum in the social world of Acts: a centurion, a female merchant, a Roman civil servant, and a synagogue president.

3. The only other narrative of household salvation in the New Testament appears at Jn 4.46-54.

4. Noted by John H. Elliott, 'Temple versus Household in Luke–Acts: A Contrast in Social Institutions', in Jerome H. Neyrey (ed.), *The Social World of*

house a convenient source of converts: 'And every day, in the temple and from house to house [κατ' οἶκον], they kept on teaching and preaching Jesus as the Christ' (5.42).[5] If the house represents a rich source of evangelistic opportunity in Acts, then the stories of household conversion proper play a positive role in Luke's overall scheme of universal salvation. As John H. Elliott observes: 'The church which grows through household conversions becomes at the same time a worldwide household of faith.'[6]

Justification of Study

As important as household conversion is to the spread of the gospel in Acts, it is surprisingly a neglected partner at the Lukan dance. No scholarly monograph presently exists that devotes singular attention to the topic, either from a literary or historical point of view.[7] The socio-historical studies dealing with the Christian household in recent years only tangentially treat the phenomenon of household conversion as such while not restricting their findings to Acts.[8] Moreover, the recent literary

Luke–Acts: Models for Interpretation (Peabody: Hendrickson Publishers, 1991), p. 226.

5. Unless otherwise noted, all scriptural citations are my own translation. It is possible to render the two Greek expressions above in a non-distributive sense ('in private homes, at home'; cf. 1 Cor. 16.19; Col. 4.15; Phlm. 2), in which case the sphere of the house as a place of evangelistic activity and growth becomes even more pronounced.

6. B. Elliott, 'Temple versus Household', p. 229.

7. A search of *Dissertation Abstracts* and *Religion Index One* reveals the paucity of material on the subject. An informative discussion, however, appears in Michael Green, *Evangelism in the Early Church* (Grand Rapids: Eerdmans, 1970), pp. 207-222. Two of the more important articles are of less recent date: Donald Wayne Riddle, 'Early Christian Hospitality: A Factor in the Gospel Transmission', *JBL* 57 (1938), pp. 141-54; Floyd V. Filson, 'The Significance of the Early House Churches', *JBL* 58 (1939), pp. 105-112. Richard J. Dillon also offers some valuable insights to the household theme in Luke and Acts (*From Eyewitnesses to Ministers of the Word: Tradition and Composition in Luke 24* [AnBib; Rome: Biblical Institute Press, 1978]).

8. Perhaps the most 'systematic' treatment of household conversion from the standpoint of social history is the work of E.A. Judge. See his *The Social Pattern of the Christian Groups in the First Century: Some Prolegomena to the Study of New Testament Ideas of Social Obligation* (London: Tyndale, 1960). More recent analyses of the Christian household include David L. Balch, *Let Wives Be Submissive: The*

studies of the conversion narratives in Acts fail to grasp the significance of the household conversion accounts precisely at the point of their uniqueness and intrigue—corporate salvation expressed in and through the believing household.[9]

By far the most extensive literature developed in connection with household conversion appears in the infant baptism debate of nearly a generation ago.[10] This debate largely centered on the meaning of the 'οἶκος formula' ('he and [all] his household', or a variation thereof) as it appears in the Old Testament and in early Christian literature.[11]

Domestic Code in 1 Peter (Chico: Scholars Press, 1981); John H. Elliott, *A Home for the Homeless: A Social-Scientific Criticism of 1 Peter, Its Situation and Strategy*, with a new introduction (Minneapolis: Fortress Press, 1990); David C. Verner, *The Household of God: The Social World of the Pastoral Epistles* (Chico, CA: Scholars Press, 1983). Other related treatments appear in Robert Banks, *Paul's Idea of Community: The Early House Churches in their Historical Setting* (Grand Rapids: Eerdmans, 1980); Abraham J. Malherbe, *Social Aspects of Early Christianity* (Philadelphia: Fortress Press, 2nd edn, 1983); and Wayne A. Meeks, *The First Urban Christians: The Social World of the Apostle Paul* (New Haven: Yale University Press, 1983). On the historical development of the house as sacred location, see Lloyd Michael White, 'Domus Ecclesiae—Domus Dei: Adaption and Development in the Setting for Early Christian Assembly' (PhD dissertation, Yale University Press, 1983).

9. See Black, 'The Conversion Stories in the Acts of the Apostles', and Robert C. Tannehill, *The Narrative Unity of Luke–Acts: A Literary Interpretation*, II (Minneapolis: Fortress Press, 1990). Beverly Roberts Gaventa provides important literary insight on the conversion of Cornelius in addition to other conversion stories in Acts (*From Darkness to Light: Aspects of Conversion in the New Testament* [Philadelphia: Fortress Press, 1986], pp. 52-129). These treatments, however, fail to recognize how the theme of household salvation creates a special typology of conversion in Acts.

10. See, for example, Joachim Jeremias, *Infant Baptism in the First Four Centuries* (trans. David Cairns; Philadelphia: Westminster Press, 1960) and *The Origins of Infant Baptism: A Further Reply to Kurt Aland* (trans. Dorothea M. Barton; Naperville: Alec R. Allenson, 1963); Kurt Aland, *Did the Early Church Baptize Infants*? (trans. G.R. Beasley-Murray; Philadelphia: Westminster Press, 1963). See also G.R. Beasley-Murray, *Baptism in the New Testament* (Grand Rapids: Eerdmans, 1962), pp. 312-20; Gerhard Delling, 'Zur Taufe von "Häusern" in Urchristentum', *NovT* 7 (1964–65), pp. 285-311.

11. A prior study that figured prominently in the debate was E. Stauffer, 'Zur Kindertaufe in der Urkirche', *Deutsches Pfarrerblatt* 49 (1949), pp. 152-54. Because of the cultic associations Stauffer attaches to this formula, Jeremias prefers to speak of 'the οἶκος phrase' (*The Origins of Infant Baptism*, p. 20). See also Peter Weigandt, 'Zur sogenannten "Oikosformel"', *NovT* 6 (1963), pp. 49-74.

Despite the fact that this formula appears almost exclusively in Acts among the writings of the New Testament (10.2; 11.14; 16.15, 31 [33-34]; 18.8; cf. Jn 4.53), concern for its doctrinal implications relating to the practice of infant baptism far outweighed any literary significance the phrase might possess for Luke. The dominance of this formula in Acts, however, did compel one of the principal players to ask whether Luke was responsible for introducing it into Christian usage.[12]

Obviously, the dearth of material relating to the subject of household salvation points to a present gap in Lukan scholarship. Since the vacuum extends to both content and method, any proposal to study the household conversion phenomena in Acts requires an innovative approach, especially if it seeks to account for their distinctively *Lukan* character. The usual procedure of extracting these stories from their literary context in Acts to argue a point of theology or doctrine strips them of their essentially literary character and divests them of any meaning that the writer may have intended for them. When studying the household conversion accounts, one does well to remember that 'exegesis cannot forget the importance of literary context for the determination of meaning'.[13]

Purpose of Study

To redress this deficiency, this book aims to develop the theme of household salvation from a distinctly literary point of view. The germ of the present proposal stems from a paper I developed for Dr Mikeal C. Parsons in a course at Baylor University on the Greek text of Acts.[14] It was there that I first began to notice a consistent pattern of household conversion centered around proclamation, baptism, and hospitality.[15]

12. Jeremias, *The Origins of Infant Baptism*, p. 21. He decides in the negative based on its independent attestation at Jn 4.53, *1 Clem.* 12.5, and numerous places in *Shepherd of Hermas* (e.g., Vision 1.1.9).

13. Luke T. Johnson, 'On Finding the Lukan Community: A Cautious Cautionary Essay', in P.J. Achtemeier (ed.), *SBLSP* (Missoula: Scholars Press, 1979), p. 92.

14. David L. Matson, 'The Role and Function of the Lukan οἶκος in the Household Conversion Stories of the Acts of the Apostles', Baylor University, Spring, 1990.

15. A more finely nuanced presentation of this pattern appears in ch. 2 of this book. Others have called attention to a household conversion 'pattern' without identifying its essential elements. In speaking of the conversion of Cornelius, for example,

That Jesus instructs the seventy-two messengers in Luke to preach salvation to households (10.5-7) was a later realization that invited the intriguing question: does Jesus' command to evangelize households in Luke provide a pre-established pattern in Acts against which to read the stories of household conversion? Does the household mission of the Seventy-two function, at the very least, as a heuristic device for interpreting a certain set of phenomena in Acts? The two-fold structure of this study (see Outline of Study below) reflects an affirmative answer to both of these questions.

The adoption of this particular reading strategy permits a more narrowly defined course of study: what are the form and the function of the household conversion narratives as they appear on the pages of Acts? By 'form' I do not mean 'form-critical', but the literary form or shape these stories assume in creative interplay with the pre-established pattern; by 'function' I mean their *literary* function, both individually and cumulatively. This two-fold purpose effectively removes the household conversion narratives from the tyranny of doctrinal or theological agendas and makes their study a creative exercise in biblical and literary interpretation.

Method of Study

The innovative approach outlined above calls for a more carefully articulated method of study. Since a literary pattern and its related functions necessarily involve both text and reader in the interpretive process, it is necessary to delineate these components more carefully below.

a. *The Text of the Reader*

To achieve its literary goals, this book employs a text-centered ('objective') type of narrative criticism that views the text as a self-sufficient story and interprets it according to its own intrinsic components.[16] It is written in the tradition of other literary-critical studies on

Howard Clark Kee writes: 'This pattern of conversion of households appears elsewhere in Acts as well' (*Good News to the End of the Earth: The Theology of Acts* [London: SCM Press, 1990], p. 51). Dillon sees in the stories of household conversion a 'reiteration of the household procedure' in Luke but he construes the elements of the pattern somewhat differently in accordance with other critical concerns (*From Eye-Witnesses to Ministers of the Word*, pp. 189-93).

16. On the various types of literary criticism currently available, see Mark Allan Powell, *What is Narrative Criticism?* (Minneapolis: Fortress Press, 1990), pp. 11-12.

the Gospels in recent years, most notably David Rhoads and Donald Michie on Mark, Jack Dean Kingsbury on Matthew and Luke, and R. Alan Culpepper on John.[17] Even more germane to this study is the two-volume work of Robert C. Tannehill, who applies a literary-critical approach to Luke–Acts as a whole.[18] Each of these studies sees meaning as residing primarily within the text itself rather than in the 'real' world of the Evangelist and his community. While it is not always possible nor desirable to distinguish so sharply between historical and narrative worlds,[19] the text itself nevertheless remains the primary referent of meaning.[20]

The 'text' of this study is the Gospel of Luke and the Book of Acts as they appear in the fourth revised edition of the United Bible Societies' Greek New Testament.[21] The tradition of observing parallels between these two texts is a long one in the history of Lukan scholarship.[22] Charles H. Talbert, one of the most noted Lukan scholars of the twentieth century,[23] regards these literary parallels as 'the primary architectonic

On the value of applying narrative criticism to the Lukan writings, see Powell, *What are they Saying about Acts?* (New York: Paulist Press, 1991), pp. 96-107 and William S. Kurz, 'Narrative Approaches to Luke–Acts', *Bib* 68 (1987), pp. 195-220.

17. See David Rhoads and Donald Michie, *Mark as Story: An Introduction to the Narrative of a Gospel* (Philadelphia: Fortress Press, 1982); Culpepper, *Anatomy of the Fourth Gospel*; Jack Dean Kingsbury, *Matthew as Story* (Philadelphia: Fortress Press, 2nd edn, 1988), *Conflict in Luke: Jesus, Authorities, Disciples* (Minneapolis: Fortress Press, 1991). A precursor to this approach appears in Luke T. Johnson, *The Literary Function of Possessions in Luke–Acts* (Missoula: Scholars Press, 1977). As this list reveals, the advent of narrative criticism in biblical studies represents a distinctly American movement.

18. Tannehill, *The Narrative Unity of Luke–Acts.*

19. The importance of this point is addressed more fully below, on p. 22.

20. To the extent that other scholars using differing methodologies illuminate features of the *text*, their insights are included throughout the course of this investigation.

21. K. Aland, *et al* (eds.), *The Greek New Testament* (Stuttgart: Biblia-Druck, 4th rev. edn, 1993). Needless to say, I am concerned with the finished form of the Alexandrian version.

22. See, for example, W. Ward Gasque, *A History of the Interpretation of the Acts of the Apostles* (Peabody: Hendrickson, 1989), pp. 21-54. Also Susan Marie Praeder, 'Jesus–Paul, Peter–Paul, and Jesus–Peter Parallelisms in Luke–Acts: A History of Reader Response', in Kent Harold Richards (ed.), *SBLSP* (Chico, CA: Scholars Press, 1984), pp. 23-39.

23. See the chapters devoted to his life and work in Mikeal C. Parsons and

pattern in Luke–Acts'.[24] While recent research now limits the way one can speak about 'Luke–Acts',[25] the similarities between them are nevertheless striking. At the same time the types of literary patterns that Talbert sees are quite diverse.[26]

Of the various types of patterns observed by Talbert, the pattern of household evangelism belongs to the category of parallel activity: wayfaring messengers in Acts convert entire households to the faith after the manner of the seventy-two messengers in Luke. As 'event', household conversion takes on a redundant character in Acts, occurring repeatedly in the course of the narrative:

11.14	and he will speak words to you [Cornelius] by which you will be saved, *you and all your household.*
16.14b-15	and the Lord opened her [Lydia] heart to give heed to the things being spoken by Paul... And when *she and her household had been baptized...*
16.31	And they said, 'Believe in the Lord Jesus and you [the jailer] will be saved, *you and your household*'.

Joseph B. Tyson, *Cadbury, Knox, and Talbert: American Contributions to the Study of Acts* (Atlanta: Scholars Press, 1992).

24. He cites thirty-two 'parallels' between the Gospel and Acts respectively. See Charles H. Talbert, *Literary Patterns, Theological Themes, and the Genre of Luke–Acts* (Missoula: Scholars Press, 1974), p. 15. Talbert writes: 'As far as we know, only Luke–Acts in early Christianity reflects the conviction that both the story of Jesus and the story of the apostolic church are incomplete without the other as complement' (p. 15).

25. The 'unity' of the Lukan writings, long cherished since the time of Henry J. Cadbury, has recently been challenged by Mikeal C. Parsons and Richard I. Pervo, *Rethinking the Unity of Luke and Acts* (Minneapolis: Fortress Press, 1993). Because of the misconceptions inherent in the phrase 'Luke–Acts', I will generally refrain from using this hyphenated expression (see Mikeal C. Parsons, 'The Unity of the Lukan Writings: Rethinking the *Opinio Communis*', in Naymond H. Keathley (ed.), *With Steadfast Purpose: Essays on Acts in Honor of Henry Jackson Flanders, Jr* [Waco: Baylor University, 1990], pp. 30-31). A discussion of the kind of 'unity' posited by the household mission awaits the conclusion of this book.

26. Talbert's 'parallels' include similar literary forms (prologues); similar activities (praying, healing, traveling, raising the dead); the same name (Theophilus); similar characters (a lame man, a centurion, widows); the same group (Pharisees); the same geographical reference (Jerusalem); numbers (four trials; three declarations of innocence; seven references to Jerusalem); similar statements; and similar themes (noted by Joseph B. Tyson, 'The Problem of Food in Acts: A Study of Literary Patterns with Particular Reference to Acts 6.1-7', in P.J. Achtemeier (ed.), *SBLSP*, p. 70).

18.8 And Crispus, the president of the synagogue, believed in the Lord *with all his household*, and many of the Corinthians, when they heard, were believing and being baptized.

These multiple occurrences of household conversion are an example of what Gérard Genette calls 'multiple-singular narration', a literary device that reports repeatedly an event that happens repeatedly.[27] The multiple nature of an event demands that the reader consider its significance more than once.[28]

The character of household conversion as a 'redundant event' in Acts invites comparison with the biblical 'type-scene', a feature for which Luke is well-known.[29] The definitive study of the biblical type-scene is that of Robert Alter, who classifies it among the various repetitive structuring devices available in Hebrew Scripture.[30] A type-scene is a 'basic situation' that recurs a number of times in a narrative, yet not in such a wooden way as to prevent variations in the development of a scene.[31] Though not bound to such, the type-scene is often marked by a recurrent term or phrase, what Alter styles a *Leitwort*.[32]

27. Gérard Genette, *Narrative Discourse: An Essay in Method* (trans. J. Lewin; Ithaca: Cornell University Press, 1980). Cited in Powell, *What is Narrative Criticism*?, p. 39.

28. Powell notes: 'Repetition usually implies some type of emphasis, for it requires the reader to consider the significance of an event more than once' (*What is Narrative Criticism*?, pp. 39-40).

29. The notion of 'type-scene' originally developed out of Homeric scholarship. For examples of type-scenes in Luke and Acts, see Tannehill (*The Narrative Unity of Luke–Acts*, I, pp. 170-72; II, pp. 201-203, 221-24). The situation of 'Jesus at meal', for example, is a typical situation in Luke's Gospel (Craig Thomas McMahan, 'Meals as Type-Scenes in the Gospel of Luke' [PhD dissertation, The Southern Baptist Theological Seminary, 1987]; cf. Kingsbury, *Conflict in Luke*, p. 8).

30. Robert Alter, *The Art of Biblical Narrative* (New York: Basic Books, 1981), p. 96. His discussion of the type-scene proper appears on pp. 47-62.

31. Tannehill, *The Narrative Unity of Luke–Acts*, I, p. 170. On the important role of variation in redundant stories, see Janice Capel Anderson, 'Double and Triple Stories, the Implied Reader, and Redundancy in Matthew', *Semeia* 31 (1985), pp. 71-89.

32. Quoting Martin Buber, Alter identifies a *Leitwort* as 'a word or word-root that recurs significantly in a text, in a continuum of texts, or in a configuration of texts' (*Werker*, II, *Schriften zur Bibel* [Munich, 1964]; cited in *The Art of Biblical Narrative*, p. 93). The use of the term '*Leitwort*' in this study applies to those words or phrases that often appear in stories of household salvation. On the occurrence of

While the notion of type-scene is potentially helpful for interpreting the household conversion phenomena in Acts, this study does not use it without qualification. Two important differences in methodology should be noted. First, the existence of a pre-established pattern of household evangelism in Luke eliminates the need to establish an 'archetypal scene' in Acts by universalizing the common elements of a household salvation story.[33] The presence of a pre-established pattern potentially allows for even greater degrees of variation to occur among repetitive stories without compromising the constancy of the pattern. Secondly, this study makes no appeal to 'convention', either oral or literary, to establish the pattern of household evangelizing; nothing exists in the literary milieu of Luke and Acts to suggest that the mission to households *had* to unfold in a certain way.[34] Rather, the authority of the pattern rests on the instructions of the Lukan Jesus, the 'Lord' of the mission to the house.

b. *The Reader of the Text*

'An act of interpretation is the work of a reader', observes Joseph B. Tyson, 'and Luke–Acts has had many different kinds of readers'.[35] The importance of this observation compels one to ask: who is the 'reader' posited in this study? Obviously, the persuasiveness of any literary-critical study increases considerably if the author is clear about the kind of reader he or she is envisioning. Many otherwise fine literary treatments of biblical narratives fail at the point of adequately defining their readers.[36]

repeated key words in Lukan type-scenes, see Tannehill, *The Narrative Unity of Luke–Acts*, I, pp. 170-71.

33. McMahan suggests this procedure as the first step in an analysis of a type-scene ('Meals as Type-Scenes in the Gospel of Luke', p. 51).

34. Alter repeatedly emphasizes the 'must' nature of the biblical type-scene according to the workings of convention. Concerning the familiar 'betrothal' scene in the Old Testament, for instance, Alter writes of the author: 'both he and his audience were aware that the scene had to unfold in particular circumstances, according to a fixed order' (*The Art of Biblical Narrative*, p. 52).

35. Joseph B. Tyson, *Images of Judaism in Luke–Acts* (Columbia: University of South Carolina, 1992), p. 19.

36. See Robert M. Fowler, 'Who is "The Reader" in Reader Response Criticism?' *Semeia* 31 (1985), pp. 5-23. See also his later book, *Let the Reader Understand: Reader-Response Criticism and the Gospel of Mark* (Minneapolis: Fortress Press, 1991). Perhaps the most recent example of one who fails to define

The primary reader presupposed throughout this investigation is the ideal implied reader of Luke and Acts.[37] The 'implied' reader, as understood in narrative criticism, is the reader 'inside' the text, as opposed to an actual flesh-and-blood reader residing 'outside' the text.[38] While the implied reader is purely a literary construct, presupposed by the text itself, this 'reader' actually provides a viable control for interpretation. As Mark Allan Powell observes: 'With regard to any proposed reading, the question may be asked, Is there anything *in the text* that indicates the reader is expected to respond in this way?'[39] For purposes of this study, the question in essence becomes, Is there anything in the text of Luke and Acts that leads the implied reader to read the household conversion stories in Acts against the pattern of household evangelizing in Luke?

As an 'ideal' reader, the implied reader is that 'imaginary person in whom the intention of the text is to be thought of as always reaching its fulfillment'.[40] This idealized implied reader 'will always be imagined to respond to the text with whatever knowledge, understanding, or emotion the text calls for at any given juncture'.[41] In encountering a story of household conversion, for example, the implied reader remembers perfectly well the instructions of Jesus to convert households and

his 'reader' adequately is Arthur A. Just, Jr, *The Ongoing Feast: Table Fellowship and Eschatology at Emmaus* (Collegeville: The Liturgical Press, 1993). By contrast, John A. Darr takes great pains to define clearly his reader (*On Character Building: The Reader and the Rhetoric of Characterization in Luke–Acts* (Louisville: Westminster Press/John Knox, 1992), pp. 16-36.

37. I offer here only a brief sketch of the reader as it pertains to this study. For a more thorough distillation of some of the more technical aspects of narrative criticism, see Powell, *What is Narrative Criticism*? The notion of an implied author and reader was originally developed by Wayne C. Booth (cf. *The Rhetoric of Fiction* [Chicago: University of Chicago Press, 2nd edn, 1983]). For a helpful discussion of Booth's early literary theory and subsequent developments by Wolfgang Iser and others, see Willem S. Vorster, 'The Reader in the Text: Narrative Material', *Semeia* 48 (1989), pp. 21-27.

38. Cf. Vorster: 'The reader in the text is a literary construct, an image of a reader which is selected by the text. It is implied by the text, and in this sense it is encoded in the text by way of linguistic, literary, cultural, and other codes' ('The Reader in the Text', p. 27).

39. Powell, *What is Narrative Criticism*?, p. 21.

40. Kingsbury, *Matthew as Story*, p. 38.

41. Kingsbury, 'Reflections on "The Reader" of Matthew's Gospel', *NTS* 34 (1988), p. 456.

can therefore detect the similarities that exist in content, language and theme as well as the variations that occur in the process of its development. This possession of sure memory[42] is also helpful to a reader who has engaged in multiple readings of the text and can therefore respond appropriately and ideally to whatever set of directions the text ultimately elicits, both in prospect and retrospect.[43] Thus, Powell observes: 'The implied reader...is not necessarily to be thought of as a first-time reader. In some instances the narrative text apparently assumes the reader will come to an understanding only after multiple readings.'[44]

Two important qualifications, however, emerge in the course of this investigation. First, this study is not strictly 'formalist' in orientation since it is helpful at times to supplement the narrative world of Acts with information that lies outside it. Susan R. Garrett, for example, observes that authors must rely on 'the culturally informed knowledge and beliefs

42. R. Robert Creech asserts that Theophilus, the 'narratee' of the Third Gospel and Acts (Lk. 1.3; Acts 1.1), 'is possessed with a sure memory of all events in the narrative of which he has been informed' ('The Most Excellent Narratee: The Significance of Theophilus in Luke–Acts', in Keathley (ed.), *With Steadfast Purpose*, p. 120). In Gospel studies, the distinction between an implied reader and a narratee is so slight as to be indistinguishable (so Kingsbury, *Matthew as Story*, p. 38).

43. This emphasis on multiple readings of the text distinguishes my method from the 'affective stylistics' of the early Stanley Fish ('Literature in the Reader: Affective Stylistics', *New Literary History* 2 [1972], pp. 123-62) and the phenomenological approach of Wolfgang Iser (*The Act of Reading: A Theory of Aesthetic Response* [Baltimore: The Johns Hopkins University Press, 1978]; *The Implied Reader: Patterns of Communication in Prose Fiction from Bunyan to Beckett* [Baltimore: The Johns Hopkins University Press, 1974]), both of which posit first-time real readers of a given text. The 'late' Fish now prefers to speak of 'interpretive communities' that embody the same reading strategy (*Is There a Text in This Class? The Authority of Interpretive Communities* [Cambridge, MA: Harvard University Press, 1980]).

44. Powell, *What is Narrative Criticism*?, p. 20. Richard I. Pervo, who attempts a first-time reading of Acts, admits that such an endeavor runs counter to the very nature of Luke–Acts: 'One of the principal pleasures in reading Luke–Acts is the discovery of its interconnectedness, the "parallels" large and small, and the cross-references within the text... Luke sprinkles his work with hints and allusions pointing forward and backward, providing a nearly inexhaustible treasure of links by which the various components illuminate one another' (*Luke's Story of Paul* [Minneapolis: Fortress Press, 1990], p. 12). In a recent article Tannehill experiments with a first-time reading strategy for Luke from the standpoint of two different first-century social locations ('"Cornelius" and "Tabitha" Encounter Luke's Jesus', *Int* 48 [1994], pp. 347-56).

of the readers to supplement the narrative world of a text, because the authors could no more explain every detail about a person or event in a narrative than could speakers define every word of every sentence spoken'.[45] Tannehill, who applies narrative criticism to a study of Luke–Acts with great profit, nevertheless considers it only one method among many, to be used in conjunction with others.[46] An understanding of historical events and first-century society, he argues, is at times necessary for understanding Acts as a *narrative*, contending that the 'study of first-century Mediterranean literature and society may illuminate unspoken assumptions behind the narrative and may also suggest specific reasons for emphases in the text'.[47]

The second qualification centers on the admission that real readers have a role to play in the construction of the implied reader: why do *I*, as the author of this book, choose to observe the textual connections that I do? Here the roles of the idealized implied reader and the 'real' reader admittedly overlap in the creative act of interpretation, blurring the distinction between them. This overlapping comes especially into view when dealing with narrative 'gaps' in Acts, which demand that a real reader fill in the missing parts of a story.[48] That the implied reader is partially the construct of real flesh-and-blood readers has led some to question the usefulness of the model.[49] While this criticism unveils a

45. Susan R. Garrett, *The Demise of the Devil: Magic and the Demonic in Luke's Writings* (Minneapolis: Fortress Press, 1989), p. 6.

46. In the introduction to his second volume he writes: 'I do not understand narrative criticism to be an exclusive method, requiring rejection of all other methods. Methodological pluralism is to be encouraged, for each method will have blind spots that can only be overcome through another approach' (*The Narrative Unity of Luke–Acts*, II, p. 4).

47. *The Narrative Unity of Luke–Acts*, II, p. 5. Kurz acknowledges the importance of other approaches when he writes: 'The original implied readers are deduced from the text read in its first-century context, which historical criticism helps to understand' (*Reading Luke–Acts: Dynamics of Biblical Narrative* [Louisville: Westminster Press/John Knox, 1993], p. 160). His notion of an 'original' implied reader, however, only clouds the issue.

48. Where gaps appear in the household conversion stories, however, textual clues exist to direct the implied reader to draw the appropriate inference. On the relation of real readers to narrative 'gaps and indeterminacies', see Iser, *The Act of Reading: A Theory of Aesthetic Response* and *The Implied Reader: Patterns of Communication in Prose Fiction from Bunyan to Beckett.* For a study of narrative gaps in the Lukan writings, see Kurz, *Reading Luke–Acts*, pp. 31-36.

49. See this criticism in Wilhelm Wuellner, 'Is There an Encoded Reader

'weak spot' in the narrative-critical approach, it also overlooks the worthy goal of reading the text from the vantage point of the implied reader, thus narrowing the 'distance' between an actual and implied reader and retaining the text as the primary (but not the sole) referent of meaning.[50]

Outline of Study

This book divides naturally into two parts, each comprised of two chapters. Part I focuses on the way the pattern of the household mission derives from both the words and deeds of Jesus as he appears on the pages of the Gospel of Luke. The first chapter (ch. 2) establishes the constituent elements of the pattern proper by noting the way they receive expression in the mission of the Seventy-two, a sending that stands unique among the four canonical Gospels. The second chapter (ch. 3) traces the source of these elements to the Lukan presentation of Jesus' earthly ministry, thus investing the pattern with dominical authority.

Part II constitutes the real focus of this study. Its purpose is to read the four accounts of household conversion in Acts against the established pattern of the seventy-two messengers in Luke. The first chapter (ch. 4) concentrates on the story of Cornelius, the first and fullest expression of the pattern in the book of Acts. The second chapter (ch. 5) takes up the remaining accounts of Lydia, the jailer, and Crispus, each of whom converts to the messianic faith after the manner of Cornelius—'with all their household'. It remains for the conclusion to this study (ch. 6) to draw out some new interpretive insights gained by this

Fallacy?', *Semeia* 48 (1989), p. 46. See also Darr, who comments: 'Readers cannot be both object and subject; that is, they cannot simultaneously be part of the text's rhetorical structure *and* respondents to it' (*On Character Building*, pp. 20-21).

50. 'To the extent that the implied reader is an idealized abstraction', remarks Powell, 'the goal of reading the text "as the implied reader" may be somewhat unattainable, but it remains a worthy goal nevertheless' (*What is Narrative Criticism*?, p. 21). That real readers are capable of resisting certain ideologies of the text (e.g., anti-Semitism or gender bias) does not detract from the ability of the text to act as the final arbiter of meaning since readers are largely conscious of when they are doing so. This view, of course, would meet with strong resistance from reader-response critics who grant reader and text equal authority in the production of meaning.

approach, including the way these stories function in Luke's overall scheme of universal salvation.

PART I
THE PATTERN ESTABLISHED: THE HOUSEHOLD MISSION IN THE GOSPEL OF LUKE

Chapter 2

The Household Mission of the Seventy-Two

Introduction

The house as a social institution plays an important evangelistic role in the book of Acts. It is primarily by means of the house that the gospel marches steadily from Jerusalem to Rome.[1] The mission of the church begins in a house (1.13; 2.2) and ends in a house (28.30), providing a coherent structure to Luke's account of an emergent and triumphant Christianity.[2]

The importance of the house for the narrative of Acts is not surprising when one considers the instructions of Jesus recorded earlier in the Gospel of Luke:

1. As John Elliott observes: 'Houses and households constitute not only the settings for the reception of the good news in Luke–Acts. As house churches, they also represent the basic social organization through which the gospel advances from Palestine to Rome' ('Temple versus Household in Luke–Acts: A Contrast in Social Institutions', in Jerome H. Neyrey (ed.), *The Social World of Luke–Acts: Models for Interpretation* [Peabody: Hendrickson, 1991], p. 226).

2. This literary *inclusio* parallels the way that the temple functions in the Gospel of Luke to frame the story of Jesus (1.5-23; 24.50-53). According to Elliott, this 'structural feature' of Luke and Acts contrasts the institutions of temple and household, a theme that receives expression elsewhere in the two volumes ('Temple versus Household', pp. 215-17). Though neither οἶκος nor οἰκία appears at 28.30, the term μίσθωμα (NIV: 'rented house') denotes a rental dwelling of some kind. The conditions of Paul's imprisonment in Rome, which allowed him to preach the gospel openly and 'unhindered' (ἀκωλύτως, 28.31), finds a certain parallel in a letter by Gaius Caligula to Piso, the prefect of Rome, at the time of Tiberius's death. It contains an order 'that Agrippa should be removed from the camp to the house [οἰκία] where he had lived before his imprisonment. After that he had no hardship to fear, for though he was still guarded and watched, yet the watch on his daily activities was relaxed' (Josephus, *Ant.* 18.235 [LCL]).

> Whatever house you enter, first say, 'Peace to this household!' And if a son of peace is there, your peace will rest on him; but if not, it will return to you. And stay in that house, eating and drinking what they give you, for the worker is worthy of his wages. Do not move from house to house (10.5-7).

This injunction to evangelize various houses, directed to seventy-two unnamed disciples, forms an important link between Luke and Acts. Household evangelism becomes the *modus operandi* of the growing church.[3]

As a missionary strategy, the instructions of Jesus to the Seventy-two serve an additional literary purpose for Luke:[4] they formally establish the pattern of household evangelizing.[5] The household mission of the unnamed disciples in Luke thus becomes a backdrop against which the household conversions of Acts can be read, creating a type-scene typical of Lukan style.[6] This use of what Robert Alter terms a repetitive

3. Historically, the formation of house churches 'was of the greatest significance for the spreading of the gospel' (Colin Brown, (ed.), *NIDNTT*, II [Grand Rapids: Zondervan, 1976], see 'house', by J. Goetzmann, p. 250). On the historical connection between the synoptic presentation of the household mission and the early church's practice of converting households, see Donald Wayne Riddle, 'Early Christian Hospitality: A Factor in the Gospel Transmission', *JBL* 57 (1938), pp. 141-54. Also Floyd V. Filson, 'The Significance of the Early House Churches', *JBL* 58 (1939), pp. 105-112. More recently, John Dominic Crossan, *The Historical Jesus: The Life of a Mediterranean Jewish Peasant* (San Francisco: Harper & Row, 1992), pp. 339-44. Riddle believes the pervasive practice of converting households in the early church was 'read back' into the teaching of Jesus ('Early Christian Hospitality', p. 153).

4. 'Luke' in this chapter refers to both the implied author and narrator of the Third Gospel without intending a major distinction between them. In the Gospels, the latter always functions as the reliable voice of the former (see Jack Dean Kingsbury, *Conflict in Luke: Jesus, Authorities, Disciples* [Minneapolis: Fortress Press, 1991], pp. 9-10).

5. Richard J. Dillon terms Lk. 10.5-7 the 'protocol for the household' consisting, in his view, primarily of the *pax* and table-fellowship motifs (*From Eye-Witnesses to Ministers of the Word: Tradition and Composition in Luke 24* [AnBib; Rome: Biblical Institute Press, 1978], p. 187). While construing the actual elements of the protocol somewhat differently, Dillon nevertheless recognizes the paradigmatic function of these verses for accounts of household salvation in Luke and Acts (pp. 190-92).

6. Robert C. Tannehill is one who has developed the type-scene with much profit for an understanding of Luke's narrative art (*The Narrative Unity of Luke–Acts: A Literary Interpretation*, I [Philadelphia: Fortress Press, 1986], pp. 18, 170-71).

structuring device enhances the reader's capacity to recognize certain characteristic elements in a story as well as to detect any departures from the established pattern.[7] Redundancy contributes to predictability but requires variation if the story is to maintain its interest.[8] Thus, the task of this chapter is to establish the typical elements of a 'household conversion', which receive varying degrees of repetition on the pages of Acts.

This method of relying on the Gospel of Luke to establish a literary pattern in Acts presupposes a narrative 'unity' between these two works, at least on some level.[9] In an influential 1974 study, Charles H. Talbert recognized the way Luke utilizes literary patterns to form parallels not only within the Gospel and Acts respectively, but between the Gospel and Acts.[10] This latter correspondence, he asserts, constitutes 'the

Craig Thomas McMahan has also applied the concept of type-scene to a study of meal scenes in Luke ('Meals as Type-Scenes in the Gospel of Luke' [PhD dissertation, The Southern Baptist Theological Seminary, 1987]).

7. Repetitive structuring devices, as Alter classifies them, may also include *Leitwort*, motif, theme, and sequence of actions. See his discussion in *The Art of Biblical Narrative* (New York: Basic Book Publishers, 1981), pp. 95-96.

8. Avoidance of boredom is only one function of variation in repetitive stories. It also permits the introduction of new information (cf. Janice Capel Anderson, 'Double and Triple Stories, the Implied Reader, and Redundancy in Matthew', *Semeia* 31 [1985], p. 85). R. Alan Culpepper notes that stories 'which have a lower degree of dissonance and a higher ratio of repetition demand less of readers than stories which have a greater level of dissonance and higher ratio of variation' ('Redundancy and the Implied Reader in Matthew: A Response to Janice Capel Anderson and Fred W. Burnett', Unpublished Seminar Response Paper, SBL, Literary Aspects of the Gospels and Acts, 1983, p. 2). Henry J. Cadbury noted long ago that variation is characteristic of Lukan verbal style ('Four Features of Lucan Style', in Leander E. Keck and J. Louis Marty (eds.), *Studies in Luke–Acts: Essays Presented in Honor of Paul Schubert* [Nashville: Abingdon Press, 1966], pp. 87-96; see esp. pp. 91-93).

9. On the recent challenge to facile assumptions regarding the 'unity' of the Lukan writings, see ch. 1, p. 15 n. 25. In a commentary soon to be published, Mikeal C. Parsons regards Luke and Acts as 'interrelated' narratives that are best read and understood in relationship with each other: 'Maintaining the individual character of each Lukan writing allows the reader to see both the similarities and the differences between Luke and Acts' (Watson Mills [ed.], *Mercer Commentary on the Bible* [Macon: Mercer University Press], 1995). The importance of this observation for the presentation of the household mission in Acts is taken up in the conclusion to this book.

10. Charles H. Talbert, *Literary Patterns, Theological Themes and the Genre of*

primary architectonic pattern in Luke–Acts'.[11] Building on Talbert's insights, Joseph B. Tyson observes how the pattern of initial acceptance and final rejection on the part of the Jewish public, formally established in the synagogue scene at Nazareth in Lk. 4.16-30, typifies Jewish response to the Christian message at key points in the Acts narrative.[12] Among other things, the pattern witnesses Luke's tendency to carry forward certain programmatic themes and patterns from his Gospel into his literary presentation in Acts.

If the household pattern of Lk. 10.5-7 is in fact significant for the narrative of Acts, as this chapter argues, the proleptic character of the second missionary discourse (10.1-16) must be credibly established, or at least reasonably shown. Talbert, for example, believes that the mission of the Seventy-two foreshadows the gentile mission in Acts, particularly the Pauline journeys.[13] Before proceeding to an analysis of the household pattern proper, therefore, it is necessary first to look for clues in the text that point to a time beyond the earthly ministry of the Lukan Jesus.

A Lukan Creation

Like his synoptic counterparts, Luke records a mission of the Twelve (Lk. 9.1-6; cf. Mt. 10.1-23; Mk 6.7-13). The Third Evangelist is unique, however, in recording an additional sending of seventy-two messengers which becomes the setting for a second, more elaborate, missionary charge by the Lukan Jesus (10.1-16). The reason for these two similar but distinct missions is not readily apparent to most commentators on Luke's Gospel.[14]

The absence of a separate commission of seventy-two disciples in the rest of the synoptic tradition has naturally raised questions regarding the historical veracity of Luke's account. Joseph A. Fitzmyer, for example,

Luke–Acts (Missoula: Scholars Press, 1974), pp. 15-22.

11. Talbert, *Literary Patterns*, p. 15.

12. Acts 13.13-52; 14.1-2; 17.1-9; 17.10-15; 19.8-10. See Joseph B. Tyson, 'The Jewish Public in Luke–Acts', *NTS* 30 (1984), pp. 574-83. According to Tyson, 'the pattern of initial acceptance followed by rejection is clearly present in Acts, both in several individual sections and in the book as a whole' (p. 580).

13. Talbert, *Literary Patterns*, p. 20.

14. Frederick W. Danker observes how Luke, 'who frequently avoids recitation of Mark's doublets, appears to have developed one of his own out of variant forms of a tradition' (*Jesus and the New Age: A Commentary on St Luke's Gospel* [Philadelphia: Fortress Press, rev. edn, 1988], p. 211).

believes Luke created this literary 'doublet' from the 'Q' material parallel to Mk 6.6b-13.[15] I. Howard Marshall, in seeking to minimize the Third Evangelist's own compositional creativity, considers it likely that the author derived the idea of two historical missions from a misunderstanding of his sources.[16] However this literary doublet may have originated, many Lukan scholars consider the mission of the Seventy-two to be largely unhistorical, either in whole or in part.[17]

A close analysis of the discourse in the wider context of the Gospel of Luke and the synoptic tradition supports the validity of the above charge. First, the mission of the Seventy-two appears in the 'journey' section of the Gospel (9.51–19.28), which is itself of artificial construction.[18] The lack of any perceptible geographical movement in this 'journey' suggests that it is essentially 'an editorial structure created by Luke', leading scholars to locate its organizing principle elsewhere.[19] Though not decisive, the artificial character of this section of the Gospel is at least suggestive of the non-historical character of Lk. 10.1-16.

Secondly, not only are the other Synoptics ignorant of a separate sending of seventy-two disciples, but much of the material that Luke addresses to the Seventy-two, Matthew addresses to the Twelve.[20] This fact alone raises suspicions regarding Luke's historical intentions. A third consideration pointing in the direction of Lukan composition is the 'fusion' of the two missions at Lk. 22.35, which contains Jesus' question

15. Joseph A. Fitzmyer, *The Gospel According to Luke X–XXIV*, II (AB; New York: Doubleday, 1985), p. 843.

16. I. Howard Marshall, *The Gospel of Luke: A Commentary on the Greek Text* (NIGTC; Grand Rapids: Eerdmans, 1978), p. 413.

17. Bruce M. Metzger includes Creed, Easton, Klostermann, Luce and Manson among those scholars who consider the sending of the Seventy-two to be another version of the sending of the Twelve ('Seventy or Seventy-two Disciples?', *NTS* 5 [1958–59], p. 302).

18. 'The mission is as artificial in conception as is the whole journey to Jerusalem' (C.F. Evans, *Saint Luke* [TPINTC; London: SCM Press, 1990], p. 446). For a detailed analysis of the Lukan Travel Narrative, see David P. Moessner, *Lord of the Banquet: The Literary and Theological Significance of the Lukan Travel Narrative* (Minneapolis: Fortress Press, 1989).

19. Fred B. Craddock, *Luke* (IBC; Louisville: John Knox, 1990), p. 138. 'Though Luke depicts Jesus himself en route to Jerusalem, he never indicates whence these disciples are dispatched or whither they return—save from Jesus and to Jesus' (Fitzmyer, *The Gospel According to Luke X–XXIV*, pp. 841-42).

20. Lk. 10.2 = Mt. 9.37-38; Lk. 10.3-12 = Mt. 10.7-16; Lk. 10.13-15 = Mt. 11.21-23; Lk. 10.16 = Mt. 10.40.

to the Twelve: 'When I sent you out without a purse, bag, or sandals, did you lack anything?' The allusion here to 'sandals' (ὑποδημάτων) is surprising since it is the Seventy-two, not the Twelve, who receive prior instructions regarding the use of footwear (10.4; cf. 9.3). The confusion evident within Luke's own Gospel testifies to the complexity these two traditions exerted in the process of their historical transmission.[21] The three points considered above argue cogently that the mission of the Seventy-two is largely the product of Luke's own creative making. F.W. Beare asserts that the discourse of Luke 10 is essentially the construction of the evangelist, not that of Jesus:

> Jesus may have supplied some or all of the words in one context or another (it is most unlikely that anything like all of them are authentic utterances of his), but it is the gospel writer who has arranged them as seemed good to him, fitting them into a pattern of his own designing, like an artist setting the tesserae into a mosaic. His tesserae are the fragments of tradition—sayings by or attributed to Jesus—but the pattern of the mosaic is the creation of the evangelist.[22]

Since, on the whole, Luke avoids literary 'doublets' of the Markan material, one still must ask what function an additional mission of seventy-two disciples serves in the course of his narrative.[23] Why does Luke juxtapose a sending of seventy-two disciples with a mission of the Twelve?

Prefigurement of the Mission in Acts

The Palestinian setting of Luke 10 has led more than one commentator to posit an essentially Jewish character to the mission of the Seventy-two. Helmuth L. Egelkraut, for example, argues that the journey motif at 10.1, linking the mission of the disciples to the Jerusalem-bound mission of Jesus, clearly fixes the geographical sphere of the charge. Their mission, he asserts, is a 'mission to Israel'.[24] Similarly, T.W. Manson

21. So Danker, *Jesus and the New Age*, p. 211.

22. F.W. Beare, 'The Mission of the Disciples and the Mission Charge: Matthew 10 and Parallels', *JBL* 89 (1970), p. 2.

23. According to Marshall, 'we must ask why Luke, who on the whole avoids "doublets", has allowed these two very similar accounts to stand in his Gospel' (*The Gospel of Luke*, p. 413). On Lukan doublets, see Fitzmyer, *The Gospel According to Luke I–IX*, pp. 81-82.

24. Helmuth L. Egelkraut, *Jesus' Mission to Jerusalem: A Redaction Critical Study of the Travel Narrative in the Gospel of Luke, Lk. 9.51–19.48* (Frankfurt:

contends that 'the errand on which these disciples were sent out was certainly no Gentile mission'.[25] Yet both Egelkraut and Manson overlook the importance of the mission to Samaria that inaugurates the journey and establishes its wider thematic scope (9.51-53), evident elsewhere in this section.[26] Moreover, the contrast between the cities of Galilee and the favorable reception of the gospel by Tyre and Sidon (10.13-14) serves 'preliminary notice' of a mission among non-Jews.[27] These two gentile cities, observes Marshall, represent the 'pagan' world.[28]

The ostensibly Jewish setting given by Luke to the mission of the Seventy-two thus in no way precludes the reader from also perceiving its deeper symbolic elements.[29] A number of 'points of contact', as Robert C. Tannehill terms them, suggests that the mission of the Seventy-two serves as a model for the later mission of the church.[30]

Peter Lang, 1976), pp. 147-48. Stephen G. Wilson, while insisting that 'in the immediate context the mission of the Seventy is clearly to Israel', nevertheless admits that 'Luke may well have had one eye on the later mission of the church' (*The Gentiles and the Gentile Mission in Luke–Acts* [Cambridge: Cambridge University Press, 1973], pp. 45-47).

25. T.W. Manson, *The Sayings of Jesus* (London: SCM Press, 1949), p. 257.

26. Ferdinand Hahn regards the stories of the Good Samaritan (10.25-37) and the cleansed leper of Samaria (17.11-19) as the 'scaffolding' that supports the travel narrative of Luke's Gospel (*Mission in the New Testament* [trans. Frank Clarke; Naperville: Alec R. Allenson, 1965], p. 129). That 'Samaritan' is equivalent to 'foreigner' (ἀλλογενής) in Luke's symbolic world (Lk. 17.16,18) increases the probability of the universalistic motif at 9.51-53. Appearing only at Lk. 17.18 in the New Testament, ἀλλογενής denotes in the Septuagint both a 'lay person' excluded from priestly service (Lev. 22.10, 12-13; Num. 16.40; 18.4, 7) and a 'stranger' in the sense of a non-Jew (Isa. 56.3,6; 60.10; 61.5). No 'stranger', for example, could eat the Passover meal (Exod. 12.43).

27. Hahn, *Mission in the New Testament*, p. 130. Earlier, Luke presents the people of Tyre and Sidon as responding eagerly to Jesus (6.17-18).

28. Marshall, *The Gospel of Luke*, p. 424. Luke's omission of Matthew's restricted mission to Israel (Mt. 10.5-6) provides further evidence of universalistic concern in Lk. 10.1-16.

29. From a purely literary point of view, of course, the Palestinian flavor of the discourse is 'realistic' to the setting in which Luke has placed it—the Palestinian-based ministry of Jesus. This factor alone places certain geographical and traditional parameters on Luke as 'literary artist'.

30. Tannehill, *The Narrative Unity of Luke–Acts*, I, p. 233. The commission of such a large number of disciples (seventy-two) as full co-workers with Jesus leads K.N. Giles to press the connection with Acts even further by concluding that 'Luke has bestowed on the disciples, in the Gospel period, a developed theological status.

Likewise, in Talbert's view, the mission envisioned in Luke 10 stretches beyond the boundaries of Israel to foreshadow the universal mission in Acts.[31] If the mission of the Twelve in Luke points to the reconstitution of the tribes of Israel (6.13; 9.1-6; 22.30),[32] it is not unlikely that the mission of the Seventy-two points to the evangelization of the Gentiles. Both missions, as Craig A. Evans astutely observes, 'represent the Jewish–Gentile foundation of the church'.[33]

In possessing this wider significance, the mission of the Seventy-two performs a dual function in the Lukan writings. As part of the Travel Section of Luke's Gospel (9.51–19.28), the discourse grounds the mission of the Seventy-two in Jesus' own mission of suffering and death. The preface at 10.1, which depicts Jesus sending the disciples 'before his face' (πρὸ προσώπου αὐτοῦ), clearly recalls the identical motif at the beginning of his journey to Jerusalem (9.51-53).[34] In both instances Jesus sends messengers before him to prepare his way and to participate in his mission of suffering and rejection (cf. 10.16).[35] As John Drury observes of Luke, 'It is not only Jesus' story that he is telling but the church's too, and in this way the Christian community is linked to the splendour and the suffering of the gospel.'[36]

He has affirmed that they are in fact the Church' ('The Church in the Gospel of Luke', *SJT* 34 [1981], p. 127). For Giles, the disciples in Luke's Gospel 'are not meant to prefigure the Church nor to represent the Church in embryo: they *are* the Church, albeit in idealised form' (p. 121).

31. Talbert, *Reading Luke: A Literary and Theological Commentary on the Third Gospel* (New York: Crossroad, 1982), p. 115.

32. Tannehill, *The Narrative Unity of Luke–Acts*, I, pp. 232-33; on the significance of the number 'twelve' in Luke's narrative, see Jacob Jervell's essay, 'The Twelve on Israel's Thrones', in his *Luke and the People of God: A New Look on Luke–Acts* (Minneapolis: Augsburg, 1972), pp. 75-112.

33. Craig A. Evans, *Luke* (NIBC; Peabody: Hendrickson Publishers, 1990), p. 169. On the other hand, the fusion of the two missions evident at 22.35 may indicate that they are not kept so clearly distinct in the narrator's mind, a fact that may explain why Peter, one of the Twelve, becomes evangelist to the house of Cornelius (Acts 10.1–11.18).

34. Commenting on 10.1, Moessner writes: 'It is evident that Luke intends the following narrative to be a continuation of the journeying-guest story' (*Lord of the Banquet*, p. 135).

35. So Tannehill, *The Narrative Unity of Luke–Acts*, I, p. 232.

36. John Drury, *The Gospel of Luke* (New York: Macmillan, 1973), p. 99. According to Giles, Luke's persistent portrayal of the disciples as fellow travelers with Jesus invites 'his audience to see what it should mean for them to be the

The mission of the Seventy-two also prepares the reader for the universal mission that transpires on the pages of Acts. In this context, 'seventy-two' takes on added importance as a figure of universal significance since it calls to mind the seventy-two nations of the world according to the Septuagint reading of Genesis 10.[37] While other allusions are perhaps possible,[38] a reference to this text best explains the vacillation between 'seventy' and 'seventy-two' disciples in the manuscript tradition.[39] The uncertainty regarding the actual number of disciples sent out by Jesus, well-established in textual studies on the New Testament,[40] only testifies to the degree of symbolic import this number

Christian community. He invites them to see themselves as a community on mission, always on the move, always on a journey, always in the presence of the Lord' ('The Church in the Gospel of Luke', p. 141).

37. 'What most clearly distinguishes Luke's reader from the vast majority of Greco-Roman readers in the late first century,' observes John A. Darr, 'is an intimate knowledge of the Jewish scriptures in Greek' (*On Character Building: The Reader and the Rhetoric of Characterization in Luke–Acts* [Louisville: Westminster Press/John Knox, 1992], p. 28). On the authority of the Jewish scriptures for both the implied author and reader of Luke, see Tyson, *Images of Judaism in Luke–Acts* (Columbia: University of South Carolina Press, 1992), p. 35.

38. See the possibilities listed in Metzger, 'Seventy or Seventy-two Disciples?', pp. 302-304. Given Luke's fondness for the Septuagint, Sidney Jellicoe argues for an allusion to the Letter of Aristeas as the basis for the gentile motif in Luke 10: 'Just as the seventy-two emissaries of Aristeas had, by their translation, brought the knowledge of the Law to the Greek-speaking world, so the Seventy(-two) are divinely commissioned to proclaim its fulfillment in the Gospel message' ('St. Luke and the Seventy[-two]', *NTS* 6 [1959–60], p. 321). A weakness with Jellicoe's position is that it requires a motif *outside* the biblical text itself. Another possibility is an allusion to the seventy(-two) helpers appointed by Moses (Num. 11), most recently advocated by Susan R. Garrett in *The Demise of the Devil: Magic and the Demonic in Luke's Writings* (Minneapolis: Fortress Press, 1989), pp. 47-48.

39. 'This vacillation of the manuscripts', Talbert asserts, 'is best explained by Genesis 10 in the Masoretic Text in which the number of the nations of the world is seventy, whereas in the LXX the number is seventy-two' (*Reading Luke*, p. 115). Even if an allusion to Numbers 11 is in view, it does not necessarily negate the symbolic value of the number for prefiguring the gentile mission in Acts. For Garrett, the placement of God's Spirit upon the helpers of Moses (Num. 11.17, 25) foreshadows 'the period of the church, when not only the twelve but *many* sons and daughters would receive the Spirit of the Lord and prophesy, and would thereby be enabled to carry out Jesus' work' (*The Demise of the Devil*, p. 48).

40. See, for example, Bruce M. Metzger, *A Textual Commentary on the Greek New Testament* (New York: United Bible Societies, corrected edition 1975),

possessed among ancient readers of Luke.[41] Modern readers, moreover, have not missed this symbolic significance.[42] By means of this numerical symbolism, the narrator anticipates the mission in Acts whose parameters extend to the 'end of the earth' (Acts 1.8; 13.47).[43]

The symbolic portrayal of the 'Seventy-two' leads one to expect further hints in Luke 10 pointing in the direction of Acts. One such clue appears in the commissioning of the seventy-two 'others' (ἑτέρους, 10.1a), a detail that serves to legitimate the role of messengers not belonging to the circle of the Twelve.[44] This widening of the missionary circle, the result of the mission's growth and movement at this stage of Luke's Gospel, finds fulfillment in the mission of the early church.[45] That these messengers are expressly sent out into the missionary harvest by the Lukan Jesus (ἀποστέλλω, 10.1b, 3) anticipates a key term in

pp. 150-51; also his earlier 'Seventy or Seventy-two Disciples?', pp. 300-302. Luke's fondness for the Septuagint, combined with the rare occurrence of '72' in the Old Testament (cf. Num. 31.38), favors an allusion to the table of nations in Genesis 10. By contrast, the number '70' enjoys wide attestation in the biblical tradition and hence more easily explains a scribal change in this direction. See Kurt Aland's dissenting note in Metzger, *A Textual Commentary on the Greek New Testament*, p. 151.

41. The observation of David L. Tiede is forceful here: 'Whether Luke wrote "70" or "72", one group of scribes apparently felt it was appropriate to "correct" the number by deferring to the scriptural or traditional number known to them. The symbolic significance of the number was clearly regarded as important' (*Luke* [ACNT; Minneapolis: Augsburg, 1988], p. 201).

42. As Frank Stagg observes, 'The symbolic character of the number seventy[-two] is recognized by nearly all interpreters of this passage' (*Studies in Luke's Gospel* [Nashville: Convention Press, 1967], p. 77).

43. Tannehill, *The Narrative Unity of Luke–Acts*, I, p. 233. Marshall sees a possible allusion to Genesis 10 in the statement at Lk. 10.3, paralleled in a rabbinic conversation c. 90 CE: 'Hadrian said to Jehoshua: "There is something great about the sheep [Israel] that can persist among 70 wolves [the nations]." He replied: "Great is the Shepherd who delivers it and watches over it and destroys them [the wolves] before them [Israel]"' (Tanchuma *tôlᵉdôṯ* 32b). Despite its late date, the conversation 'raises the question whether a current saying about Israel among the nations has been reapplied by Jesus to the true Israel...' (Marshall, *The Gospel of Luke*, p. 417).

44. Danker, *Jesus and the New Age*, p. 212.

45. Cf. R. Alan Culpepper: 'As Jesus turns toward Jerusalem, he is still preaching the kingdom of God, but now the kingdom is being preached not just by Jesus and the Twelve. In that sense, this commissioning foreshadows the mission of the early church and establishes the pattern for those who are sent out' (*The Gospel of Luke* [NIB; Nashville: Abingdon Press, forthcoming]). I wish to thank Professor Culpepper for furnishing me with an early draft of his commentary.

Acts marking the inauguration of mission at strategic points in the narrative.[46] The practice of traveling in pairs (10.1b), absent from the charge to the Twelve (9.2), as well as the theme of repentance marking the reception of the gospel (μετανοέω, 10.13), receive further expression on the pages of Luke's second volume.[47] Moreover, like their counterparts in Luke (10.9, 11), messengers in Acts regularly engage in healing and proclaiming the kingdom of God in the course of their missionary activity (8.12; 19.8; 20.25; 28.23, 31).

The acceptance or rejection of missionaries, a prominent theme in Jesus' missionary discourse (δέχομαι, 10.8, 10), constitutes yet another key theme in Acts.[48] According to the protocol of the Seventy-two, rejected messengers are to wipe away the dust from their feet in symbolic protest against an unbelieving city (10.11), a practice later instituted by Paul and Barnabas at Antioch of Pisidia (13.51; cf. 18.6). A further anticipation of Acts occurs at the conclusion of the mission when the Seventy-two return to Jesus with the happy news that 'even the demons are subject to us in your name!' (10.17), foreshadowing that power and authority by which messengers in Acts regularly achieve victory over magic and the demonic.[49] If the narrator skips over the actual itinerary of the mission trip, as the abrupt transition at 10.16-17 makes clear, it is

46. Acts 8.14; 9.17; 10.8, 17, 20, 36; 11.11, 13, 30; 15.27; 19.22; 26.17; 28.28. On the use of πέμπω, its virtual equivalent, see 10.5, 32, 33; 15.22, 25. Linkage of this sending language with the household mission appears in the commission to Ananias, who is sent (ἀποστέλλω) to the house (οἰκία) of Judas to convert the persecutor Saul (9.17).

47. Examples of pairs traveling include Peter and John (Acts 8.14), Barnabas and Saul (Acts 13.2), Judas and Silas (Acts 15.22, 32-33), Barnabas and Mark (Acts 15.39), and Paul and Silas (Acts 15.40). Repentance (μετάνοια/μετανοέω) becomes a technical expression for conversion when linked to faith and the forgiveness of sins (Acts 2.38; 5.31; 26.18, 20). On the importance of both these themes to Acts, see Hahn, *Mission in the New Testament*, p. 131.

48. Various forms of the δεχ root are popular in Acts: δέχομαι (8.14; 11.1; 17.11), ἀποδέχομαι (2.41; 18.27; 21.17), παραδέχομαι (15.4; 22.18), ὑποδέχομαι (17.7), ἀναδέχομαι (28.7). On the technical character of this root, see Abraham J. Malherbe, 'The Inhospitality of Diotrephes', in *God's Christ and His People: Studies in Honor of Nils Alstrup Dahl* (ed. Jacob Jervell and Wayne A. Meeks; Oslo: Universitetsforlaget, 1977), pp. 223, 230, n. 11.

49. Garrett, *The Demise of the Devil*, pp. 46-57. Garrett sees the victory achieved over Satan at Lk. 10.17-20 'as having an ongoing, even future effect', best exemplified in the Acts mission (p. 50).

inconsequential to a mission that is proleptic of the universal mission in Acts.

Of particular interest to this study are the two principal spheres of missionary activity targeted by the Lukan Jesus, namely, the house (οἶκος/οἰκία, 10.5-7) and the city (πόλις, 10.8-12).[50] P. Hoffmann considers the city mission here in Luke to be an anticipation of the city mission in Acts.[51] Only recently have scholars begun focusing on Luke's interest in urban settings as the locus of mission.[52] In Acts, messengers regularly target the πόλις (Acts 15.36; 16.4), such as Samaria (Acts 8.5, 8), Azotus and the towns of Judea (Acts 8.40), Antioch of Pisidia (Acts 13.14, 44, 48), Iconium (Acts 14.1, 4), Lystra (Acts 14.20-21), Thessalonica (Acts 17.1, 5-8), Corinth (Acts 18.10), and Ephesus (Acts 19.26, 29), to mention but a few. Like the Seventy-two before them, their task is 'to proclaim the gospel to the city' (cf. Acts 14.21).[53]

If the city constitutes the larger geo-political space of the Acts mission, the house constitutes a more strategic architectural location within it. In

50. Otto Michel observes that πόλις and οἰκία often appear together in Hellenistic literature (Gerhard Kittel, (ed.), *TDNT*, V see, 'οἶκος', by Otto Michel, p. 131).

51. P. Hoffmann, 'Lk. 10.5-11 in der Instruktionsrede der Logienquelle', *Evangelisch Katholischer Kommentar, Vorarbeiten*, III (Neukirchen–Vluyn: Neukirchener Verlag, 1971), p. 45. Martin Hengel notes on a historical level that 'the Pauline mission was exclusively limited to cities, and hardly reached country people... The Christian faith, like all the missionary religions in antiquity, remained predominantly a city religion' (*Property and Riches in the Early Church: Aspects of a Social History of Early Christianity* [trans. John Bowden; Philadelphia: Fortress Press, 1974], p. 37).

52. See especially Harvie M. Conn, 'Lucan Perspectives and the City', *Missiology* 13 (1985), pp. 409-428. Citing the lack of Lukan materials on the city, Conn seeks 'to conscientize the scholarly community to one perspective that needs study' (p. 410). A more recent treatment by Richard L. Rohrbaugh fills the gap somewhat, though without alluding to the study by Conn ('The Pre-industrial City in Luke–Acts: Urban Social Relations', in *The Social World of Luke–Acts*, pp. 125-49). Much of this material also appears in 'The City in the Second Testament', *BTB* 21 (1991), pp. 67-75.

53. Of the more than 160 references to πόλις in the New Testament, nearly half come from the Lukan writings, equally distributed between Luke and Acts (Rohrbaugh, 'The City in the Second Testament', p. 67). See Conn, 'Lucan Perspectives and the City' (pp. 409-428) for Luke's redactional interests in the city. He notes that even Lukan rural settings, such as that of the sending of the Seventy-two, tend toward urban coloring (p. 414).

the household conversion stories of Acts, the two spheres often overlap, the latter appearing as a more specific category of the former (10.1, 24; 11.11; 16.12; 16.20, 39; 18.1, 10).[54] Moreover, while city evangelism tends to be general and collective, house evangelism is reserved by the narrator for the salvation of individual characters and their households, including Cornelius (10.1–11.18), Lydia (16.14-15), the Roman jailer (16.22-34) and Crispus (18.8).[55] The household mission in Acts thus fulfills Jesus' instructions to the Seventy-two: his messengers go to both house and city.

Structure and Analysis of Discourse

The surface structure of the second missionary discourse reflects the importance of these two spheres of missionary activity. Following the preface of Lk. 10.1, the prayer for additional harvesters (10.2), the commissioning of workers (10.3), and the list of *impedimenta* (10.4), the main body of the discourse centers on instructions for entering both house (10.5-7) and city (10.8-12).[56] It is expressly in these locations that the Lukan Jesus expects the gospel to be preached and conversions to occur. The 'woes' pronounced against the cities of Galilee (10.13-16), which conclude the discourse proper, offer a fitting warning to any city failing to heed the message of the kingdom. While the discourse reflects an assortment of disparate material, Luke has clearly structured it around the importance of the house and city as principal spheres of missionary activity.[57]

54. See also Lk. 9.4-5 in which the Twelve enter the house (οἰκία) but take leave of the city (πόλις). The overlapping of house and city in Luke and Acts accords well with the social demographics in ancient agrarian society: 'In biblical times most houses were in cities, towns, or villages. The agricultural population had houses in settlements from which members went out to cultivate their fields or tend their flocks' (George A. Buttrick, (ed.), *IDB*, II [New York: Abingdon Press, 1962], see 'House', by O.R. Sellers, p. 657).

55. While the city mission anticipates a corporate rather than individual response (so Egelkraut, *Jesus' Message to Jerusalem*, p. 148), the household salvation stories incorporate both motifs within their scope.

56. Culpepper sees the instructions regarding house (10.5-7) and city (10.8-9) as part of a balanced structure of paired sayings in the discourse, including two proverbs (10.2, 3), positive and negative responses (10.5-9, 10-11), and dual announcements of the kingdom's imminence (10.9, 11). See his forthcoming *The Gospel of Luke*.

57. According to Fitzmyer, 'Luke is concerned more about the literary

The narrator divides the main section of the discourse into three sayings of Jesus, each beginning with a similar introductory formula.[58] The first saying directs the disciples to enter a house (εἰς ἣν δ' ἂν εἰσέλθητε οἰκίαν) and speak words of salvific peace to the respective household (10.5-7). If the message meets a positive welcome by the 'son of peace' (v. 6), the messengers must remain in the house, rightfully enjoying the hospitality of the household without raising questions about food or drink (v. 7).

The second saying concerns messengers who enter a city (εἰς ἣν ἂν πόλιν εἰσέρχησθε) and receive a positive welcome there (10.8-9). Like their reception in the house, they must partake of food without concern for dietary restrictions. In addition, they are to heal the sick and proclaim the nearness of the kingdom. The third saying, like the second, speaks of messengers entering a city (εἰς ἣν δ' ἂν πόλιν εἰσέλθητε) with the news of the kingdom's imminence. Yet this time an inhospitable welcome requires that they enact a symbolic protest against the unbelieving city (10.10-11). This lack of a positive welcome accorded to the wayfaring messengers of Jesus conjures up a picture of Sodom for Luke, a city of notorious inhospitality (10.12; cf. Gen. 19).

The repetitive use of εἰσέρχομαι in the above sayings reflects a rhetorical attempt to highlight the two principal spheres of the Lukan mission. The result is that the reader of Acts clearly expects emissaries of the Lord to 'enter' both house and city in the course of their missionary activity.[59] The prescriptive nature of the discourse further contributes to this overall expectation: the disciples have explicit instructions to follow and the reader can see whether they carry them out in a consistent fashion! The placement of the household protocol before city protocol in Luke may also reflect its special interest in the house as a center of missionary activity, particularly since Matthew appears to preserve the more natural order (cf. 10.11-13).

concatenation of sayings than about their historical or plausible transitions' (*The Gospel According to Luke X–XXIV*, p. 842).

58. Hahn believes that Luke's arrangement reflects the original form of the 'Q' material (*Mission in the New Testament*, p. 33) whereas Manson regards vv. 4-7 as an extract from Luke's special source (*Sayings*, p. 74). Whatever the point of origin, Luke's literary structure, including the reversal of Matthew's order (10.11-12), is of clear rhetorical significance.

59. In Acts, missionaries regularly enter both house (1.13; 9.12, 17; 10.3, 25, 27; 11.3, 12; 16.15, 32, 40; 18.7; 20.29[?]; 21.8; 28.8) and city (9.6; 10.24; 11.20; 14.20).

The Pattern of the Household Mission

That the house constitutes a key spatial location of evangelistic activity for the Lukan narrator is apparent from its central position in the two missionary discourses of the Lukan Jesus. Both the Twelve (9.4) and the Seventy-two (10.5-7) base their evangelistic endeavors in the house; to the house they go, from the house they depart. The house, as David Moessner observes, is 'both the starting point and the ultimate destination of the messengers' special mission'.[60]

Since the sending of the Seventy-two is the occasion for a more extensive discourse in Luke, it provides the fullest expression of the household missionary pattern.[61] This pattern, unique to the Third Gospel, centers on the way the house functions in three essential capacities: as the location of the gospel's proclamation, as the personified object of the messenger's salvific appeal and as the unique sphere of inclusive table-fellowship in the kingdom of God.

'Whatever House You Enter'

The first element of the household pattern centers on the house (οἰκία) as the place of proclamation and acceptance of the gospel. In sending out the Seventy-two, the Lukan Jesus directs his messengers to enter (εἰσέρχομαι) houses with the message of salvific peace (Lk. 10.5a).[62] The architectural sense of οἰκία evident here is a particularly fond one for Luke, who employs both οἶκος and οἰκία interchangeably on the pages of his two volumes to denote physical space.[63] This emphasis on

60. Moessner, *Lord of the Banquet*, p. 137.

61. Helmut Flender attributes the longer discourse of Luke 10 to the Evangelist's method of 'climactic parallelism'. See his *St Luke: Theologian of Redemptive History* (trans. Reginald H. and Ilse Fuller; Philadelphia: Fortress Press, 1967), pp. 20-27.

62. The house thus functions as the 'architectural mode' of the household messengers (cf. Elizabeth Struthers Malbon, *Narrative Space and Mythic Meaning in Mark* [San Francisco: Harper & Row, 1986], pp. 106-140). 'Εισέρχομαι often has a close association with houses in both Luke (1.40; 4.38; 6.4; 7.6, 36, 44-45; 8.41, 51; 9.4; 10.38; 11.37; 14.23; 15.28; 17.7; 19.7; 24.29) and Acts (1.13, 21; 5.7, 10; 9.12, 17; 10.3, 25, 27; 11.3, 12; 16.15, 40; 21.8; 28.8).

63. Malbon regards these terms as 'architectural synonyms' (*Narrative Space*, pp. 107-108). Note how Luke uses these terms within the same story to denote the same physical location (Lk. 7.6, 10; Acts 10.6, 17, 32; 11.11[cf. 10.22, 30], 12-13). In Attic law, οἶκος originally denoted the whole estate and οἰκία the house itself

the household is striking in light of the role domestic space plays in the mission in Acts: the house, not the temple or synagogue, becomes 'the typical location of the gospel's reception and the church's growth'.[64]

Two characteristic features of the household mission are perceptible here that emerge later in Acts. First, in directing his messengers to enter homes large enough to accommodate them and their work, the Lukan Jesus targets householders of some economic and social means. Paul, for example, will often seek to establish a new work in Acts by attracting a 'man of means' with a home 'large enough to serve as a center of Christian activity'.[65] That the wayfaring messengers of Jesus are not to move 'from house to house' (Lk. 10.7c) but must depend upon a single household for their provisions and support[66] presupposes both a physical domestic structure[67] and household economy[68] capable of sustaining the

(Xenophon, *Economics* 1.5; cf. Herodotus 7.224), but this distinction gradually disappears in later Greek.

64. Elliott, 'Temple versus Household', p. 225.

65. Filson, 'The Significance of the Early House Churches', p. 111. On the same page he notes that 'homes large enough to house a considerable number of Christians in one assembly must have been owned by persons of some means' (see also Malherbe, 'Diotrephes', p. 224). Biblical writers, of course, are familiar with large and affluent houses containing, for example, 'many rooms' (Jn 14.2) and 'many utensils' (2 Tim. 2.20). While it is doubtful that Luke has these great houses in mind, the household mission in Acts does require sufficiently large houses to accommodate the founding of new believing communities. The house of Lydia, for example, is large enough to provide a place of meeting for the upstart church in Philippi (Acts 16.40; cf. v. 15).

66. The wayfaring messengers arrive at the doorstep totally bereft of material goods (Lk. 10.4). It becomes clear later in Luke (22.35) that the support rendered by the household extended beyond shelter to possessions (Luke T. Johnson, *The Literary Function of Possessions in Luke–Acts* [Missoula: Scholar's Press, 1977], p. 164). While the ability to travel in the Roman world was usually the prerogative of the wealthier upper classes (cf. Malherbe, *Social Aspects of Early Christianity* [Philadelphia: Fortress Press, 2nd edn, 1983], p. 73), the household messengers of Jesus do so at the expense of their generous hosts.

67. Though little is known about houses in Roman times, excavations from second-century Ostia reveal that typical housing for the masses consisted of one and two bedroom apartments (*insulae*) containing neither kitchen nor latrine facilities, hardly the kind of house envisioned by Luke (see David C. Verner, *The Household of God: The Social World of the Pastoral Epistles* [Chico: Scholars Press, 1983], p. 57, who relies on a study of James E. Packer, 'Housing and Population in Imperial Ostia and Rome', *JRS* 57 [1967], pp. 80-95). Since these dwellings were too small for socializing with friends, Verner surmises that 'their inhabitants must

needs of the household and its guests over an extended period of time. Targeting economically established (or modestly so) owners of houses as a strategic component of the missionary enterprise thus tips Luke's hand on one form the household mission will assume on the pages of his second volume.

The strategic role accorded to economically viable households in propagating and sustaining the mission presents Luke with a basic tension in his 'theology of the poor'. Elsewhere he condemns the rich (Lk. 1.51-53; 16.19-31) and encourages Christians to sell all that they own (Lk. 14.33; 18.22-25; Acts 2.44-45), including houses (Acts 4.34-35). Yet in the practice of the household mission, converts, such as the tax collector Zacchaeus (Lk. 19.1-10) and the later householders in Acts, typically do not sell their houses but use their houses to advance the missionary cause.[69] Luke's more general interest in the conversion of socially prominent individuals is, of course, well-known.[70]

have done most of their eating, drinking, and socializing in public places' (*The Household of God*, p. 57). A.G. McKay further argues that this type of dwelling existed in the eastern cities of the Empire as well (*Houses, Villas, and Palaces in the Roman World* [Ithaca: Cornell University Press, 1975], cited in Verner, *The Household of God*, pp. 58-59). Luke's knowledge of physical house structures ranges from a Hellenistic house with tiled roof (Lk. 5.19) and basement (Lk. 6.48) to a Palestinian peasant's house consisting of one room (Lk. 15.8). On the history of dwellings in Palestine, see H. Keith Beebe, 'Ancient Palestinian Dwellings', *BA* 31 (1968), pp. 38-58.

68. Douglas E. Oakman notes that the pre-industrial economies as reflected in the Bible were essentially household-based. 'Industry was normally small-scale and conducted by families and their slaves' ('The Ancient Economy in the Bible', Unpublished Paper, Westar Meeting, October, 1989, p. 3). He notes how the word 'economy' itself derives from 'household [*oikou*] management [*nomia*]' (p. 2).

69. On Luke's ambiguous stance toward possessions, see Luke T. Johnson, *Sharing Possessions: Mandate and Symbol of Faith* (Philadelphia: Fortress Press, 1981), pp. 11-29. See esp. pp. 17-20. Hengel remarks that Luke 'did not feel it a contradiction that he should dedicate his two-volume work to the well-born Theophilus and take special pleasure in enumerating prominent people who joined Jesus and his community' (*Property and Riches*, p. 64 n. 46).

70. Malherbe, for example, notes 'Luke's tendency to mention socially prominent and economically well-off converts' (*Paul and the Thessalonians: The Philosophic Tradition of Pastoral Care* [Philadelphia: Fortress Press, 1987], p. 16). Adolf Harnack calls attention to the way Acts records the conversion of the 'cultured classes', including the proconsul Sergius Paulus (8.7-12), Dionysius the Areopagite (17.34), certain prominent women of Thessalonica (17.4) and Berea (17.12), and Priscilla, whom Harnack also assigns to this category (*The Expansion of Christianity*

A second and, from the standpoint of Acts, more significant characteristic of the household mission is its total disregard for racial and ethnic distinctions. The implicit command to enter a house (εἰς ἣν δ' ἂν εἰσέλθητε οἰκίαν) is indiscriminate (10.5a), blurring the demarcations between clean and unclean! While this directive, in its present Palestinian context, may envision entry into homes of ritually impure Jews,[71] in light of Acts it can only anticipate the most unclean people of all—Gentiles. As the social world of Luke and Acts prohibited a Jew from entering the house of a Gentile,[72] so in their symbolic world it is unlawful (ἀθέμιτος) for a Jew to visit a Gentile in a Gentile's house, especially to eat there (Acts 10.28; 11.3,12; cf. Lk. 7.6). Thus, the command to eat and drink in the house without regard for dietary restrictions (Lk. 10.7) signals the radically inclusive scope of the mission.[73] As Jerome H. Neyrey observes:

> What is striking is the injunction to the missionaries that they 'eat and drink what they (the hosts) provide' (Lk. 10.7) and 'eat what is set before you' (10.8). No concern is to be given to whether foods are clean or unclean, for such distinctions function to separate peoples. Jesus signals an inclusive sense of mission by breaking down distinguishing food concerns.[74]

in the First Three Centuries [trans. James Moffatt, II; New York: G.P. Putnam's Sons, 1905], p. 184). See Acts 6.7; 8.26; 10.1; 18.8.

71. The 'son of peace' who hears the message is a typically Jewish expression.

72. According to the Mishnah, 'The dwelling places of Gentiles are unclean' (*Ohol.* 18.7). In Jn 18.28, the Jews refuse to enter the Praetorium (a Gentile's residence) for fear of becoming defiled. Mt. 18.17 presupposes no social contact between Jew and Gentile, and this fact would particularly extend to one's house. See also *Jub.* 22.16; *Jos. Asen.* 7.1; Jdt. 12.2, 7-9. For an excellent survey of the historical evidence, including a recent defense of the intensity with which Jews observed the purity laws in the New Testament period, see Philip Francis Esler, *Community and Gospel in Luke–Acts: The Social and Political Motivations of Lucan Theology* (Cambridge: Cambridge University Press, 1987), pp. 76-86.

73. That the messengers must be instructed to 'eat what they set before you' establishes the 'Jewish' identity of the Seventy-two. They are additional workers (cf. ἑτέρους, 10.1) in the missionary harvest with the Twelve (9.1-6).

74. Jerome H. Neyrey, 'Ceremonies in Luke–Acts: The Case of Meals and Table Fellowship', in *The Social World of Luke–Acts*, p. 381. Eduard Schweizer likewise comments: 'The missionaries are therefore not to worry about food that is cultically unclean, which was forbidden the Jews' (*The Good News According to Luke* [trans. David E. Green; Atlanta: John Knox, 1984], pp. 175-76).

The radical nature of the Lukan presentation is particularly revealing in a comparison with Matthew.[75]

The household mission of the Seventy-two thus anticipates the erasure of ethnic distinctions in Acts that occurs when Peter 'enters' the house of the gentile Cornelius and eats with him and his household (10.25, 27; 11.3).[76] Since the mission of the Seventy-two respects no barriers of a racial or ethnic kind, Luke subtly prepares the reader for the conversion of the first 'official' Gentile, who converts in a house with his entire household.

'First Say, "Peace to this Household!"'

Upon entering a house, the messengers of Jesus bring a salvific word of greeting to its inhabitants: 'Peace to this household!' (10.5b).[77] The Lukan pattern now shifts from 'house' as a spatial location to 'house' in the figurative sense of 'family'.[78] It is this personified house (οἶκος), the

75. John B. Mathews interprets the reference to a 'worthy' host at Mt. 10.11 as the attempt to discern in advance who is clean and unclean so as to avoid the latter. Thus, he contends that this verse, like Lk. 10.7, pertains to Jewish purity laws but from the opposite point of view ('Hospitality and the New Testament Church: An Historical and Exegetical Study' [ThD dissertation, Princeton Theological Seminary, 1964], pp. 202-203 n. 3).

76. Luke's three-fold emphasis on entering (εἰσέρχομαι) the house of Cornelius highlights the momentous step of invading Gentile 'space': 'By entering', Gerhard A. Krodel observes, 'Peter is blurring the distinction between Jew and Gentile' (*Acts*, [ACNT; Minneapolis: Augsburg, 1986], p. 193).

77. It is grammatically possible to understand the adverb *proton* as denoting the sense of 'before' in which case the greeting of peace occurs prior to the messenger entering the house (so NCV). This interpretation, however, turns the 'greeting' into a quasi-magical formula since it is not actually addressed to members of the household (for a recent treatment of Luke's negative view of magic, see Garrett, *The Demise of the Devil*). For this reason it is better to understand *proton* in the more natural sense of 'first' as rendered, for example, by the translators of the Revised English Bible: 'When you go into a house, let your first words be...' (cf. NRSV, NIV, NAS). In this case the stress is upon the primacy of extending the word of salvific peace to the household. See, A.T. Robertson and W. Hersey Davis, *A New Short Grammar of the Greek Testament* (Grand Rapids: Baker, 1977), pp. 206-207.

78. See *BAGD*, 'οἶκος', p. 560. The almost universal practice of rendering οἶκος in Lk. 10.5 as 'house' (e.g., NRSV, REB, NIV, NASB) only obscures its intended figurative meaning of 'family' or 'household' (so also Lk. 19.9). The clear sense of the passage is: 'I wish peace to all this family' (Robert G. Bratcher, *A Translator's Guide to the Gospel of Luke* [New York: United Bible Societies, 1982],

'household', which here becomes the object of the messenger's salvific appeal. The peace that the messenger offers is more than a simple greeting: 'it confronts the people of the house with God's salvation and authority'.[79] In Lukan terms, 'peace' is a metaphor for salvation (Lk. 7.50; 8.48).[80]

The personification of the οἶκος at Lk. 10.5b, while representing a subtle rhetorical move from its more basic sense of an architectural dwelling,[81] is significant for the presentation of the household mission in Acts. It occurs in a stylized formula whenever entire families convert to the Christian faith (Acts 10.2; 11.14; 16.15, 31 [33-34]; 18.8).[82] Moreover, whereas both οἰκία and οἶκος are terms of spatial location for Luke, only the latter carries the figurative sense of 'family' as such.[83]

Reflecting the social psychology of his day, Luke closely identifies the response of the household with that of the householder.[84] Messengers

p. 175). See also Joachim Jeremias, *The Origins of Infant Baptism: A Further Reply to Kurt Aland* (Naperville: Allenson, 1963), p. 17.

79. Tiede, *Luke*, p. 202. The household conversion stories in Acts stress the speaking (λαλέω) and/or hearing (ἀκούω) of the word of salvation, the gospel message. In listening to the word of the messenger, the household is really listening to the word of Jesus and ultimately God (ἀκούω, Lk. 10.16).

80. See also Lk. 1.79; 2.14; 24.36; Acts 10.36. According to Fitzmyer, the proffering of the peace 'first' indicates the kind of salvific effect that the messenger is to have on the occupants of the house (*The Gospel according to Luke I–IX*, p. 225).

81. See the listing in *BAGD*, see 'οἶκος', p. 560.

82. The formula, with some variation, is 'and/with (all) his/her household'. For the secondary literature relating to this formula, see ch. 1, p. 13 n. 11.

83. This figurative sense of οἶκος is relatively rare in the New Testament. Jeremias can cite only twelve instances where it occurs (Lk. 10.5; 19.9; Acts 10.2; 11.14; 16.15, 31; 18.8; 1 Cor. 1.16; 2 Tim. 1.16; 4.19; Tit. 1.11; Heb. 11.7; see *The Origins of Infant Baptism*, p. 17 n. 1). One should also add the other passages listed in *BAGD* (1 Tim. 3.4-5, 12; 5.4; Heb. 3.6b). Whereas οἰκία sometimes carries this figurative sense (Mt. 12.25; 13.57; Mk 3.25; 6.4; Jn 4.53; 1 Cor. 16.15), none of the instances appears in the Lukan writings. The Lukan emphasis on the οἶκος as the special object of salvation shares some affinity with the *Shepherd of Hermas*: 'But it is not for this that God is angry with you, but in order that you should convert your family [οἶκόν], which has sinned against the Lord, and against you, their parents' (*Herm. Vis.* 1.3.1; see also 1.1.9; 1.3.2; 2.3.1; *Herm. Man.* 2.7; 5.1.7; 12.3.6; *Herm. Sim.* 5.3.9; 7.2; 7.5-7).

84. For the way in which a person of Luke's original audience would have arrived at certain decisions, religious or otherwise, see Bruce J. Malina and Jerome H. Neyrey, 'First-Century Personality: Dyadic, Not Individual', in *The Social World*

direct their message to the household (v. 5b), but the 'son of peace' (υἱὸς εἰρήνης) determines its salvific response (v. 6). The expression 'son of peace' is a Semitic idiom meaning a 'peaceful person' or, better, 'a person destined for peace'.[85] While it may describe an individual member of the household, it more probably denotes the owner of the house.[86] In the immediate context of the discourse, the son of peace represents a potential convert to the messianic faith.[87] When the householder accepts the peace of the messengers (10.6a, ἐπ' αὐτὸν), the entire household reciprocates with its offer of food and drink (10.7a, ἐσθίοντες καὶ πίνοντες τὰ παρ' αὐτῶν). In this way the faith of one becomes the faith of all. This religious solidarity of the household receives further expression in Acts where, as Otto Michel observes, it 'is explicitly emphasized that the conversion of a man leads his whole family to faith'.[88]

At the same time, the possibility of rejection by the household, though not as pronounced as that by the city (cf. Lk. 10.10-12), is one with which the messengers must ultimately reckon. In this case, the salvific peace returns to the ones who brought it (10.6b). Here, however, a basic

of Luke–Acts, pp. 67-96. 'For people of that time and place, the basic, most elementary unit of social analysis is not the individual person but the dyad, a person in relation with and connected to at least one other social unit, in particular, the family' (pp. 72-73).

85. So Marshall, *The Gospel of Luke*, p. 420. Luke is fond of employing the figurative use of υἱός: 5.34 ('sons of the bridegroom'), 16.8 ('sons of this age' and 'sons of light'), 20.34 ('sons of this age'), 20.36 ('sons of the resurrection'). See Frederick W. Danker, 'The υἱός Phrases in the New Testament', *NTS* 7 (1960–61), p. 94, who calls attention to the idiom's wider Greek usage.

86. So R.C.H. Lenski: 'Jesus is speaking of the head of the house, the man who owns the home and thus decides who shall be its guests' (*The Interpretation of St Luke's Gospel* [Minneapolis: Augsburg, 1946], p. 571). Also, Moessner, *Lord of the Banquet*, pp. 136-37. For the 'son of peace' as an individual member of the household, see C.F. Evans, *Saint Luke*, p. 447.

87. The potential status of the convert, already suggested by ἐὰν ᾖ at 10.6a, is indicated by a number of factors: 1. the mission has still to arrive at the household (cf. 10.1); 2. Jesus emphasizes the bringing of salvific peace by his household messengers and the possibility of their rejection (10.5b, 6b); 3. in Acts, salvation always comes *to* the household; Cornelius, Lydia, the Roman jailer, and Crispus are potential converts to Christianity. See also Marshall, *The Gospel of Luke*, p. 420.

88. Michel, 'οἶκος', *TDNT*, V, p. 130. Michel's emphasis on the male head of house fails to consider the case of Lydia, a *woman* of some prominence who converts along with her respective household (Acts 16.15).

tension in the narrative 'unity' of Luke and Acts emerges, since the latter knows nothing of an unreceptive household.[89] Moreover, the picture of a household responding in tandem with the faith of the householder bears tension at times within the Gospel itself, which contains strong statements about the division Jesus brings to households (12.49-53; cf. 9.61; 18.28-30). The implications of this disparity for the presentation of the household mission in Acts must await the conclusion to this study.

'Stay in that House, Eating and Drinking what they Give you'

The third element of the household mission highlights the role of the house in providing 'space' for the new inclusive community: 'Stay in that house, eating and drinking whatever they give you' (10.7a).[90] The reciprocal principle that 'the worker is worthy of his wages' (10.7b) establishes the right of the messengers to expect a hospitable stay in the house of the newly converted household.[91] That the household offers ritually unclean food is no matter; messengers must not go 'from house to house' in search of ritually prepared food (10.7c).[92] Inclusive table-fellowship in the house that received their message thus forms the fitting conclusion to the household mission proper.[93]

89. In Acts, as Carolyn Osiek notes, there is only 'idyllic household unity' ('The Lukan *oikos*: An Exercise in Symbolic Universe', unpublished paper, Social Facets Seminar, Spring, 1987, p. 1).

90. In the Gospel of Luke, μένω ('stay') appears only in relation to time spent in a house, either stated (1.40, 56; 8.27; 9.4; 10.7; 19.5) or implied (24.29). This same connection to a house exists throughout Acts as well (9.43; 16.15; 18.3, 18, 20; 20.5; 21.7-8; 28.16, 30). By contrast, the Gospel of John accords the term a more spiritualized sense (1.32-33; 3.36; 5.38; 6.27, 56; 8.31; 12.46; 14.16-17, 25; 15.4-7, 9-11, 16) in addition to its usual spatial connotations (1.38-39; 2.12; 4.40; 10.40; 11.6).

91. Cf. Mathews, 'Hospitality and the New Testament Church', p. 202. Robert Karris notes in this passage the intimate connection between the sharing of food and the sharing of the gospel (*Luke: Artist and Theologian* [New York: Paulist Press, 1985], p. 50).

92. So Arthur A. Just, Jr, *The Ongoing Feast: Table Fellowship and Eschatology at Emmaus* (Collegeville: Liturgical Press, 1993), p. 165.

93. The intensive pronoun αὐτός at 10.7a possesses demonstrative force, highlighting the physical locale of inclusive table-fellowship: the messengers must stay 'in that house' (see N. Turner, *A Grammar of New Testament Greek*. III. *Syntax* [Edinburgh: T. & T. Clark, 1963], p. 194; on construing αὐτός as an adjective ['the same house'], see C.F.D. Moule, *An Idiom Book of New Testament Greek*

In directing his messengers to stay in houses, the Lukan Jesus anticipates the emergence of a new 'sacred space' for the new inclusive people of God.[94] The result of the household protocol is that the house effectively becomes the house church.[95] A physical structure that formerly bears no relationship to a religious setting is now set apart as the distinct locale for eucharistic 'eating and drinking', an act sealing 'the acceptance of the gospel by the receptive household'.[96] The third element in the household pattern thus anticipates the practice of the church in Acts whose messengers often stay in a house, providing the

[London: Cambridge University Press, 2nd edn, 1957], p. 93). If the goal of the Lukan mission were to evangelize as many houses as possible, 'then the messengers should not tarry too long at one household... But it is clear that this kind of movement is not envisioned. Rather, the activities within or through this house constitute a primary end in themselves' (Moessner, *Lord of the Banquet*, pp. 137-38). Unlike Matthew, Luke never entertains the thought of the messengers leaving the house (cf. Mt. 10.14: ἐξερχόμενοι ἔξω τῆς οἰκίας).

94. I use this phrase only in a qualified sense of space that is transformed when the community gathers for eucharistic table-fellowship, a phenomenon observable elsewhere in the New Testament. The different estimation accorded by Paul to houses at 1 Corinthians 11.22 and 34, for example, leads Lloyd Michael White to conclude that 'the assembled community, already in Paul, creates a special (dare we say "sacred") space, an inviolable sphere, in even the most ordinary of physical settings' ('Domus Ecclesiae—Domus Dei: Adaption and Development in the Setting for Early Christian Assembly', [PhD dissertation, Yale University, 1983], p. 601 n. 271). See also Jerome H. Neyrey, *Paul in Other Words: A Cultural Reading of His Letters* (Louisville: Westminster Press/ John Knox, 1990), pp. 50-51. On the sacred character of a house from a social science perspective, see Bruce J. Malina, *The New Testament World: Insights from Cultural Anthropology* (Atlanta: John Knox, 1981), pp. 122-25.

95. This phenomenon appears elsewhere in the New Testament, most notably in the Johannine writings where οἰκία and ἐκκλησία are equated (2 Jn 10 = 3 Jn 10). On this close correspondence, White writes: 'In some measure, then, the boundaries of the religious community have become defined by the physical setting; the walls of the house demarcate the limits of the church as much as the individuals assembled within it' (Domus Ecclesiae—Domus Dei', pp. 605-606).

96. Marshall, *The Gospel of Luke*, p. 421. The phrase 'eating and drinking', a common one in Luke (5.30, 33; 7.33-34; 12.45; 17.27-28), carries definite eucharistic connotations at 22.30 in a passage unique to the Third Evangelist: 'that you may eat and drink (ἵνα ἔσθητε καὶ πίνητε) at my table in my kingdom...' (cf. 22.16, 18). Moessner sees in Lk. 10.7 hints of the messianic banquet motif, declaring that the table-fellowship 'is ipso facto no ordinary eating and drinking! At the very least, it represents a fellowship of those in the saving presence of the Kingdom of God' (*Lord of the Banquet*, p. 137).

locus for a distinctively Christian worship apart from the institutions of temple and synagogue.[97]

In the above ways Lk. 10.5-7 furnishes a pattern of household evangelism which, this book contends, appears within the narrative of Acts as a repetitive structuring device. As a result of the mission of the Seventy-two, the reader expects accredited messengers of Jesus to enter the homes of economically established (gentile) householders, there present the word of salvation to the household, and stay in the house eating and drinking as an expression of inclusive table-fellowship. This pattern constitutes the essential 'plot' of a household salvation story and the characteristic elements that establish its 'type-scene'.

Recurrent terminology, what Robert Alter styles '*Leitwort*',[98] includes the personified οἶκος as the special recipient of salvation. Other motifs, such as entering (εἰσέρχομαι) and staying (μένω) in a house, also help to comprise the pattern, which may at times include related terms or images expressive of Christian hospitality. The way in which Luke subjects one or more of these elements to degrees of variation in Acts is indicative of his immense gifts as a literary artist.[99] Yet the household conversion stories in Acts share enough of these elements to suggest that they conform to the pattern established by the mission of the Seventy-two.[100]

97. Filson, 'The Significance of the Early House Churches', p. 109. E. Jane Via notes how historically 'from the beginning the [eucharistic] meal was celebrated as part of the Christian ritual, apparently independently of the synagogue and Temple' ('Women, the Discipleship of Service, and the Early Christian Ritual Meal in the Gospel of Luke', *Saint Luke Journal of Theology* 29 [1985], p. 59).

98. On the concept of *Leitwort*, as well as the qualified notion of type-scene in this study, see ch. 1, pp. 16-17.

99. On the more recent recognition of Luke's narrative artistry, see the discussion in Mark Allan Powell's *What Are They Saying About Luke*? (New York: Paulist Press, 1989), pp. 10-14.

100. In dealing with literary patterns or parallels, particularly between Luke and Acts, it is important to bear in mind the observation of Jack T. Sanders, who comments on Luke's literary treatment of the Jews: 'Parallels are not, of course, photocopies, so that the behavior of "the Jews" in the Acts is not exactly the same as that in the Gospel; nevertheless, there are enough similarities that we can see that Luke was consciously conforming the two narratives to each other in this respect—as, of course, in others' ('The Jewish People in Luke–Acts', in *Luke–Acts and the Jewish People: Eight Critical Perspectives* [ed. Joseph B. Tyson; Minneapolis: Augsburg, 1988], p. 70).

Strategies of the Lukan Narrator

One of the chief distinctions of the household conversion 'type-scene' is its lack of reliance on literary or oral convention to create expectations in the mind of the reader. Instead, the pattern of 'household conversion' is essentially a literary creation of Luke, who places it on the lips of his Gospel's chief protagonist. What reasons exist to suggest that the pattern of household evangelizing is to continue on the pages of Acts?

Besides the proleptic nature of the discourse in which the pattern appears, three additional rhetorical strategies promote a continuation of the household missionary pattern. First, the pattern is grounded in the authority of Jesus himself. As 'the Lord' (ὁ κύριος) who appoints messengers to the house (10.1), Jesus possesses the lordship that belongs to God. While Acts often employs this title of the exalted Jesus (for example, 2.36), Luke is the only Gospel to apply it directly to Jesus during the course of his earthly career.[101] As 'the Lord of the harvest' (10.2),[102] sent by God (10.16), Jesus speaks with authority and his words elicit obedience. According to David B. Gowler, three voices of absolute authority ring out on the pages of Luke: the reliable narrator, the voice from heaven, and Jesus.[103]

In response to the authority of Jesus, the band of seventy-two disciples faithfully carries out his words of household commissioning. That Jesus

101. While Matthew and Mark only use κύριος in a non-technical (vocative) sense, it is a common designation for the Lukan Jesus during the course of his earthly career (7.13, 19; 10.1, 39, 41; 11.39; 12.42; 13.15; 16.8; 17.5, 6; 18.6; 19.8, 31, 34; 22.61; 24.3, 34). Marshall points out how this title appears always in non-Markan sections of Luke's Gospel (*Luke: Historian and Theologian* [Exeter: Paternoster Press, 1970], p. 166). 'Lord' is also a common designation in stories of household salvation: Lk. 19.8; Acts 10.33, 36; 11.16-17; 16.14-15; 16.31-32; 18.8-9.

102. Most commentators understand this description at 10.2 in reference to God. Since Jesus is the one who actually sends out workers into the harvest (10.3), answering, in effect, his own prayer, Luke may intend a cryptic allusion to Jesus. See E. Earle Ellis, who understands this title here of both God and Jesus (*The Gospel of Luke* [NCB; Grand Rapids: Eerdmans, 1966], p. 156). As a description for God, 'Lord of the harvest' has no known parallel in ancient literature (Evans, *Saint Luke*, p. 446).

103. David B. Gowler, *Host, Guest, Enemy, and Friend: Portraits of the Pharisees in Luke and Acts* (Emory Studies in Early Christianity; New York: Peter Lang, 1991), p. 181.

appoints them to their task makes these disciples fully 'reliable' to carry out the defeat of Satan, a point underscored at the conclusion to their journey (Lk. 10.17-20). As emissaries, they are the Lord's special representatives, the rejection of which is tantamount to the rejection of Jesus himself and ultimately God (10.16). Because the Seventy-two are clearly symbolic of the future mission of the church, the reader can reasonably expect all fully accredited house messengers of Jesus to implement his words of household commissioning.

A second strategy of the narrator links the mission of Luke 10 to the example of Jesus, who sends the disciples ahead 'to every city and place where he himself was going to come' (10.1b). By 'place' (τόπον) the reader of the discourse understands 'house'.[104] In sending the disciples on a preparatory mission to both house and city, the Lukan Jesus anticipates his own ministry there on his way to Jerusalem, a journey that culminates in the conversion of Zacchaeus and his household (19.1-9).[105] Thus, if Jesus brings salvation to the house, his messengers in Acts will do the same: a disciple, 'after he has been fully trained, will be like his teacher' (Lk. 6.40).

A third rhetorical strategy appears in the opening logion of Jesus: 'The harvest is plentiful, but the laborers are few' (10.2). Whereas the Matthean Jesus utters these words in response to the people's lack of a shepherd (9.36-38), in Luke the μὲν...δέ clause serves to stir a sense of urgency in the Seventy-two for their given appointment. Thus, if the first two strategies center on the authority and imitation of Jesus respectively, the third elicits wonder and desperation at the greatness of the missionary task. Because the people of the house and city constitute so great (πολύς) a harvest, not even the Seventy-two constitute a sufficient number in and of themselves. They must pray that the Lord will send additional workers into the harvest.[106] The answer to the prayer of the Seventy-two comes in Acts, whose missionaries succeed in bringing the gospel to 'the end of the earth' (1.8; 13.47). In Acts, prayer often

104. Reading the discourse strictly in its context leads one to equate πόλις and τόπος (10.1) with οἰκία/οἶκος (10.5-7) and πόλις (10.8-12) in reverse order. On the identification of τόπος with οἶκος, see Acts 7.49. For this identification outside the New Testament, see Helmut Koester, 'τόπος', *TDNT*, VIII, p. 188.

105. During the course of this 'journey', Jesus often engages the house in mission (10.38; 11.37; 14.1; 19.5).

106. 'As workers in this harvest, they are to pray that more be added to the "few"; because the harvest is "great", not even Seventy(-two) are nearly enough' (Moessner, *Lord of the Banquet*, p. 135).

accompanies the missionary enterprise (4.31; 8.14-15; 13.1-3), and is a particular feature of household evangelism (10.2, 9, 30; 11.5; 16.13, 25).[107]

Conclusion

The sending of the seventy-two disciples in Luke begins the fulfillment of an expectation created at the outset of the Gospel: Jesus comes to reign over the 'house' (1.33).[108] As the locus for the gospel's reception, the house will become a key factor in the growth of the church as depicted in Acts. There it functions as the venue for proclaiming Jesus as the Christ (5.42; 10.22, 33, 44b; 18.5, 7) as well as for the four characteristic activities of the growing community outlined in 2.42: teaching (18.11; 20.7, 11), fellowship/hospitality (21.8, 10, 16), celebration of the eucharist (2.46; 20.7, 11), and prayer (1.14; 12.12). One cannot minimize the role of the house as the setting for the life and worship of the early church.[109]

If the household comprises a key element in the spread of an 'unhindered gospel',[110] its pattern of evangelization provides the framework for those stories in Acts depicting the gospel's success in the fullest terms—those termed 'household conversions'. Until now the form and function of these stories have not received the attention from Lukan scholars that they deserve. Reading these stories against the backdrop of the pattern of the Seventy-two provides the model necessary for embarking on such a task. Before proceeding to that task, however, it remains to consider how Luke relates the household mission to the life and ministry of Jesus, his Gospel's chief protagonist.

107. Robert F. O'Toole notes how Luke employs the prayer motif at decisive junctures in his narrative (*The Unity of Luke's Theology: An Analysis of Luke–Acts* [Wilmington: Michael Glazier, 1984], pp. 72-73).

108. More specifically, Jesus reigns over the 'house of Jacob' which, according to O'Toole, is a Lukan description of the church under the lordship of the risen Christ (*The Unity of Luke's Theology*, p. 18).

109. Jeremias sees Acts 2.42 as reflecting the sequence of an early Christian worship service (*The Eucharistic Words of Jesus* [trans. Norman Perrin; London: SCM Press, 1966], pp. 118-20). If such is the case, the house functions as the important locale for early liturgical activity.

110. According to Frank Stagg, 'unhindered' (ἀκωλύτως) at Acts 28.31 summarizes the very theme of the book (*The Book of Acts: The Early Struggle for an Unhindered Gospel* [Nashville: Broadman Press, 1955]).

Chapter 3

THE HOUSEHOLD MISSION OF THE LUKAN JESUS

Introduction

Interest in places of lodging, and household settings in particular, has long been recognized as a unique feature of the Third Evangelist. Though characteristic of his writings as a whole, it becomes especially evident in his literary presentation of Jesus's life and ministry. Henry J. Cadbury, in a lexical study published over fifty years ago, first drew attention to the way in which the Third Gospel

> contains many allusions if not to the houses in which Jesus lodged at least to various forms of hospitality. He is pictured often under the Pharisees' roof. He is entertained by Simon the Pharisee and also by Zacchaeus the publican and by Mary and Martha in their homes. Jesus on several occasions discusses hospitality. The parable of Dives and Lazarus seems to turn about the question of inhospitality, while in another parable the shrewd business manager is chiefly concerned that when he is discharged he should have friends who would receive him into their houses...[1]

These passages, notes Cadbury, are unique to the composition of Third Evangelist.[2]

The house as a setting for hospitality occupies more than a minor interest of Luke. Eight of the nine meal scenes depicted in his Gospel involve an explicit use of the household setting.[3] Moreover, the Lukan Jesus depends upon the receptivity of households to direct and sustain

1. Henry J. Cadbury, 'Lexical Notes on Luke–Acts: Luke's Interest in Lodging', *JBL* 45 (1926), p. 308.

2. Cadbury, 'Lexical Notes on Luke–Acts', p. 309.

3. See 5.29-32; 7.36-50; 10.38-42; 11.37-54; 14.1-24; 19.1-10; 22.7-38; 24.13-35. The only exception appears at 9.10-17, the feeding of the multitude in a 'desolate place' (cf. v. 12). Cf. Arthur A. Just, Jr, *The Ongoing Feast: Table Fellowship and Eschatology at Emmaus* (Collegeville: The Liturgical Press, 1993), p. 172.

the work of his itinerant band of missionaries (9.4; 10.5-7), and his own ministry largely rests upon it.[4] Thus, the post-resurrection words of Peter recall the significance of houses for the ministry of Jesus with the disciples: 'he went in and out among us' (Acts 1.21).[5]

Throughout the Gospel of Luke, Jesus is conscious of being on a mission from God (Lk. 10.16). It is as one who is himself 'sent' that Jesus sends the Seventy-two to both house and city, places where 'he himself intended to go' (Lk. 10.1; cf. v. 3). At one or more points in his ministry, Jesus enters the homes of prominent householders and societal outcasts, brings salvation to a wealthy householder and his household, and stays in houses 'eating and drinking' what the household provides. As the author and exemplar of the household evangelizing pattern, Jesus obeys his own missionary directive.[6] Comparison with Matthew and Mark[7] reveals just how distinctive these three elements are in Luke's presentation of the ministry of the Lord Jesus.[8] The goal of this chapter,

4. G. Stählin, 'ξέωος', in *TDNT*, V, pp. 22-23.

5. The verb εἰσέρχομαι ('enter, go in') often depicts Jesus' movement into houses in Luke (4.38; 7.6, 36, 44-45; 8.41, 51; 10.38; 11.37 [14.1]; 19.7; 24.29), therefore providing an apt summary of the public ministry of the Lukan Jesus.

6. Richard J. Dillon sees this motif as particularly evident in the Emmaus narrative of Luke 24 where Jesus appears in 'the role of proto-missionary following the steps of his own prescription for the households' (*From Eye-Witnesses to Ministers of the Word: Tradition and Composition in Luke 24* [AnBib; Rome: Biblical Institute Press, 1978], p. 189).

7. A limited use of redaction criticism appears throughout this chapter to bring out points that are distinctively Lukan and to show emphasis or contrast. Where redactional comments are employed, Markan priority is assumed. Compare Robert C. Tannehill, who combines a judicious amount of redaction criticism with literary analysis (*The Narrative Unity of Luke–Acts: A Literary Interpretation*, I [Philadelphia: Fortress Press, 1986], p. 6).

8. Entering (εἰσέρχομαι) the house is Luke's almost universal way of denoting Jesus' movement into domestic space (4.38; 7.6, 36, 44-45; 8.41, 51; 10.38; 11.37; cf. 14.1). Matthew uses the term only once in this way (8.8; cf. 17.25) and Mark four times (5.39; 7.17, 24; 9.28), but with a decidedly non-programmatic character: the Markan Jesus wants no one to know of it! (Mk 7.24; cf. 7.17; 9.28). In addition, only Luke records the conversion of Zacchaeus's οἶκος (19.1-10) as well as the Lord's stay (μένω) with the disciples of Emmaus (24.13-35), stories to which Luke attaches prime importance. Matthew and Mark, by contrast, never picture Jesus' conversion of a household or 'stay' in a house. The expression, 'eating and drinking', is also distinctly Lukan, evident from the number of its occurrences in Luke (5.30, 33; 7.33-34; 10.7; 12.45; 17.27-28; 22.16, 18, 30) in comparison to Mark (2.16) and Matthew respectively (11.18-19; 24.29).

then, is to trace the typical elements of the household evangelizing pattern as they receive expression in the life and mission of the Lukan Jesus. These elements provide the actual 'raw material' out of which Luke constructs the mission of the Seventy-two. That these elements coalesce to form a sequential order of missionary activity only in the sending of the Seventy-two requires a slight methodological shift in this chapter to account adequately for the evidence.[9] In fashioning the pattern this way, Luke thrusts his chief protagonist into the role of paradigmatic missionary, whose experiences in houses anticipate many of the key themes in the household mission of Acts.

Jesus Enters the House

The Gospel of Luke depicts Jesus' entry (εἰσέρχομαι) into houses throughout the course of his ministry.[10] Unlike Matthew and Mark, εἰσέρχεσθαι εἰς τὸν οἶκον is 'a virtual technical term in Lucan literature to denote the act in which the guest enters into and accepts the hospitality offered by his host'.[11] In contexts of hospitality, the independent use of εἰσέρχομαι carries essentially the same meaning.[12] Only at 14.1, where Jesus dines in the house of a prominent Pharisee, does Luke depart from his usual practice and then, only slightly.[13]

Healing in the House

Three instances of miraculous healing occur when Jesus enters a house on the pages of Luke's Gospel: the mother-in-law of Simon (4.38-41),

9. All three elemental motifs of the household protocol are present in the story of Zacchaeus but in a slightly different sequence. To appreciate the fullness of Luke's literary matrix, therefore, it is necessary to peruse a number of related 'house' texts rather than focus upon a single text.

10. Luke only rarely speaks of Jesus' entry (εἰσέρχομαι) into the synagogue (4.16; 6.6) or temple (19.45). When Jesus enters a village or city (7.1; 9.52; 10.38; 17.12; 19.1), it often leads to a mission to houses (7.1; 10.38; 19.1).

11. John B. Mathews, 'Hospitality and the New Testament Church: An Historical and Exegetical Study' (ThD dissertation, Princeton Theological Seminary, 1964), pp. 171-72. See Lk. 1.40; 4.38; 7.36; 9.4 [= 10.5]; Acts 16.15; 21.8.

12. Mathews, 'Hospitality and the New Testament Church', p. 172 n. 1. See Lk. 6.4; 10.38; 11.26, 37; 19.7; 24.29. Note those instances where the independent use of εἰσέρχομαι occurs in the immediate context of a house (7.44-45; 11.24, 26; 19.5,7; 10.38).

13. The Greek text of Lk. 14.1 reads: ἐν τῷ ἐλθεῖν αὐτὸν εἰς οἶκόν.

the slave of the gentile centurion (7.1-10), and the daughter of Jairus, the president of the synagogue (8.41-42, 49-56).

a. *Simon's Mother-in-Law (4.38-41).* The first act of physical healing performed by the Lukan Jesus occurs in the house of Simon at Capernaum (4.38-41). After leaving the synagogue, Jesus 'entered' (εἰσῆλθεν) the house to heal Simon's mother-in-law of a dangerously high fever (4.38).[14] The phrase, 'the house of Simon' (τὴν οἰκίαν Σίμωνος), which identifies the place of healing, naturally points to Simon as the owner of the house.[15] That the narrator later identifies this same Simon as the owner of a fishing boat in a commercial fishing business (5.3) adds to his status as a person of some economic means on the pages of Luke's Gospel.[16]

Luke's account of the healing of Simon's mother-in-law follows in the main the Markan outline of events (1.29-31), with certain modifications of detail.[17] Whereas in Mark the disciples James and John accompany Jesus into the house, in Luke Jesus appears as a solitary messenger. The Lukan Jesus alone enters the house of the yet unknown Simon.[18] While Luke's distinctive chronology of events no doubt accounts for this particular emphasis,[19] such a portrayal serves to heighten the focus on Jesus as the first missionary to the house.

Luke accords the household a strategic role in the healing of Simon's mother-in-law. Whereas in Mark the disciples explicitly make request on her behalf (1.30), in Luke this role belongs to the members of Simon's household (ἠρώτησαν αὐτὸν περὶ αὐτῆς, 4.38b).[20] This request by

14. Here Luke slightly modifies Mark's ἦλθον εἰς (Mk 1.29).

15. By omitting the mention of Andrew, along with James and John (cf. Mk 1.29), Luke makes the house of Capernaum Simon's unique possession. See Eduard Schweizer, *The Good News According to Luke* (trans. David E. Green; Atlanta: John Knox, 1984), p. 99.

16. Luke depicts Simon as a partner in a fishing business (5.7, 10) who has 'left everything' (πάντα) to follow Jesus (5.11; cf. 18.28).

17. See Joseph A. Fitzmyer, *The Gospel According to Luke I–IX* (AB; New York: Doubleday, 1985), p. 548.

18. That Simon appears in the narrative without introduction suggests that he is known to the implied reader of Luke (see Joseph B. Tyson, *Images of Judaism in Luke–Acts* [Columbia: University of South Carolina Press, 1992], p. 27).

19. Simon, along with James and John, does not receive his call to discipleship until 5.1-11, a modification of the Markan sequence (Mk 1.16-20).

20. As John Nolland observes, 'Luke's earlier omissions leave the "they"

the household elicits a dramatic response from Jesus, whose rebuke of the fever (4.39) recalls his earlier expulsion of the demon at the synagogue in Capernaum (4.35). It is 'a living creature, the fever demon' that Jesus casts out of the woman.[21] Only in Luke does Jesus rebuke the fever that has seized her.[22] This rebuke of the demonic fever provides a further illustration of Jesus' powerful word that is present in this section of Luke.[23] As a result, the house of Simon becomes the scene for further healings and exorcisms (4.40-41),[24] the place for proclaiming release to Satan's captives (cf. 4.18-19).[25]

If Simon's house becomes the locus for the healing of his mother-in-law, she reciprocates accordingly by serving Jesus and Simon's household as her guests (ἀναστᾶσα διηκόνει αὐτοῖς, 4.39b).[26] Healing issues in the celebration of food and drink.[27] Of particular significance

without possible antecedent. Presumably the members of the household are intended', *Luke 1–9.20* (WBC; Dallas: Word Books, 1989), pp. 211-12; also Fitzmyer, *The Gospel According to Luke I–IX*, p. 550.

21. Joseph Dillersberger, *The Gospel of St Luke* (Philadelphia: Westminster Press, 1958), p. 190, cited in George E. Rice, 'Luke 4.31-44: Release for the Captives', *AUSS* 20 (1982), p. 26. Note the common use of ἐπιτιμάω ('rebuke') in these two stories (4.35, 39) as well as its occurrence at 4.41. That Luke considers demonic possession a form of sickness is evident from Acts 10.38.

22. In Matthew, Jesus heals the woman by simply touching her hand (8.15); in Mark, he does so by raising her up and taking hold of her hand (1.31).

23. Note the repeated emphasis on the λόγος of Jesus at 4.22, 32, 36. See Tannehill, *The Narrative Unity of Luke–Acts*, I, p. 84.

24. The immediate context in Luke suggests that it is the house of Simon to which the people bring the sick for healing (ἤγαγον αὐτοὺς πρὸς αὐτόν, 4.40), a connection that Mark makes more explicitly (1.33).

25. Rice notes the programmatic significance of 4.18-19 for the events that follow ('Release for the Captives', pp. 23-28).

26. In Matthew, she serves only Jesus, not the household (8.15). On the reciprocal relations between Jesus and women, see Halvor Moxnes, 'Patron-Client Relations and the New Community in Luke–Acts', in *The Social World of Luke–Acts*, pp. 261-63.

27. 'Serve' (διακονέω), in this context, is 'to be understood in terms of the food and drink she would offer her guests' (Robert G. Bratcher, *A Translator's Guide to the Gospel of Luke* [New York: United Bible Societies, 1982], p. 72). Craig Thomas McMahan, while recognizing this meaning of the term here, argues that it later functions as a metaphor for discipleship ('Meals as Type-Scenes in the Gospel of Luke' [PhD dissertation, The Southern Baptist Theological Seminary, 1987], p. 72). On the use of διακονέω in Luke's depiction of women, see E. Jane Via, 'Women, the Discipleship of Service, and the Early Christian Ritual Meal in the

here is the relation of the adverb παραχρῆμα to the rest of the clause in 4.39b: release from Satan's control issues 'immediately' in her act of hospitality.[28] Upon being restored to a full and vigorous health, the woman resumes the normal domestic activity of the household.[29]

b. *The Centurion's Servant (7.1-10).* A second instance of healing in a house occurs when Jesus heals the slave of a gentile centurion in Capernaum (7.1-10).[30] As a patron to the local Jews, one who 'built for us our synagogue', the centurion appears in Luke as a gentile 'God-fearer' as well as a person of some means (v. 5).[31] In the Lukan version of the story, Jesus and the military official never meet, nor does Jesus actually enter his house.[32] That the centurion expressly refers to Jesus'

Gospel of Luke', *Saint Luke Journal of Theology* 29 (1985), pp. 37-45. She notes how Luke often employs this term for the preparation and distribution of food (Lk. 4.34; 8.3; 10.40; 12.37; 17.8; 22.26-27[3X]; Acts 6.2; 17.22).

28. Does Satan stand opposed to the act of hospitality, a subject of immense theological importance for Luke?

29. In a study on the taxonomy of sickness in Luke and Acts, John J. Pilch assigns the healing of Simon's mother-in-law to the symbolic body-zone of the hands and feet, 'the zone of purposeful activity' ('Sickness and Healing in Luke–Acts', in Jerome H. Neyrey (ed.), *The Social World of Luke–Acts: Models for Interpretation* [Peabody: Hendrickson, 1991], p. 205). Taxonomy, according to Pilch, is '[t]he identification, classification, and clustering of illnesses into culturally meaningful categories' (p. 200).

30. Tannehill classifies this episode form-critically as a 'quest story', a more specific category of the pronouncement story (*The Narrative Unity of Luke–Acts*, II, p. 111). My concern in this chapter, however, is the way in which this and other stories contribute to the overall literary picture of Jesus as missionary to the house. Thus, the categories I employ make no claim as to form-critical considerations.

31. On his status as a God-fearer, see Joseph B. Tyson, *Images of Judaism in Luke–Acts*, pp. 37-39. For Tyson, this centurion stands, along with Cornelius (Acts 10.1-11.18), as an intratextual representation of the implied reader. I.H. Marshall notes that, as the primary benefactor of the Jewish community, the centurion of Capernaum could have possessed ample resources since '[t]he opportunities for personal enrichment in the police force were good, even for an honest man...' (*The Gospel of Luke: A Commentary on the Greek Text*, [NIGTC; Grand Rapids: Eerdmans, 1978], p. 280, citing B.S. Easton, *The Gospel According to St Luke* [Edinburgh, 1926], p. 95). According to David Kennedy, a centurion could expect to receive some sixteen times the basic legionary salary and thus possessed 'both considerable military and social status and wealth' (David Noel Freedman, (ed.), *ABD*, V [New York: Doubleday, 1992], see 'Roman Army', p. 791).

32. In Luke, the centurion works solely through emissaries composed of Jewish

entering (εἰσέρχομαι) under the roof of his house (v. 6), however, suggests that the narrator intends this episode to be read within the wider framework of Jesus' household mission. Entering the house of the centurion official, or the failure of Jesus to do so, constitutes a key element in the story.[33]

After hearing the plea of certain Jewish elders to come and heal the slave of the centurion (7.3-5), Jesus 'started on his way with them', fully intending to enter the centurion's house (7.6a).[34] While Jesus was 'not far from the house' (v. 6a), however, he was met by a delegation of messengers, who informed Jesus of the centurion's deep-felt unworthiness to have Jesus enter under his roof (v. 6b).[35] The centurion's hesitancy to receive Jesus into his home shows a sensitivity to Jewish purity laws, which forbade Jews from entering the house of a Gentile lest they incur ritual defilement.[36] By refusing Jesus admittance into his home, the centurion spares exposing Jesus to any undue criticism on the part of the Jewish authorities.[37] It is the house of another gentile centurion, Cornelius of Caesarea, that later becomes the scene of the conversion of the first Gentile (Acts 10.1–11.18), a mission largely foreshadowed by

elders and friends (7.3, 6). The Matthean centurion, however, makes it a point to meet Jesus personally (8.5). In seeking to harmonize the two accounts, Zane Hodges attempts to place the events of Lk. 7.1-8 before Mt. 8.5b-9 ('The Centurion's Faith in Matthew and Luke', *BSac* 121 [1964], pp. 321-32).

33. The lack of physical contact between Jesus and the centurion 'heightens the sense of spatial separation that constitutes the problem with which the story is working' (Tannehill, *The Narrative Unity of Luke–Acts*, I, p. 115).

34. The imperfect ἐπορεύετο is inceptive, stressing the initiation of the action.

35. According to Mathews, ὑπὸ τὴν στέγην μου εἰσέλθῃς at 7.6b is equivalent to εἰσέρχεσθαι εἰς τὸν οἶκον, contending that 'an act of hospitality and fellowship seems definitely to be at issue here in the centurion's affirmation that he is not worthy to have Jesus enter his house, i.e., not worthy to afford hospitality to Jesus' ('Hospitality and the New Testament Church', pp. 171-72).

36. So Nolland, *Luke 1–9.20*, pp. 317,19. 'The very careful and courteous way in which Jesus is being treated,' writes Tannehill, 'results from the shared assumption that help for a Gentile requires special negotiations because of a major social barrier' (*The Narrative Unity of Luke–Acts*, I, p. 114). On the strong Jewish antipathy toward gentile contact during this period, see Philip Francis Esler, *Community and Gospel in Luke–Acts: The Social and Political Motivations of Lucan Theology* (Cambridge: Cambridge University Press, 1987), pp. 76-86.

37. Frederick W. Danker, *Jesus and the New Age: A Commentary on St Luke's Gospel* (Philadelphia: Fortress Press, 1988), p. 159.

Jesus' dealings with the centurion of Capernaum.[38]

The failure of Jesus to enter the house of the centurion results in a miraculous healing performed at a distance. Jesus need only 'speak the word' (εἰπὲ λόγῳ, 7.7), says the centurion, and his servant will be healed. Like Jesus, the centurion himself is a man whose word of authority results in effective action (7.8).[39] That the messengers return to the house to find the servant healed and in good health (7.10) means that the house functions once again as the scene of Jesus' healing activity. Jesus' word is operative in the house, though he himself is absent. In the particular context in which Luke has placed this story, the centurion of Capernaum functions as one whose great faith (cf. 7.9) leads him to build his house upon the solid foundation of Jesus' word (6.46-49).[40]

c. *The Daughter of Jairus (8.41-42, 49-56)*

The next miraculous healing reserved for the domestic setting occurs in the house of a synagogue president, one Jairus by name, whose only daughter lay deathly ill (8.41-42, 49-56).[41] Only in Luke's Gospel does Jairus expressly exhort Jesus to enter his house (παρεκάλει αὐτὸν εἰσελθεῖν εἰς τὸν οἶκον αὐτοῦ, 8.41).[42] This invitation takes the place of the more explicit request for healing recorded in the Gospels of Matthew (9.18) and Mark (5.23). Luke thus presents Jairus as one who

38. 'In his dealings with Gentiles,' says Nolland, 'Jesus stays within the limits of Jewish propriety. By contrast, what is to happen in the case of the centurion Cornelius in Acts 10–11 clearly transgresses the bounds of traditional Jewish acceptability. The implicit paralleling of the two centurions is a quiet apologetic for the later gentile mission' (*Luke 1–9.20*, p. 316). According to O.C. Edwards, the lack of direct contact between Jesus and Gentiles in Luke reserves the gentile mission proper for Acts (*Luke's Story of Jesus* [Philadelphia: Fortress Press, 1981], p. 43).

39. On the historical relation of the centurion to his post at Capernaum, see J.A.G. Haslam, 'The Centurion at Capernaum: Luke 7.1-10', *ExpTim* 96 (1985), pp. 109-110.

40. 'The man who hears and does is safe against every crisis,' remarks G.B. Caird, including, one might add, the death of a trusted slave (*Saint Luke* [Philadelphia: Westminster Press, 1963], p. 107). Note the verbal connections between the two accounts: κύριος (6.46; 7.6), οἰκία (6.48,49; 7.6, 10[οἶκος]), ἀκούω (6.47, 49; 7.1, 3), λόγος (6.47; 7.7), ὁ ἐρχόμενος πρός με (6.47), πρὸς σὲ ἐλθεῖν (7.7).

41. Luke's inclusion of μονογενὴς ('only') at v. 42 adds poignancy to Jairus's request (cf. Mk 5.23; Mt. 9.18).

42. Both Matthew and Mark appear to downplay the house motif in their respective stories.

is well aware of the healing powers of Jesus that are operative in the house.[43]

Jairus appears in Luke as a person of considerable social standing. By characterizing him as a 'ruler of the synagogue' (ἄρχων τῆς συναγωγῆς, 8.41; cf. ἀρχισυναγώγου, 8.49),[44] 'Luke stresses Jairus' dignity and place in the Jewish social "establishment"'.[45] Synagogue rulers generally possessed the responsibility of maintaining the building and making arrangements for public worship, including the reading of Scripture and sermon (cf. Acts 13.15).[46] Ancient inscriptions reveal that the office was at times hereditary or simply honorary for esteemed members of the community.[47] Since the Lukan narrator shows a keen interest in the position of synagogue leaders (Lk. 13.14; Acts 13.15; 18.8, 17), the story of Jairus may anticipate the conversion of Crispus, the president of the synagogue at Corinth (Acts 18.7-8), in much the same way that the centurion at Capernaum foreshadows the conversion of Cornelius.

Following the Markan arrangement, the healing that occurs in the home of Jairus is delayed by the encroachment of the woman with an issue of blood (8.43-48).[48] The interruption serves to build anticipation and heighten interest in the story.[49] Two additional obstacles stand in the

43. An explicit request for healing in Matthew and Mark is therefore equivalent to a request to enter the house in Luke.

44. The shift between the two forms is curious (see Fitzmyer, *The Gospel According to Luke I–IX*, p. 745).

45. Nolland, *Luke 1–9.20*, p. 419. On the position of synagogue presidents in the social world of Luke's day, see Gerd Theissen, *The Social Setting of Pauline Christianity: Essays on Corinth* (ed. and trans. John H. Schutz; Philadelphia: Fortress Press, 1982), pp. 73-75.

46. While the synagogue president had charge over these functions, it was the ὑπηρέτης who performed the actual tasks (cf. Lk. 4.20). See Marshall's discussion, *The Gospel of Luke,* p. 343. The role of the synagogue president usually required a person of some economic means: 'Since upkeep of the synagogue required money, there was reason to entrust this office to a wealthy man who would be in a position, should the occasion arise, to supplement the community's funds with his own contribution' (Theissen, *The Social Setting of Pauline Christianity*, p. 74).

47. See the inscriptions in Theissen (*The Social Setting of Pauline Christianity*, pp. 74-75).

48. Mark's intercalation of these two stories is allowed to stand in Luke's Gospel. References to the number 'twelve' (8.42, 43) and 'daughter' (8.42, 48) provide literary points of contact between the two encounters.

49. Fred B. Craddock, *Luke* (IBC; Louisville: John Knox Press, 1990), p. 116.

way of Jesus' mission to the house: the pressure of the crowd, which impedes Jesus' progress (v. 42b), and the death of Jairus's daughter, which renders the trip unnecessary (v. 49).[50] These obstacles, typical of Luke's method elsewhere (for example, 5.17-26; 18.35-43), increase the reader's involvement in the plight of the sick and the suffering.[51] At the same time, they show the strong determinism underlying Jesus' mission. Taking time to heal the woman with the hemorrhage may delay Jesus' movement to the house of Jairus, but it does not stop it.[52]

In coming to the house of Jairus, Jesus permits no one to enter with him except Peter, John and James, in addition to the girl's parents (8.51).[53] Once again Luke alters the Markan language to reflect his preferred verbal expression.[54] Once inside the house, Jesus calls the young girl forth (8.54), and the power of his word causes the girl's spirit to return (8.55a). 'She is asked to do what a dead person cannot do', remarks John Nolland, 'but the powerful word of Jesus enables what it demands'.[55] Upon being healed, the girl arises immediately (παραχρῆμα) and receives something to eat in accordance with Jesus' command (8.55).[56] As in the case of Simon's mother-in-law, healing issues in the celebration of food and drink.[57] Jesus' word restores not only the girl's health but her participation in the daily activities of the household.[58] Salvation thus results in a full and normal domestic life (8.50).[59]

50. 'The basis for the journey begun in v. 42 now collapses. Death steps forward as the final barrier to all action' (Nolland, *Luke 1–9.20*, p. 421).

51. Tannehill, *The Narrative Unity of Luke–Acts*, I, pp. 92-93.

52. Cf. Leon Morris, *The Gospel According to St Luke: An Introduction and Commentary* (TNTC; Grand Rapids: Eerdmans, 1974), p. 160.

53. It is not altogether clear whether Luke regards the band of professional mourners, present at 8.52, as already in the house, as is the case in Mark (5.40).

54. Luke modifies Mark's συνακολουθῆσαι (Mk 5.37) to εἰσελθεῖν (Lk. 8.51).

55. Nolland, *Luke 1–9.20*, p. 422.

56. With the use of διέταξεν ('he ordered'), the Lukan Jesus is more insistent on hospitality than the Markan (εἶπεν, 5.43).

57. The parallel here to the healing of Simon's mother-in-law consists of the same temporal element (παραχρῆμα), a raising up of one who is sick (ἀνίστημι), and a subsequent meal (cf. 4.39; 8.55).

58. Luke's presentation includes a double stress on the power of Jesus' word—in the act of healing (ἐφώνησεν, 8.54) and in the act of hospitality (διέταξεν, 8.55).

59. Both Luke and Mark (5.23) attach an explicit salvific theme to Jesus' actions in the house of the synagogue official.

Dining in the House

The Gospel of Luke features three occasions when Jesus entered the house of a Pharisee to dine (7.36-50; 11.37-54; 14.1-24). On each occasion Jesus is present at the invitation of his Pharisaic host (7.36; 11.37; 14.12). The preponderance of these stories suggests it was customary for Jesus to dine with Pharisees.[60] Each reflects in some way a distinctively Lukan interest or setting, adding deeper dimensions to the narrator's presentation of the household ministry of Jesus.

a. *The House of Simon the Pharisee (7.36-50).* In the first story, Jesus enters the house of Simon the Pharisee for the purpose of dining with him (7.36). Jesus' act of reclining at table in v. 36b (κατεκλίθη) is suggestive of a rather elaborate occasion since normally this word was reserved for festive banquets in ancient Palestine.[61] Such an expensive dinner would indicate something of Simon's economic position as host.[62]

The similarities of this story with those in the other Synoptics (Mt. 26.6-13; Mk 14.3-9) and John (12.1-8) are well-known.[63] In Luke's version the actions of Simon are perplexing, since he invites Jesus to enter his home but fails to show him the finer gestures of hospitality. The appearance of a woman who is a sinner (ἁμαρτωλός, 7.37, 39), however, serves to offset this oversight since she extends to Jesus those gestures that Simon has overlooked (7.37b-38). By allowing public contact with this sinful woman, 'Jesus becomes unclean in the eyes of his host'.[64] Such hospitable actions on the part of the woman not only recall Jesus' association with sinners in the immediate context of the

60. On Jesus' meals with Pharisees as constituting a Lukan type-scene, see McMahan, 'Meals as Type-Scenes', pp. 160-211. That Luke can work within the elements of one type-scene in the process of forming another is indicative of his literary sophistication.

61. See Fitzmyer, *The Gospel According to Luke I–IX*, p. 688.

62. That Simon owned a spacious home, capable of housing a large number of guests, is evident in the way that a woman of notorious reputation could enter in (7.37), apparently unnoticed in the crowd.

63. See the standard commentaries for an analysis of the problem. Form-critically assessed, Luke's story of the sinful woman consists of both pronouncement story and parable (see Fitzmyer, *The Gospel According to Luke I–IX*, p. 684).

64. Bruce J. Malina and Richard L. Rohrbaugh, *Social-Science Commentary on the Synoptic Gospels* (Minneapolis: Fortress Press, 1992), p. 331.

story ('a friend of tax-gatherers and sinners', 7.34), but compel Jesus to recall his entry into Simon's home:

> And after turning toward the woman, he said to Simon, 'Do you see this woman? I entered [εἰσῆλθόν] your house; you gave me no water for my feet, but she bathed my feet with her tears and dried them with her hair' (7.44).
>
> 'You gave me no kiss, but from the time I entered [εἰσῆλθον] she has not ceased kissing my feet' (7.45).

The latter verse is particularly striking since it is the woman's entry, not that of Jesus, that best suits the context of the passage.[65]

Jesus' references to the woman's heart-felt actions above, coupled with the Parable of the Two Debtors that forms part of Jesus' response to Simon (7.40-43), suggest that the woman experienced forgiveness *prior* to her appearance in Simon's house; 'her ministrations to Jesus...seem to be a consequence rather than a cause of pardon'.[66] While this omission in the story may provide an example of a 'textual gap' that the reader must fill,[67] the two-fold stress on the entry motif calls attention to the house as the place where the woman's forgiveness is both hospitably expressed and proclaimed. The woman enters the hostile space of a Pharisee's house, but even he cannot prevent his house from becoming the venue for the 'cleansing' of despised sinners and outcasts.[68] Jesus concludes his encounter with the woman by declaring: 'Your faith has saved you; go in peace' (7.50). The woman thus leaves the house with the peace (εἰρήνη) bestowed on her by the messenger to the house.[69]

65. Some minor variants read εἰσῆλθεν ('she entered') instead of εἰσῆλθον ('I entered') at 7.45, reflecting the tension.

66. Noted by John A. Darr, *On Character Building: The Reader and the Rhetoric of Characterization in Luke–Acts* (Louisville: Westminster Press/John Knox, 1992), p. 19.

67. Darr, *On Character Building*, pp. 17-20.

68. Tannehill notes that 'the Pharisee was the person of status in the community and was presumably in control of events in his own house. The woman was a despised sinner in the town, who had made herself especially vulnerable by her presence and behavior in the Pharisee's house' (*The Narrative Unity of Luke–Acts*, I, p. 117).

69. The same 'peace' proclaimed by the Seventy-two (10.5)! This concluding statement by Jesus directly links the dual themes of salvation and peace. While 'go in peace' is a common dismissal in the Old Testament (1 Sam. 1.17; 20.42; 29.7), Luke no doubt invests peace here with salvific significance, as evidenced elsewhere in his

b. *The House of the Unnamed Pharisee (11.37-54)*. The second dinner scene involving Jesus and a Pharisee occurs, like the first, in response to an invitation. After Jesus had finished speaking, he 'entered' (εἰσελθὼν) and 'reclined' (ἀνέπεσεν) at the table of an unnamed Pharisee (11.37). The series of woes[70] directed against the Pharisees (vv. 42-44) and their lawyers (vv. 46-52) is instigated on this occasion[71] by a notable break with Pharisaic protocol: Jesus does not first ceremonially wash before the meal (v. 38)! As on the previous occasion in a Pharisee's home, ritual distinctions between clean and unclean become the subject of 'table talk' during the course of a meal.[72] How could Jesus, as the 'Teacher' of Israel (cf. 11.45), ignore such distinctions?[73]

The response of Jesus to his Pharisaic host is as sharp as it is striking: the Pharisees, Jesus declares, 'clean' (καθαρίζετε) the outside of the cup and of the platter but disregard the important matters of internal purity (11.39-40); if they give 'the things inside' (τὰ ἐνόντα) as alms, then 'all things' (πάντα) are 'clean' (καθαρὰ) for them (11.41). While

writings (Lk. 8.48; 10.5; Acts 10.36). See Fitzmyer, *The Gospel According to Luke I–IX*, pp. 224-25.

70. Craddock observes how Luke, in contrast to Matthew who places much of the 'woe' material during the interrogations at Jerusalem near the close of Jesus' ministry (23.1-36), reserves Jesus' rebuke for 'the home of a Pharisee where Jesus is dinner guest' (*Luke*, p. 156).

71. 'The teachings which follow, and which include a collection of sayings against the Pharisees, are placed in the setting of a meal and, by means of this literary device, are tied together' (Smith, 'Table Fellowship as a Literary Motif', p. 623; on the presence of the symposium tradition here, see below, n. 72). The teaching of Jesus forms part of the table-fellowship matrix in Luke's Gospel (so Just, *The Ongoing Feast*, p. 89 n. 15). Both here (11.45) and in the previous instance of dining with a Pharisee (7.40) Jesus is addressed as 'Teacher', offering an apt description of Jesus' actions on both occasions.

72. Luke alone places the events of 11.37-41 in the house of a Pharisee (cf. Mk 7.17-23; noted by Smith, 'Table Fellowship as a Literary Motif', p. 623). Smith sees in 11.37-54 as a whole a reflection of the symposium tradition, evident elsewhere in Luke (7.36-50; 14.1-24). The symposium, he says, 'was the second course of the traditional banquet, or drinking party that followed the meal proper. It was during the drinking party that the entertainment of the evening was traditionally presented. In the philosophical tradition, this tended to consist of elevated conversation on a topic of interest to all in the group' (p. 614).

73. David L. Tiede, *Luke* (ACNT; Minneapolis: Augsburg, 1988), p. 222.

the meaning of τὰ ἐνόντα here is ambiguous,[74] it is perhaps best to take the expression as an accusative of direct object, referring to what is inside the vessels; when the Pharisees give their food 'as alms' (ἐλεημοσύνην), all things become clean.[75] Seen in this way, 'almsgiving takes on a new importance through its relationship to purity'.[76]

This disregard for Jewish purity concerns, apparent earlier in Jesus' charge to the Seventy-two (Lk. 10.5a, 7), anticipates the events transpiring in the house of Cornelius, a righteous but unclean Gentile who is unfit for table-fellowship with Jews (Acts 11.3).[77] Commensurate with Jesus' declaration in the house of the unnamed Pharisee is the fact that Cornelius appears as a generous giver of alms (ποιῶν ἐλεημοσύνας πολλὰς τῷ λαῷ, 10.2), of which even God takes notice (10.4)! The cleansing of Cornelius, therefore, illustrates a new kind of 'purity' consisting of a proper attitude toward wealth (10.15, 28).[78]

Jesus' departure from the house occasions a stern reaction from the scribes and Pharisees: 'And after leaving there, the scribes and the Pharisees began to be exceedingly hostile and to question him closely concerning many things, lying in wait to catch him in something he might say' (11.53-54).[79] This development reveals a 'new level of opposition to Jesus on the part of the Jewish authorities.[80] In Luke, Jesus

74. See the possibilities in William F. Arndt, *The Gospel According to St Luke* (Saint Louis: Concordia Publishing House, 1956), pp. 306-307.

75. Most recently, Robert H. Stein, *Luke* (NAC; Nashville: Broadman Press, 1992), p. 340.

76. Halvor Moxnes, *The Economy of the Kingdom: Social Conflict and Economic Relations in Luke's Gospel* (Philadelphia: Fortress Press, 1988), p. 121. Moxnes notes that the transformation of purity here, from a ritual concept to a concept of societal solidarity expressed in and through almsgiving, means a break with first-century Jewish society's structures and boundaries (p. 121).

77. Moxnes, *The Economy of the Kingdom*, pp. 121-22. It seems that Lukan scholarship has not fully recognized the importance of Lk. 11.41 as an anticipation of Peter's vision in Acts declaring all foods clean (10.12, 15).

78. Cf. Moxnes: 'The demand for purity was not set aside. It was merely qualified in a new way' (*The Economy of the Kingdom*, p. 122).

79. Entry into (11.37) and departure out of (11.53) the house thus 'bracket' the story, providing a rare depiction of Jesus' physical movement in this section of Luke's Gospel (cf. Fitzmyer, *The Gospel According to Luke X–XXIV*, p. 951).

80. Tannehill, *The Narrative Unity of Luke–Acts*, I, p. 180. He notes the use of ἤρξαντο ('they began') in 11.53 with present infinitives of continuous or repeated action, suggesting that 'this heightened opposition begins at this point and will

indeed will get himself crucified by the way he eats.[81] The next time Jesus enters the house of a Pharisee to eat, they watch him closely for the purpose of trapping him (14.1).

c. *The House of the Prominent Pharisee (14.1-24)*

The narrator reserves the third and final act of Jesus' entry into the house of a Pharisee for the festive occasion recorded at 14.1. The reference to a host in v. 12 indicates that Jesus is once again the recipient of Pharisaic invitation, this time by a leader (ἄρχων) of the Pharisees.[82] By now the reader recognizes Jesus' invitation to enter the home of influential Pharisees as a 'stock situation' in Luke's Gospel.[83]

The rather benign character of the two previous invitations is, not surprisingly, absent here from the third. The Pharisees invite Jesus to dinner for the expressed purpose of watching him (14.1b).[84] The close scrutiny exhibited on this occasion, according to Tannehill, should 'be understood as the continuation of the sharpened opposition reported in 11.53-54'.[85] This connection between the two episodes reveals the sophistication of a narrator who is consciously aware of prior turning-points in the story.[86]

The healing of the man with dropsy in the house of a leading Pharisee, taking place on a Sabbath day (14.1-6), becomes the immediate occasion for three table discourses of Jesus, each of which treats the theme of

continue' (p. 180). David P. Moessner calls 11.37-54 the 'climax to this watershed of rejection in the Central Section' of the Gospel (*Lord of the Banquet: The Literary and Theological Significance of the Lukan Travel Narrative* [Minneapolis: Fortress Press, 1989], p. 197), noting the use of the three aorist verbs in 11.52 (ἤρατε, εἰσήλθατε, ἐκωλύσατε) to describe 'a definitive influence which at this stage in the plot is portrayed as irrevocable' (p. 255 n. 408).

81. Robert J. Karris, *Luke: Artist and Theologian* (New York: Paulist Press, 1985), p. 47.

82. The precise meaning of this term in 14.1 is not certain. Marshall points to three possibilities: rulers who belonged to the Pharisaic party (cf. Jn 3.1); rulers of the synagogues (cf. Lk. 8.41); or, leading rulers among the Pharisees (*The Gospel of Luke*, p. 578).

83. Tannehill, *The Narrative Unity of Luke–Acts*, I, p. 180.

84. In view of the events of 11.53-54, one must consider the likelihood of a 'set up' to see if Jesus will violate rules of purity or Sabbath observance.

85. Tannehill, *The Narrative Unity of Luke–Acts*, I, pp. 182-83.

86. Tannehill, *The Narrative Unity of Luke–Acts*, I, p. 183; *contra* Fitzmyer: 'The Lucan Jesus seems to be unaware of what was recorded in 11.53-54' (*The Gospel According to Luke X–XXIV*, p. 1040).

invitation to dinner.[87] If previously the Pharisees criticize Jesus for the way he eats, he now criticizes them for the way they eat.[88] The first discourse addresses the practice of invited guests who seek out places of honor (14.7-11). The second challenges a self-serving host who, in inviting his rich friends and neighbors to dinner, expects recompense in return (14.12-14). The third discourse contains the Parable of the Great Banquet in which a householder throws open the hospitality of his house to those persons on the highways and byways of society's margins (14.15-24). This last discourse is significant for the way the house becomes the sphere of universal salvation expressed in table-fellowship: 'Go out into the highways and along the hedges, and compel them to come in, that my house may be filled' (v. 23, NASB). Bo Reicke is doubtless correct in seeing here an anticipation of the gentile mission in Acts.[89] The 'two-stage' program of mission observable in vv. 21-23 makes this connection all the more probable.[90] Thus, even the Gentiles form part of the 'whoever' (ὅστις) that 'shall eat bread in the kingdom of God' (14.15).[91]

Teaching in the House

The preceding stories of Jesus' dining in the house of Pharisees all result in an occasion for his teaching. This combination of meal and instruction

87. Note the common use of καλέω in these sections: 14.7, 8[2×], 9, 10[2×], 12[2×], 13, 16, 17, 24. On the 'symposium' character of this story, see the article by Smith, 'Table Fellowship as a Literary Motif'.

88. As Tannehill observes, each of these discourses presupposes persons of wealth and substance who naturally expect to receive and extend such invitations: 'The scribes and Pharisees whom Jesus meets at dinner parties are understood to be persons of wealth who need instruction in their social responsibility for the poor' (Tannehill, *The Narrative Unity of Luke–Acts*, I, p. 183).

89. Bo Reicke, *The Gospel of Luke* (Richmond: John Knox, 1962), p. 81.

90. Cf. Dillon: 'The "great banquet" parable, which climaxes the dominical instruction in the meal scene of Lk. 14, becomes in its Lucan version an allegory of the two-stage Christian *mission*: to the despised and disinherited of Judaism, then to the Gentile outsiders' (*From Eye-Witnesses to Ministers of the Word*, p. 202, emphasis Dillon). On differing possibilities for interpreting the two groups represented in the parable, see Marshall, *The Gospel of Luke*, pp. 584-87.

91. In the parable one thus sees a reflection of Jesus' own table-fellowship practice with tax-collectors and sinners. The emphasis is not so much 'on the refusal of the guests to come, but on the readiness of the host to fill the table' (paraphrasing F. Hahn, Marshall, *The Gospel of Luke*, p. 585).

represents a distinctive feature of Luke and Acts.[92] In the story of the two sisters, Mary and Martha, this same combination of word and meal appears, emphasizing the essential connection between the two.

Mary and Martha (10.38-42). The opening verse poses great thematic significant for Luke, linking the Jerusalem journey motif to the household mission of Jesus. It was while 'they were going along' that Martha welcomed Jesus into her home (10.38). This reference to travel recalls the start of the journey at 9.51-53, presenting Jesus as the wayfaring messenger to the house. The twin acts of entering (εἰσῆλθεν) the village and being welcomed (ὑπεδέξατο αὐτόν) into Martha's house[93] suggest that they are inseparable for Luke. Entering the village is, in this instance, tantamount to entering the house.[94]

Once inside the house, Jesus begins to teach. Mary, the sister of Martha, 'was listening [ἤκουεν] to his word', seated at Jesus' feet (10.39). By assuming this posture, Mary was assuming the role of rabbinical disciple, a position traditionally restricted to men.[95] Jesus' gentle rebuke of Martha's request for help (10.40-42) indicates that Jesus accepted Mary's act of discipleship, breaking down the barrier of gender.[96] The 'one thing' needful is for Martha, like her sister, to listen

92. Tannehill, *The Narrative Unity of Luke–Acts*, I, pp. 290-91. See also Via, 'Women and the Early Christian Ritual Meal', pp. 51-52, who sees the combination of teaching and meal as theologically significant in Luke.

93. On the uncertain reading εἰς τὸν οἶκον αὐτῆς ('into her house'), see Bruce M. Metzger, *A Textual Commentary on the Greek New Testament* (New York: United Bible Societies, 1971), p. 153. The context of the passage, with its emphasis on hospitality in a familial setting (cf. ὑπεδέξατο, v. 38), clearly implies a household setting (cf. 19.6; Acts 17.7).

94. Of those instances in which Jesus expressly 'enters' a village or city on the pages of Luke's Gospel (7.1 [Capernaum]; 9.52; 17.12 [unnamed village]; 19.1 [Jericho]), only at 10.38 is the connection so close as to make them virtually one and the same.

95. Via, 'Women and the Early Christian Ritual Meal', p. 39.

96. R. Alan Culpepper cites *m. Abot* 1.4-5: 'Let thy house be a meeting-house for the Sages and sit amid the dust of their feet and drink in their words with thirst... [but] talk not much with womankind' (see his *The Gospel of Luke* [NIB; Nashville: Abingdon Press, forthcoming]). Culpepper himself comments: 'By sitting at Jesus' feet, Mary was acting like a male. She was neglecting her duty to assist her sister in the preparation of the meal, and by violating a clear social boundary she was bringing shame upon her house.' I wish to thank Professor Culpepper for allowing me to see an earlier draft of his commentary.

to the Lord's word (v. 42). Meal without word has no lasting affect.[97] In this way, Jesus anticipates the conversion of Lydia, a gentile woman whose heart is opened as she 'was listening' (ἤκουεν) to the word of Paul (Acts 16.14).[98]

Jesus Converts a Household: The Story of Zacchaeus (19.1-10)

The story of Zacchaeus, recounted in Lk. 19.1-10, has traditionally received little interest on the part of Lukan scholarship. As William P. Loewe remarks, 'Commentators give the pericope short shrift, clarifying this or that detail...before generalizing its meaning'.[99] When scholars do attend to the story in greater detail, they disagree over how to classify its literary form: is it biographical apophthegm (Bultmann), personal legend (Dibelius), a Story about Jesus (Taylor) or, more recently, a quest story (Tannehill)?[100]

Apart from these form-critical concerns, which so often fail to address the story's wider literary function, is there any other way to read the story of Zacchaeus that would unfold its meaning for Luke? One way of reading the story, I suggest, is to view it against the background of the mission of the Seventy-two.[101] In converting the household of Zacchaeus, Jesus is functioning in his proto-typical role as missionary to the house.

Conversion or Apologia?

The encounter with Zacchaeus occurs as Jesus 'was passing through' (διήρχετο) the city of Jericho (19.1; cf. διέρχεσθαι, v. 4). The theme of journey once again attends Jesus' mission to the house. The strategic placement of this story at the conclusion of the journey to Jerusalem

97. 'A *diakonia* [10.40] that bypasses the word is one that will never have lasting character; whereas listening to Jesus' word is the lasting "good" that will not be taken away from the listener' (Fitzmyer, *The Gospel According to Luke X–XXIV*, p. 892).

98. Lydia offers hospitality to Paul only *after* receiving the 'word' (Acts 16.15).

99. William P. Loewe, 'Towards an Interpretation of Lk. 19.1-10', *CBQ* 36 (1974), p. 321.

100. On the various attempts to classify the Zacchaeus story form-critically, see Robert F. O'Toole, 'The Literary Form of Luke 19.1-10', *JBL* 110 (1991), pp. 107-116.

101. See the table at the conclusion of this chapter to observe the remarkable parallels between the two accounts.

suggests that it is in some way definitive for Jesus' ministry on the pages of Luke.[102] David P. Moessner believes Zacchaeus 'represents that person for whom Jesus the Lord is sent on his journey and who receives this Lord as guest and Lord of the household when he comes'.[103]

The narrator introduces Zacchaeus with a succinct use of epithetical characterization (10.2). Most striking is Zacchaeus's identification as a 'chief tax-collector' (ἀρχιτελώνης), a term that appears only here in all of Greek literature.[104] Its close association with πλούσιος in the same verse suggests that Zacchaeus is 'rich' precisely on account of his occupation.[105] As one existing on the very periphery of Judaism, Zacchaeus is a proto-type of the Gentiles, who later become the object of the church's missionary concern.[106]

Because Zacchaeus was small in stature, he runs on ahead of Jesus and climbs up into a sycamore tree (19.4), for 'he was seeking [ἐζήτει] to see who Jesus was' (19.3). That Jesus sums up his own mission to Zacchaeus's house as coming 'to seek [ζητῆσαι] and to save the lost' (19.10), however, effectively turns this episode into a story of Jesus seeking Zacchaeus.[107] Jesus seizes the salvific initiative when he turns to the chief tax-collector and says: 'Zacchaeus, hurry and come down, for today I must stay [δεῖ με μεῖναι] in your house' (19.5). Zacchaeus responds by receiving Jesus gladly (ὑπεδέξατο, 19.6), a term Luke uses elsewhere to describe an act of hospitality (10.38; Acts 17.7). To stay

102. According to Just, 'Luke has located this story at the end of Jesus' journey to Jerusalem to bring to conclusion the themes of Jesus' Galilean ministry and travel account' (*The Ongoing Feast*, p. 185).

103. Moessner, *Lord of the Banquet*, p. 170.

104. LSJ, see 'ἀρχιτελώνης', p. 253.

105. The notorious dishonesty of tax-collectors is evident in John the Baptist's injunction to 'collect no more than the amount prescribed for you' (Lk. 3.13).

106. Argued by Jack T. Sanders, *The Jews in Luke–Acts* (Philadelphia: Fortress Press, 1987), pp. 207-208: 'It is among the outcasts, in the periphery, that Jesus finds appropriate response, and this periphery is to be the springboard to the Gentile mission.' See also his essay, 'The Jewish People in Luke–Acts', in Joseph B. Tyson, (ed.), *Luke–Acts and the Jewish People: Eight Critical Perspectives* (Minneapolis: Augsburg, 1988), pp. 51-75. 'He has gone [εἰσῆλθεν] to be the guest of one who is a sinner' (Lk. 19.7) foreshadows the charge levelled against Peter in Acts: 'You went [εἰσῆλθες] to uncircumcised men and ate with them' (11.3).

107. According to Tannehill, Jesus' statement of purpose at 19.10 'invites us to reread the story of Zacchaeus not as a story of Zacchaeus seeking Jesus but as a story of Jesus seeking Zacchaeus, since this is what "the Son of Man came" to do' (*The Narrative Unity of Luke–Acts*, I, p. 125).

in someone's house (μένω) implies that a meal would be eaten (cf. Lk. 10.7).[108] That Jesus 'must' (δεῖ) stay with Zacchaeus underscores the determinism resting behind Jesus' mission to the house.[109] Jesus' decision to stay in the home of a chief tax-collector prompts criticism on the part of the crowd: 'And when they saw this, they all began to complain, saying, "He has gone to lodge with a sinful man"' (19.7). Criticism of Jesus' eating habits on this particular occasion derives not from the 'Pharisees' per se but from 'all' (πάντες). Here καταλῦσαι ('to lodge') is synonymous with μεῖναι in v. 5 to suggest that Jesus 'is more than a guest at Zacchaeus' table, he is a guest in his home'.[110] Indeed, the complaint levelled against Jesus focuses attention on his very act of entry into the house: 'he has gone' (εἰσῆλθεν) to be the guest of a notorious sinner.

While in the house, Zacchaeus stood up from the table (σταθεὶς) and announced: 'Look, half of my possessions, Lord, I will give [δίδωμι] to the poor; and if I have cheated anyone out of anything, I will pay back [ἀποδίδωμι] four times as much' (19.8). The problem for commentators is how to understand the meaning of δίδωμι and ἀποδίδωμι here, both of which appear in the Greek text of Luke in the present tense. As futuristic presents, these verbs suggest that Zacchaeus is now rejecting his unjust practices of the past and converting to a new way of life; as iterative presents, they portray a Zacchaeus who defends himself against unjust charges by appealing to past exemplary conduct. That the noted grammarian A.T. Robertson could discuss these verbs under both classifications reflects his own ambiguity on the issue.[111]

108. Just, *The Ongoing Feast*, p. 188. Jesus' stay in the house of Zacchaeus recalls the meal ('eating and drinking') that Jesus shares in the house of the tax-collector Levi (5.29-32). So Smith, 'Table Fellowship as a Literary Motif', p. 636.

109. The theological import this term carries for Luke is well-known. Whereas previous studies stress the note of divine providence, Charles Cosgrove also insists on the human side of its accomplishment. He notes that 'Jesus is no passive pawn of divine necessity in Luke's Gospel; he is executor of that necessity' ('The Divine ΔΕΙ in Luke–Acts: Investigations into the Lukan Understanding of God's Providence', *NovT* 26 [1984], p. 169). Cosgrove's comments on the δεῖ of Lk. 19.5 are likewise instructive: 'Jesus determines that he must stay at Zacchaeus' house in order to fulfill an aspect of the mission: "The Son of Man came to seek and save the lost" (19.10)' (p. 175).

110. McMahan, 'Meals as Type-Scenes in the Gospel of Luke', p. 134 n. 65.

111. A.T. Robertson, *A Grammar of the Greek New Testament in the Light of Historical Research* (New York: C.H. Doran, 1914), pp. 869-70, 880. On the use of

This latter view finds able exposition in the commentary of Joseph A. Fitzmyer and, more recently, in an insightful article by Alan C. Mitchell. Both argue that Jesus brings vindication, rather than conversion, to Zacchaeus.[112] This view finds a further proponent in Richard C. White who, in subjecting the Zacchaeus story to a form-critical analysis, deems it deficient as a Lukan salvation story.[113] Among other things, the story lacks an expressed reference to Zacchaeus's contrition as well as to his faith and subsequent forgiveness. Yet White's conclusions have themselves been questioned on form-critical grounds.[114]

A majority of Lukan scholars has supported the first view above by reading δίδωμι and ἀποδίδωμι as futuristic presents, thus regarding the episode as the conversion of a chief tax-collector.[115] It is difficult, for example, to envision the giving away of half of one's possessions as anything more than a one-time act.[116] Moreover, Zacchaeus's address of Jesus as κύριος most likely signals his reception of the 'Lord' of the house.[117] Even more determinative is the pronouncement of Jesus at the conclusion of the pericope: 'For the Son of Man came to seek out and to save the lost' (v. 10). Whatever the origins of this statement,[118] it serves in the context of the story to identify Zacchaeus as one of the

the futuristic present, see F. Blass and A. DeBrunner, *A Greek Grammar of the New Testament and Other Early Christian Literature* (trans. Robert W. Funk; Chicago: University of Chicago Press, 1961), p. 167. The futuristic present appears in 'confident assertions regarding the future' (p. 168). See Mt. 11.3; 24.43; Mk 14.1; Lk. 12.54-55; 14.19; Jn 8.14.

112. See Fitzmyer, *The Gospel According to Luke X–XXIV*, pp. 1220-221. Alan C. Mitchell, 'Zacchaeus Revisited: Luke 19.8 as a Defense', *Bib* 71 (1990), pp. 153-76.

113. Richard C. White, 'Vindication for Zacchaeus?', *ExpTim* 91 (1979–80), p. 21. White hypothesizes the existence of a Lukan salvation story against which he measures the Zacchaeus episode.

114. See Dennis Hamm, 'Luke 19.8 Once Again: Does Zacchaeus Defend or Resolve?', *JBL* 107 (1988), pp. 431-37, esp. p. 434.

115. So Marshall, Ellis, Creed, Plummer, Schmid.

116. For proponents of the 'defense' theory, 'it becomes almost imperative to translate τῶν ὑπαρχόντων at 19.8 as "income", whereas its normal meaning is "possessions", "property", "means", "capital"' (Nigel M. Watson, 'Was Zacchaeus Really Reforming?', *ExpTim* 77 [1965–66], p. 282).

117. Moessner, *Lord of the Banquet*, p. 169.

118. See Rudolf Bultmann, *The History of the Synoptic Tradition* (trans. John Marsh; New York: Harper & Row, 1963), p. 155, who considers it a Hellenistic product and hence a 'late formulation'.

'lost' whom Jesus came to save.[119] These considerations make it likely that the story of Zacchaeus is in fact a story of conversion.

Household Salvation

Lending support to this view is a critical piece of evidence overlooked by most commentators, namely, the corporate character of Zacchaeus's conversion. Jesus responds to Zacchaeus's appeal by declaring that 'today salvation has come to this household [τῷ οἴκῳ τούτῳ]' (19.9)! Marshall regards this reference to Zacchaeus's household as 'surprising', correctly perceiving its linkage to the household salvation stories in Acts (10.2; 11.14; 16.15, 31; 18.8).[120] The story of Zacchaeus recounts not only a conversion but a particular kind of conversion—the bestowal of salvation to the personified οἶκος by the Lukan Jesus.[121]

Jesus' declaration to Zacchaeus highlights the sphere of the house as the place for the restoration and cleansing of 'sinners'. The repetitive use of the temporal element 'today' (σήμερον) makes this connection clear: 'today' salvation comes to Zacchaeus (19.9) because 'today' Jesus has stayed in Zacchaeus's house (19.5).[122] 'To have Jesus as one's guest', notes Robert F. O'Toole, 'is to be host to salvation.'[123]

The basis for the salvation of Zacchaeus's household appears in the second half of Jesus' declaration: 'because he, too, is a son of Abraham' (19.9b). The close connection between αὐτός here and οἶκος in the first half of the sentence illustrates the strong sense of familial solidarity in the ancient world. The 'household' receives salvation because 'he' (= Zacchaeus) is a son Abraham, that is, one who brings forth works in keeping with repentance (cf. Lk. 3.8).[124] This phenomenon becomes

119. As Watson observes, these words 'clearly imply that Zacchaeus is one of the lost sheep of the house of Israel whom the Son of Man has come to save' ('Was Zacchaeus Really Reforming?' p. 283).

120. Marshall, *The Gospel of Luke*, p. 698.

121. The mention of Zacchaeus's household indicates that 'the whole family of Zacchaeus turned to God in true repentance... Thus Jesus Himself, as later the Apostles, could behold the spread of the Good News through association provided in family life' (Arndt, *The Gospel According to St Luke*, p. 390).

122. The appearance of σήμερον elsewhere in Luke signifies the immediacy of the saving act (2.11; 5.26; 13.32-33; 23.43; 24.21).

123. O'Toole, 'The Literary Form of Luke 19.1-10', p. 110. A similar salvific 'embodiment' motif occurs in the story of the aged Simeon, who sees the σωτήριον of God as he beholds the infant Jesus in his arms (Lk. 2.28-30).

124. Cf. Loewe: 'Repentance replaces physical descent as the criterion' for relation

readily observable in Acts when entire households convert to the Christian faith on the basis of the faith of the householder.[125] As Frederick W. Danker observes of Zacchaeus, 'His entire household is the beneficiary...[W]ith him they were implicated in his guilt...and with him they share the benefits of the Kingdom.'[126] As a true 'son of Abraham', Zacchaeus becomes a true 'son of peace' by virtue of his hospitable reception of Jesus in the house (cf. Lk. 10.6).[127]

The story of Zacchaeus furnishes the only synoptic account of a conversion of a household. Its strategic placement in Luke suggests that the narrator regards this story as the climactic fulfillment of Jesus' journey to Jerusalem. A mission that begins with the sending of the Seventy-two to the houses and cities of Israel (10.1-16) concludes with Jesus' conversion of a household in the city of Jericho (19.1-10). Like the messengers whom he himself sends, Jesus converts a household by entering and staying in the house of a proto-typical Gentile. Though the poetic sequence of these actions varies,[128] the Zacchaeus account succeeds in showing how Jesus enacts his own pattern of mission to households.

Jesus Stays in the House

The third element of the household missionary pattern receiving unique expression in Luke's Gospel is the motif of staying in a house. Comparison with the Gospels of Matthew and Mark reveals Luke's special interest in μένω (and compounds) to denote acts of hospitality.[129]

to Abraham ('Towards an Interpretation of Luke 19.1-10', p. 326). See also Ellis, *The Gospel of Luke*, pp. 220-21.

125. Particularly in the story of the Roman jailer, who rejoices with all his household (πανοικεὶ) because *he* believed in God (πεπιστευκὼς, 16.34)!

126. Danker, *Jesus and the New Age*, p. 306.

127. See also Moessner, *Lord of the Banquet*, p. 124.

128. On the difference between poetic and referential sequencing, see Norman R. Petersen, *Rediscovering Paul: Philemon and the Sociology of Paul's Narrative World* (Philadelphia: Fortress Press, 1985), pp. 43-53. Poetic sequence, according to Petersen, is the order of events as it appears in the narrative itself; referential action refers to the actual chronological order of events (p. 48).

129. Matthew employs μένω once for hospitality in a house (10.11) and Mark similarly once (6.10); Luke, by contrast, uses the term in this way seven times in his Gospel (1.56; 8.27; 9.4; 10.7; 19.5; 24.29[2×]) and ten times in Acts (9.43; 16.15; 18.3, 20; 20.5, 15; 21.7-8; 28.16, 30). Luke also is fond of the related compound ἐπιμένω in Acts (10.48; 15.34; 21.4, 10; 28.12, 14).

Besides the key appearance of this term in the story of Zacchaeus, time spent in a house constitutes a significant theme in the encounter of the risen Jesus with the disciples on the road to Emmaus (24.13-35), a story peculiar to the Third Evangelist. Here taking up residence in a house is no ordinary act; the house becomes the distinctive setting for the recognition of Jesus as the risen Christ.

Breaking Bread: Table Fellowship at Emmaus (24.13-35)

Luke 24 records two appearances of the risen Jesus, one to the disciples on the road to Emmaus (vv. 13-35) and the other to the band of disciples gathered in Jerusalem (vv. 36-43). Of the two, the Emmaus narrative clearly functions as the climax of the Third Gospel, bringing to fulfillment the theme of Jesus' table-fellowship with his disciples as a manifestation of the eschatological kingdom.[130] That Jesus appears to 'two' disciples on the road to Emmaus ('two of them', 24.13) has led some to identify these disciples as members of the Seventy-two, who likewise travel 'two by two' (10.1).[131]

The story of Jesus' appearance to the disciples on the road to Emmaus reflects considerable literary artistry. Part of the author's skill is manifest in the way the road and the house function as places of divine disclosure. The narrative begins with two disciples journeying on the road to Emmaus during which the mysterious stranger opens up the scriptures (24.13-27; cf. v. 32). It concludes with the journey of the disciples back to Jerusalem after their recognition of Jesus in the breaking of bread (24.28-35). In the course of the story, these two settings, a public road and a private home, converge to form 'closely connected parts of a single sequence of events'.[132] The recapitulation of events at 24.35 makes this convergence clear: 'Then they told what had happened

130. See, most recently, Just, *The Ongoing Feast.* Just believes the Emmaus account of Lk. 24 provides the key to reading the entire Gospel: 'If one sees the Emmaus meal as the climax of Luke's Gospel, then it is possible to recognize *at the end* that the table fellowship of Jesus with his people was *from the first* a manifestation of the eschatological kingdom' (p. 2).

131. Dillon says that 'it may not be inappropriate to consider the travelers to Emmaus representatives of the "Seventy-two", thus participants in the proleptic world-mission of Luke 10...' (*From Eye-Witnesses to Ministers of the Word*, p. 277). Just notes that this interpretation was common among the early Church Fathers (Just, *The Ongoing Feast*, p. 34 n. 2).

132. Tannehill, *The Narrative Unity of Luke–Acts*, I, p. 290.

on the road, and how he had been made known to them in the breaking of the bread' (NRSV).

In this fascinating portrayal of divine encounter, the Lukan Jesus once again appears in his role as proto-typical missionary to the house. Three missional motifs underscore this presentation. The first is the theme of travel, which figures prominently in the narrative. The disciples are going to Emmaus, about seven miles from Jerusalem (24.13), when the risen Jesus begins traveling with them (24.15). Jesus asks them specifically what they are talking about as they are 'walking' (24.17). Together, they approach the village where they are going (24.28a), though Jesus acts as if he intends to go farther (24.28b). Later, after their eyes are opened, the two disciples reflect on their experience with Jesus 'on the road' (24.32) and subsequently relate this experience 'on the road' to the disciples in Jerusalem (24.35). Whatever else this journey theme may convey,[133] it certainly presents a peripatetic Christ who journeys to open the eyes of the blind.

Alongside this travel motif is the theme of Jesus the teacher/missionary. Hans Dieter Betz notices how in the course of the narrative the role of Jesus shifts, from one instructed by the disciples (24.19b-24) to one who instructs them (24.25-27).[134] Jesus' instruction on the road takes the form of an inspired Scripture theology that interprets the prophetic scriptures of himself and of his death (v. 27; cf. vv. 44-46). 'The Lucan Christ catechizes the disciples,' observes Fitzmyer, 'setting their hearts afire with his interpretation of OT Scriptures.'[135]

The third motif directly links the Emmaus account to the mission to households. When Jesus pretended to go farther, the disciples 'urged him strongly, saying, "Stay [μεῖνον] with us..." So he entered [εἰσῆλθεν] to stay [τοῦ μεῖναι] with them' (24.29). 'Entering' and 'staying' are distinctive vocabulary recalling the protocol of the Seventy-two (10.5, 7). Though the express mention of a house οἶκος/οἰκία) is

133. On the theme of travel, see Robert J. Karris, 'Luke 24.13-35', *Int* 41 (1987), pp. 57-58; B.P. Robinson, 'The Place of the Emmaus Story in Luke–Acts', *NTS* 30 (1984), pp. 482-83.

134. Hans Dieter Betz, 'The Origin and Nature of Christian Faith According to the Emmaus Legend (Luke 24.13-32)', *Int* 23 (1969), p. 40. He comments: 'In the first phase of the discussion on the road to Emmaus he is the one who raises questions; in the further course of the discussion he more and more becomes the one who teaches and uncovers ignorance and unbelief on the part of the disciples.'

135. Fitzmyer, *The Gospel According to Luke X–XXIV*, p. 1558.

lacking at 24.29, constituting a narrative 'gap',[136] Luke's language practically demands it.[137] Both Fitzmyer and Eduard Schweizer, for example, suppose that Jesus entered a house belonging to one of the disciples.[138]

The importance of the house as the setting for Jesus' revelatory activity is underscored by the two appearances of μένω at Lk. 24.29. Both function rhetorically to emphasize the domestic flavor of the account. The first, which appears in the imperative mood, occurs on the lips of the two disciples when they say to Jesus: 'stay [μεῖνον] with us'. The command is ironic. Previously Jesus commanded his disciples to 'stay' in the house (10.7); now they command him.[139] The second use of μένω occurs in an articular infinitive construction expressing purpose: Jesus enters the house for the purpose of staying there (εἰσῆλθεν τοῦ μεῖναι σὺν αὐτοῖς).[140] This infinitive of purpose underscores 'Jesus' intent to be present with the disciples at the meal at Emmaus. This was for him the ultimate reason for journeying with them.'[141]

While reclining at table in the house, Jesus 'took the bread, blessed

136. For a recent treatment of narrative gaps in Luke's writings, see William S. Kurz, *Reading Luke–Acts: Dynamics of Biblical Narrative* (Louisville: Westminster Press/John Knox, 1993), pp. 17-36.

137. In situations of hospitality, εἰσέρχομαι is usually expressly associated with a house in the immediate or larger context (1.40; 4.38; 7.6, 36; 8.41, 51; 10.7, 38; [14.1]; Acts 1.13; 9.11-12, 17; 10.3, 25, 27; 11.3, 12; 16.15, 40; 18.7; 20.29; 21.8). Likewise, μένω and compounds: Lk. 1.56; 8.27; 10.7; 19.5; Acts 9.43; 16.15; 21.7-8; [28.16, 30]. These textual considerations help the implied reader to fill in the 'gap' correctly.

138. Fitzmyer, *The Gospel According to Luke X–XXIV*, p. 1567; Eduard Schweizer, *The Good News According to Luke*, p. 371. Just also locates the Emmaus meal in the home of the two disciples (*The Ongoing Feast*, p. 69 n. 1). Even more emphatic is Leon Morris, who believes it 'scarcely' possible that some other structure, such as an inn, is in view (*The Gospel According to St Luke*, p. 339).

139. By 'pretending to go farther' (24.28b), Jesus invites the imperative response on the part of the disciples (see Marshall, *The Gospel of Luke*, p. 897). Fitzmyer calls this action a 'literary foil' encouraging the disciples to 'react out of a motive of hospitality for a stranger' (*The Gospel According to St. Luke X–XXIV*, p. 1567).

140. 'The wanderer,' says Betz, 'accepts the invitation and enters into the house with them, "in order to remain with them" as the words mysteriously read' ('The Origin and Nature of Christian Faith', p. 37). In light of Jesus' proto-typical mission, are the words so mysterious?

141. Just, *The Ongoing Feast*, pp. 222-23.

and broke it, and gave it to them' (24.30), actions that recall the celebration of the Last Supper in the upper room of a house in Jerusalem (22.10-11, 19). By means of these actions the role of Jesus shifts yet again, this time from being the guest of the disciples to being their host.[142] The immediate result is clearly a moment of revelation for the disciples: 'their eyes were opened, and they recognized him' (24.31). While this revelation actually begins on the road to Emmaus when Jesus 'opens up the Scriptures' (24.32b), reserving the dramatic moment of disclosure for the breaking of bread allows Jesus 'to combine the instruction he has given the two disciples with the sharing of table fellowship'.[143] Teaching and table-fellowship often form two parts of the same act for Luke. Thus, the teaching that begins on the road via the exposition of the Scriptures culminates in the house via the breaking of bread.

The uniquely Lukan phrase that denotes the meal on this occasion (τῇ κλάσει τοῦ ἄρτου, 24.35) suggests that the meal was no ordinary one. 'Breaking bread' is Luke's common designation in Acts for the celebration of the Eucharist (2.42, 46; 20.7; 27.35).[144] That Luke intends a eucharistic connotation here is apparent from the similarities at 24.30 and 22.19.[145] At the same time, the eschatological character of the Supper, as an anticipation of the future kingdom of God (22.16, 18, 30), is clearly present and may invest the Emmaus meal with similar significance. As B.P. Robinson argues, all meals involving Jesus and the disciples in Luke are proleptic celebrations of the future kingdom of God.[146]

142. On the significance of Jesus as host, see Robinson, 'The Place of the Emmaus Story in Luke–Acts', p. 486.

143. Jack Dean Kingsbury, *Conflict in Luke: Jesus, Authorities, Disciples* (Minneapolis: Fortress Press, 1991), p. 135.

144. This phrase does not appear in secular Greek literature except in the Paris magic papyri bearing Jewish Hellenistic and Christian influence (see Johannes Behm, 'κλάω', *TDNT*, III, p. 728). While the phrase denotes a simple meal in the Greek Old Testament (cf. Jer. 16.7; Lam. 4.4), Luke invests it with eucharistic significance (cf. 1 Cor. 10.16). In some of the later Christian writings, it becomes a technical designation for the Lord's Supper (*Did.* 14.1; Ign. *Eph.* 20.2).

145. The 'longer' reading of the Lukan Lord's Supper, which includes 22.19cd, is assumed here. See the extended discussion in Bruce M. Metzger, *A Textual Commentary on the Greek New Testament*, pp. 173-77.

146. See Robinson, 'The Place of the Emmaus Story in Luke–Acts', pp. 492-94, though he questions the eucharistic meaning of the meal at Emmaus. One who

Eating and Drinking

A concomitant feature of staying in a house, according to the protocol of Lk. 10.7, is the act of 'eating and drinking' that defines the messenger's stay there more clearly. A study of this motif in Luke's Gospel reveals once again a uniquely Lukan interest. Appearing only once in Mark (2.16) and three times in Matthew (11.18-19; 24.29), the phrase occurs regularly in Luke to describe the act of table-fellowship (5.30, 33; 7.33-34; 10.7; 12.45; 17.27-28; 22.30). At times Luke modifies the Markan tradition to include this precise phrasing in his account.[147] Three passages in Luke's Gospel particularly reveal the significance of the eating and drinking motif to the household ministry of Jesus.

a. *With Tax-Collectors and Sinners (7.33-34).* In response to the Pharisees and lawyers who rejected John's baptism for themselves, Jesus offers the following comparison at Lk. 7.33-34:

> For John the Baptist has come eating [ἐσθίων] no bread and drinking [πίνων] no wine, and you say, 'He has a demon'; the Son of Man has come eating and drinking [ἐσθίων καὶ πίνων], and you say, 'Look, a glutton and a drunkard, a friend of tax collectors and sinners' (NRSV).

In contrast to John, whose ministry was not characterized by 'eating and drinking', Jesus affirms its central role in his mission from God: the Son of Man 'has come' to eat and drink with tax collectors and sinners (cf. 5.27-32; 19.1-10).

A characteristic feature of Jesus' household mission in Luke, as seen at various points throughout this study, is its utter disregard for Jewish purity rules. By eating with the sinful and the unclean, the Lukan Jesus radically redefines the boundaries of the people of God. Craddock succeeds in putting the contrast between Jesus and John in its proper purity perspective:

> When, therefore, critics of John say that he eats with *no one* they are saying that he has removed himself from the covenant fellowship of God's people. When the critics say of Jesus that he eats with *anyone* they

develops the eschatological theme of the Emmaus narrative with great profit is Just in *The Ongoing Feast.* 'Eschatological fulfillment,' observes Tannehill, 'and specifically sharing in God's reign, is repeatedly pictured in terms of a festive meal in Luke' (*The Narrative Unity of Luke–Acts*, I, p. 218).

147. See, for example, 5.30, 33 where Luke adds his characteristic 'drinking'; noted by Via, 'Women and the Early Christian Ritual Meal', pp. 45-46.

> are saying that he violates the sacred distinctions as to who is and who is not within the covenant fellowship.[148]

The radical re-defining of the covenant community anticipated in Jesus' eating practices awaits its full implementation in the conversion of the household of Cornelius, which culminates in unbridled table-fellowship between Peter and the Gentiles (Acts 10.48; 11.3).

b. *In the House of Levi (5.29-32).* A second appearance of the 'eating and drinking' motif occurs in the story of Levi, a tax collector who throws a party for Jesus in his house (5.29-32). Luke clearly presents Jesus as staying in a house owned by Levi, clarifying Mark's ambiguity on the issue (Lk. 5.29).[149] This instance of eating with a tax-collector (τελώνης) no doubt foreshadows Jesus' hospitable stay in the house of Zacchaeus, an ἀρχιτελώνης. Moreover, in the Lukan account, the *disciples*, not Jesus, become the target of Pharisaic objectors: 'Why do you eat and drink [ἐσθίετε καὶ πίνετε] with tax collectors and sinners?' (5.30).[150] Since the Lukan principle is that every disciple 'will be like his teacher' (Lk. 6.40), the book of Acts will record a similar charge against Peter, an accredited messenger of Jesus who eats and drinks with unclean Gentiles in a house (11.3).

c. *At the Last Supper (22.14-38).* Perhaps the most striking instance of the 'eating and drinking' motif appears in the Last Supper discourse. Here, in a passage unique to the Third Evangelist, Jesus confers on the Twelve a kingdom 'just as my Father conferred on me a kingdom, in order that you might eat and drink [ἔσθητε καὶ πίνητε] at my table in my kingdom' (22.30). The passage distinctly recalls the words of Jesus given earlier during the celebration of supper:

> for I tell you, I will not eat [φάγω] it until it is fulfilled in the kingdom of God (22.16, NRSV).

148. Craddock, *Luke*, p. 101 (emphasis mine).

149. The αὐτοῦ in Mark's ἐν τῇ οἰκίᾳ αὐτοῦ (2.15a) is ambiguous. Elizabeth Struthers Malbon argues that the house in Mark's presentation actually belongs to *Jesus*, not Levi ('ΤΗ ΟΙΚΙΑ ΑΥΤΟΥ: Mk 2.15 in Context', *NTS* 31 [1985], pp. 282-92). She contends (pp. 283-84) that most commentators 'who identify "his house" at Mk 2.15 as Levi's house do so under the influence of the Lukan redaction (Lk. 5.29)'.

150. Both Mark (2.16) and Matthew (9.11) make Jesus the subject of the Pharisees' complaint.

> for I tell you that from now on I will not drink [πίω] of the fruit of the vine until the kingdom of God comes (22.18, NRSV).

That Luke intends these two statements to comprise yet another instance of Jesus' 'eating and drinking' in a house (cf. οἰκία, 22.11) is clear from the way they stand in parallel relationship to each other, possessing an identical ground of action ('for I tell you') and a common perspective toward the future rooted in the coming 'kingdom of God'.[151] This parallel suggests that the eating and drinking motif possesses eschatological significance for Luke. Tannehill observes how 22.30 'speaks of an eschatological meal which is a *messianic* meal, for Jesus speaks of the table as his table and the kingdom as his kingdom'.[152]

Conclusion

Part One of this book attempts to locate the origin of the pattern of household evangelizing in both the words and actions of Jesus, Luke's chief protagonist. If, on the pages of Luke, Jesus instructs his messengers to enter houses, bring salvation to households, and stay in houses for table-fellowship, it is because his own ministry enacts these elements at various points throughout the Gospel. This convergence of word and deed undergirds the pattern at the two levels of 'telling' and 'showing'. That all three elements coalesce in the sending of the Seventy-two to form a unified 'plot' of evangelistic activity owes to the literary creativity of the Third Evangelist, who, in investing the pattern with dominical authority and precedent, leaves an example for all accredited messengers to follow. In this way, Jesus 'goes before' those messengers in Acts who succeed in converting entire households to the messianic faith.

151. Fitzmyer, *The Gospel According to Luke X–XXIV*, p. 1389.
152. Tannehill, *The Narrative Unity of Luke–Acts*, I, p. 218 (emphasis his).

Luke 10	*Luke 19*
1) Jesus is called 'the Lord' (v. 1)	1) Jesus is called 'the Lord' (v. 8)
2) Messengers go to city; enter the city (vv. 1, 8, 10)	2) Jesus enters city of Jericho (v. 1)
3) Messengers come (ἔρχομαι) to the place (τόπος) (v. 1)	3) Jesus comes (ἔρχομαι) to the place (τόπος) (v. 5)
4) Jesus is about (ἤμελλεν) to come (v. 1)	Jesus is about (ἤμελλεν) to pass by (v. 4)
5) Messengers enter (εἰσέρχομαι) house indiscriminately (v. 5)	Jesus enters (εἰσέρχομαι) house of 'sinner' (v. 7)
6) Messengers extend salvific peace to household (οἶκος) (v. 5)	6) Jesus brings salvation to (οἶκος) (v. 9)
7) 'Son of peace' receives messengers of Jesus (v. 6)	7) 'Son of Abraham' receives Jesus (v. 9b)
8) Messengers stay (μένω) in house for hospitality indiscriminately (v. 7)	8) Jesus stays (μένω) in house of sinner (v. 5)

Table 1. *Verbal and Thematic Links between Zacchaeus and the Seventy-Two*

PART II

THE PATTERN IMPLEMENTED: HOUSEHOLD CONVERSIONS IN THE ACTS OF THE APOSTLES

Chapter 4

THE HOUSEHOLD CONVERSION OF CORNELIUS

Introduction

The first conversion of a household in the book of Acts is the story of Cornelius, the centurion at Caesarea (Acts 10.1–11.18). While nearly all commentators recognize the importance of Cornelius's conversion, which represents a decisive turning point in the narrative of Acts, few have appreciated sufficiently the corporate significance of the account: baptism of the first Gentile results in the baptism of a congregation.[1] The angel appearing in Cornelius's house instructs Cornelius to send for Peter, who 'will speak words to you by which you will be saved, you and all your household' (11.14).

That the salvation of households plays an important role in Acts is clear from the way the narrator[2] merges the inaugural mission to the Gentiles with the first mission to the household. When, at the Council in Jerusalem, James resorts to precedent by noting how 'Simeon has recounted how God first concerned himself to take from among the Gentiles a people for his name' (Acts 15.14), he alludes to Cornelius and the baptism of his household. By means of Peter's witness in the house,

1. Ernst Haenchen, *The Acts of the Apostles: A Commentary* (trans. Bernard Noble and Gerald Shinn; Philadelphia: Westminster Press, 1971), p. 361.

2. In this chapter and the next, this term denotes only the narrator of Acts in distinction from Luke. For the sake of tradition and convenience, I will still call him 'Luke'. While Luke and Acts almost certainly come from the same hand, they may in fact employ different narrators in the telling of their stories. See Mikeal C. Parsons, 'The Unity of the Lukan Writings: Rethinking the *Opinio Communis*', in Naymond H. Keathley (ed.), *With Steadfast Purpose: Essays on Acts in Honor of Henry Jackson Flanders, Jr*, (Waco: Baylor University, 1990), pp. 38-45. For Parsons, the issue is: 'Can the same author produce two distinct narrators?' (p. 38). On the more complex question of narrative levels in relation to the unity of the Lukan writings, see Mikeal C. Parsons and Richard I. Pervo, *Rethinking the Unity of Luke and Acts* (Minneapolis: Fortress Press, 1993), pp. 45-83.

the 'household' (οἶκος) of Cornelius becomes the gentile 'people' (λαός) of God.[3] Despite the crucial presence of the household in the story of Cornelius, few scholars have made the corporate aspect of salvation a key element in their interpretation.[4]

Preliminary Considerations

Because this chapter begins the study of the household conversion stories proper, some preliminary considerations are in order. Two important issues are the methodological parameters governing this second section of the study and the justification for devoting a separate chapter to the story of Cornelius.

The Issue of Method

The goal of this study, as set forth in ch. 1 of this book, is to read the stories of household conversions in Acts against the pattern of the seventy-two missionaries in Luke. In this way one can adequately account for the 'household' character of these stories.[5] Before proceeding to the actual methodological procedures for doing so, it is first necessary to ask what rhetorical strategies are available in the text that make such a reading possible.

Common to each story of household salvation is the presence of the 'οἶκος formula' ('and/with [all] his/her household'), a phrase that Hans Conzelmann considers a 'Lukan schematic formulation'.[6] Its significance

3. Peter's speech (Acts 15.7-11) and the reference to 'first' (πρῶτον) in 15.14 point unmistakably to the household of Cornelius, though he is nowhere mentioned by name. Scholars generally fail to notice the equation between λαός and οἶκος made possible by the story of Acts (cf. Nils A. Dahl, 'A People for His Name', *NTS* 4 [1958], pp. 319-27).

4. See, for example, Robert Allen Black, 'The Conversion Stories in the Acts of the Apostles' (PhD dissertation, Emory University, 1986), pp. 149-61, and Beverly Roberts Gaventa, *From Darkness to Light: Aspects of Conversion in the New Testament* (Philadelphia: Fortress Press, 1989), pp. 96-122. While much insight is to be gained from these studies, both fail to account adequately for the presence of the household. See also Robert C. Tannehill, *The Narrative Unity of Luke–Acts: A Literary Interpretation*, II (Minneapolis: Fortress Press, 1990), pp. 128-45.

5. See ch. 1, pp. 12-17.

6. Hans Conzelmann, *Acts of the Apostles* (trans. James Limburg, A. Thomas Kraabel, and Donald H. Juel; ed. Eldon Jay Epp with Christopher A. Matthews; Hermeneia; Philadelphia: Fortress Press, 1987), p. 152.

has, up until now, been analyzed only in connection with the infant baptism debate, particularly its usage in the Greek Old Testament and in early Christian literature.[7] That the narrator reserves this formula for only a few select moments in the story of Acts, however, contributes to its effectiveness as a rhetorical marker.[8]

The formula, it seems, performs two important rhetorical tasks for the reader.[9] First, it creates a 'moment of recognition' that leads the implied reader to recall other stories in Acts depicting the same phenomenon, both in prospect and retrospect. Lydia (16.15), the Roman jailer (16.31, 34), and Crispus (18.8) are householders in Acts who convert in the same manner as Cornelius, that is, with 'all their household'. That the formula is limited almost exclusively to these accounts results in a distinct typology of conversion deriving from a single cluster of repetitive stories.[10]

Second, the formula engages the implied reader's memory by recalling the command of the Lukan Jesus to convert households (Lk. 10.5-7). Because of the authority of Jesus and the proleptic mission of the Seventy-two, the reader naturally expects the pattern of household evangelizing to be carried into Acts, contributing to the emergence of a Lukan 'type-scene'.[11] The special focus on the personified οἶκος, shared

7. On the important literature relating to this phrase, see ch. 1, pp. 11-12.

8. The overuse of a word or phrase may actually detract from its rhetorical impact over the course of a narrative. Of the repetitive use of 'Jesus', for example, in the Gospel of Matthew, R. Alan Culpepper observes: 'Would not reserving its use for a few, select settings in the gospel give it even greater meaning?' ('Redundancy and the Implied Reader in Matthew: A Response to Janice Capel Anderson and Fred W. Burnett', An Unpublished Seminar Response Paper, SBL Literary Aspects of the Gospels and Acts, 1983, p. 3).

9. On the primary 'reader' presupposed throughout this investigation, see ch. 1, pp. 17-21.

10. The phrase also appears in Stephen's speech where it denotes the property and possessions of Pharaoh over which Joseph was put in charge (ὅλον τὸν οἶκον αὐτοῦ, Acts 7.10; cf. Gen. 41.40; see *BAGD*, see 'οἶκος', p. 561). The context is so markedly different (a speech rehearsing the history of Israel), however, that the phrase retains its power to call only a certain cluster of stories to mind. Outside of Acts, the formula appears in the New Testament only at Jn 4.53 (with οἰκία).

11. The formative study of the biblical type-scene is that of Robert Alter, *The Art of Biblical Narrative* (New York: Basic Book Publishers, 1981), pp. 47-62. According to Alter, 'a recurrent term or phrase may help mark the presence of a particular type-scene' (p. 96). On the qualified notion of type-scene employed in this study, see ch. 1, pp. 15-17.

by both the mission of the Seventy-two and the household conversion stories proper, makes the textual connection between them explicit.[12] By means of these two rhetorical strategies, then, the implied reader of Acts is encouraged to understand the stories of household conversion against the backdrop of the household mission in Luke, to see how, and in what ways, the command of the Lukan Jesus is being fulfilled by faithful messengers.

Because the stories of household conversion belong together, the actual procedures of investigation are the same. The first task is simply to locate each story in the narrative of Acts by noting both its proximate and global context. 'Proximate', in this study, refers to the portion of the text that brackets a particular narrative unit; 'global' takes into account a story's verbal and thematic connections to the narrative as a whole.[13] In this way, the full range of a story's contextual parameters is taken into account. As Luke T. Johnson writes: 'The context of a pericope in Luke–Acts is established not only by what happens immediately before and after, but as well by the way a whole series of passages flow from and illuminate statements within the narrative.'[14] This emphasis on context, particularly global, is part and parcel of the narratological method:

12. According to Joachim Jeremias, the meaning of οἶκος as 'family' appears in the Lukan writings only at Lk. 10.5; 19.9; Acts 10.2; 11.14; 16.15; 16.31; 18.8 (*The Origins of Infant Baptism: A Further Study in Reply to Kurt Aland* [trans. Dorothea M. Barton; Naperville: Alec R. Allenson, 1963], p. 17 n. 1; cf. Lk. 11.17[?]; 12.52[?]). A shared focus on the household brings these accounts together in much the same way that the theme of magic connects portions of Luke to certain stories in Acts (see Susan R. Garrett, *The Demise of the Devil: Magic and the Demonic in Luke's Writings* [Minneapolis: Fortress Press, 1989]).

13. On the importance of global and proximate contexts for understanding type-scenes, see McMahan, 'Meals as Type-Scenes in the Gospel of Luke', pp. 64-66. Compare Anderson's 'focal' and 'global' expectations in 'Double and Triple Stories, the Implied Reader, and Redundancy in Matthew', *Semeia* 31 (1985), p. 83. Drawing on Anderson's insights, Tannehill writes: 'Reading is a constant process of forming and revising expectations, both "focal expectations" in the immediate context and "global expectations", stretching over large sections of work' (*The Narrative Unity of Luke–Acts*, II, p. 75).

14. Luke T. Johnson, 'On Finding the Lukan Community: A Cautious Cautionary Essay', in P.J. Achtemeier (ed.), *SBLSP* (Missoula: Scholars Press, 1979), p. 93.

> The significance of particular features of an episode may only appear when we note connections with other sections of Luke–Acts. The work as a whole is the best guide to the special perspectives and values of the implied author.[15]

The second task is to read each household salvation story in Acts against the backdrop of the household mission of the Seventy-two in Luke. This approach, the result of following the rhetorical strategies in the text, involves paying close attention to how each story both repeats and modifies the established pattern in its narrative context. In shifting the household mission away from the Palestinian-based ministry of Jesus to the mission of the church in the Diaspora, Luke invests the pattern with new and, in some cases, unexpected twists. Thus, while redundancy is critical to the recognition of a literary pattern, variation permits the introduction of vitally new information.[16]

Building on the first two procedures, the third task is to determine the literary function of each story by observing the creative interplay between pattern and context. In an insightful study of the conversion stories in Acts, Robert Allen Black outlines three primary considerations for determining the literary function of a given story: 1. how the story relates to expectations created by the previous narrative, 2. how the story resonates with other stories as repetitions of a particular theme or pattern, and 3. how the story relates to subsequent events in the narrative.[17] In light of these parameters, one best arrives at an understanding of a household conversion story by observing how both repetition and variation of the pattern resonate with and contribute to certain developments in the text. Thus, the caveat of Johnson observed in ch. 1 of this book holds true: 'exegesis cannot forget the importance of literary context for the determination of meaning.'[18]

The Issue of Primacy

Since one of the results of this study is the development of a literary rationale for treating the stories of household conversion together, on

15. Tannehill, 'The Composition of Acts 3–5: Narrative Development and Echo Effect', in K.H. Richards (ed.), *SBLSP* (Chico, CA: Scholars Press, 1984), p. 217.

16. On the relation of redundancy and variation in repetitive stories, see Anderson, 'Double and Triple Stories, the Implied Reader, and Redundancy in Matthew', pp. 84-85. More generally, Ronald H. Carpenter, 'Stylistic Redundancy and Function in Discourse', *Language and Style* 3 (1970), pp. 62-63.

17. Black, 'The Conversion Stories in the Acts of the Apostles', p. 219.

18. Johnson, 'On Finding the Lukan Community', p. 92.

what basis does the study justify a separate chapter devoted to the story of Cornelius? Surely one reason is the sheer length of the story, which forms one of the longest continuous narratives in the book of Acts (10.1–11.18).[19] That the Cornelius event appears twice more in the course of the narrative (15.7-11, 13-21) is indicative of its immense importance for Acts. Of course, not only the length but the location and theme of the story also contribute to its critical significance.[20]

Important as these considerations are, they miss the more precise rationale of this study. Rarely have scholars recognized the way in which the Cornelius narrative stands at the head of a distinct class of conversion experiences in Acts.[21] Haenchen makes the almost rudimentary but important observation that 'in the Cornelius story it is not only one person who is converted, but an entire (Gentile!) congregation is founded'.[22] In their eagerness to focus on Cornelius as the first Gentile admitted into the church,[23] scholars lose sight of the fact that not just an individual but an entire household receives salvation at the preaching of Peter.[24]

This inadequacy in prior treatments of the Cornelius story means that little effort has been made to see this account in relationship to the other stories of household conversion in the book of Acts—Lydia (16.11-15), the Roman jailer (16.25-34) and Crispus (18.5-11). As the first and the longest of these stories, containing the most pregnant implications for the gentile mission, the conversion of Cornelius's household performs a paradigmatic role that justifies a separate treatment in this book. In performing this task, the story not only replicates the standard *Leitwörter*

19. As Gerhard A. Krodel observes, the sixty-six verses devoted to the conversion of Cornelius are more than the three conversion accounts of Paul combined (forty-three verses). See his *Acts* (ACNT; Minneapolis: Augsburg, 1986), p. 187.

20. Noted by John H. Elliott, 'Household and Meals vs. Temple Purity: Replication Patterns in Luke–Acts', *BTB* 21 (1991), p. 105.

21. Richard J. Dillon is almost alone in observing that 'the Cornelius sequence is full of resonances of the dominical program for the mission to the households' (*From Eye-Witnesses to Ministers of the Word* [AnBib; Rome: Biblical Institute Press, 1978], p. 190).

22. Haenchen, *The Acts of the Apostles*, p. 361.

23. So Stephen G. Wilson: 'According to Luke, Cornelius was the first and decisive convert from the Gentile world' (*The Gentiles and the Gentile Mission in Luke–Acts* [Cambridge: Cambridge University Press, 1973], p. 259).

24. Is this oversight the result of Western readers with a view of conversion that is overly individualistic in conception?

drawn from the pattern of the Seventy-two, it adds new ones to the literary landscape as well. Seen in this way, the story of Cornelius becomes the fullest expression of the household mission in Acts, anticipating and informing the subsequent stories of household conversion.

Narrative Context

The story of Cornelius stands in a strategic position in the narrative of Acts. Globally, it constitutes the climax to the first half of Acts, with 11.19–15.35 forming the denouement.[25] Proximately, the story follows closely the persecution of the synagogue and the Judean ministry of Peter, both of which inform the story of Cornelius in different but important ways. Both the global and proximate context receive more detailed attention below.

Global Context: The Mission to the Gentiles

That the conversion of Cornelius and his household inaugurates a mission to Gentiles is clear from the report of Acts 11.1. As a result of Cornelius's acceptance of the preaching of Peter, 'the Gentiles' (τὰ ἔθνη) receive the word of God. The language suggests that a fundamental turning point has occurred in the narrative of Acts.[26] The reaction of the Jerusalem community to Peter's re-telling of the story is equally conclusive: God has granted 'to the Gentiles' [τοῖς ἔθνεσιν] repentance that leads to life (11.18). For his part, Cornelius represents the kind of person 'in every nation' (ἐν παντὶ ἔθνει) acceptable to God (10.35), his conversion occasioning the first dramatic outpouring of the Holy Spirit upon 'the Gentiles' (τὰ ἔθνη, 10.45). Judging from the speech of James at the Jerusalem Council, it is clear that Luke regards the household of Cornelius as the 'first' (πρῶτον) group of Gentiles (ἐξ ἐθνῶν) to be visited with salvation (15.14). Thus, it is only after the Cornelius event that Luke feels free to narrate the systematic spread of the gospel to the Gentiles at Antioch (11.19-21), though little causal connection exists between them.[27]

25. Gaventa, *From Darkness to Light*, p. 122.

26. Haenchen, *The Acts of the Apostles*, p. 354. Nearly identical language occurs at Acts 8.14 to signify the penetration of the gospel into Samaria (ἀκούσαντες δὲ...ὅτι δέδεκται ἡ Σαμάρεια τὸν λόγον τοῦ θεοῦ).

27. Gaventa, *From Darkness to Light*, p. 122. The textual discrepancy at 11.20 is in favor of reading Ἕλληνας here (Greeks, not Hellenistic Jews), particularly

The above observations make it clear that the conversion of τὰ ἔθνη lies at the heart of the Cornelius story. Black is certainly not guilty of overstatement when he asserts that 'virtually every aspect of the story as well as the role it plays in chs. 11 and 15 indicates that it functions primarily in connection with the Gentile mission'.[28] Similarly, Joseph B. Tyson calls the Cornelius narrative the 'centerpiece' of Luke's treatment of the Gentile mission.[29] This emphasis on the salvation of τὰ ἔθνη makes it easier to locate the verbal and thematic connections in the global context of Acts 10.1–11.18.

As the seminal event in a document well-known for its universalism,[30] the conversion of Cornelius, with its implications of radical inclusiveness, does not come upon the reader unexpectedly. Already at the beginning of his Gospel, Luke sounds the note of universalism: 'all flesh will see the salvation of God' (Lk. 3.6).[31] This promise begins the process of concrete realization when the Lukan Jesus commands his messengers to preach repentance and forgiveness of sins to 'all the nations' (πάντα τὰ ἔθνη, Lk. 24.47), a theme that reappears at the beginning of Acts when Jesus re-commissions the apostles to bear witness in Jerusalem, in all Judea and Samaria, and to the ends of the earth (1.8). Luke depicts this gradual expansion of the church's mission primarily by means of conversion stories, of which Cornelius's clearly is one.[32]

Standing in the global context of Acts 10.1–11.18 are four stories of

given the contrast with 'the Jews' at 11.19 (see Luke T. Johnson, *The Acts of the Apostles* [Collegeville: The Liturgical Press, 1992], p. 203).

28. Black, 'The Conversion Stories in the Acts of the Apostles', p. 149.

29. Joseph B. Tyson, 'The Gentile Mission and the Authority of Scripture in Acts', *NTS* (1987), p. 624.

30. See, for example, John Navonne, *Themes of St Luke* (Rome: Gregorian University Press, 1978).

31. The universalist motif of Lk. 3.6 provides for Tannehill the unifying principle tying together both Luke and Acts. In noting τὸ σωτήριον τοῦ θεοῦ both here and at Acts 28.28, he says: 'The end of the work reminds us of the divine purpose which was disclosed at the beginning and which remains central throughout' (*The Narrative Unity of Luke–Acts*, I, p. 40).

32. Linda M. Maloney objects to speaking of the 'conversion' of Cornelius because of his acceptance with God *prior* to his 'Christianization' (10.2, 4). See her *'All that God had Done with Them': The Narration of the Works of God in the Early Christian Community as Described in the Acts of the Apostles* (New York: Peter Lang, 1991), p. 83. I will continue to speak of the 'conversion' of Cornelius because 1. Luke clearly regards it as such, and 2. there is more than one type of conversion depicted in Acts (see Gaventa's discussion in *From Darkness to Light*, pp. 1-16).

conversion, each of which prepares for and anticipates the conversion of Cornelius. These conversions include the three thousand Jews on the day of Pentecost (2.1-47), the people of Samaria (8.5-25), the Ethiopian eunuch (8.26-40), and Saul, the arch persecutor of the church (9.1-19a). Not only are these stories preparatory for the mission soon to commence in Cornelius's house, they also serve to widen the geographical parameters of the church's mission in accordance with the missional program of Acts 1.8.[33]

The story of Pentecost marks the beginnings of the church's witness in Jerusalem (Acts 2.5, 14; cf. Lk. 24.47; Acts 1.8a). While the converts on this occasion are unquestionably Jews from among the 'house of Israel' (2.36-41), certain hints point beyond the parameters of Israel. The narrator emphasizes, for example, the presence of Jews from 'every nation [παντὸς ἔθνους] under heaven' (2.5), including proselytes from among the Gentiles (2.11). Even more explicit are two lines from the prophet Joel cited in the sermon of Peter. The first declares that God would in the last days pour out his Spirit upon 'all flesh' (πᾶσαν σάρκα, 2.17; cf. Joel 2.28 [LXX]), an expression that directly recalls the universal promise of Lk. 3.6. Though Peter does not yet perceive the radical implications of these words, the narrator most likely intends them to adumbrate the gentile mission.[34] The second equally stresses the availability of salvation for all: 'everyone who calls on the name of the Lord shall be saved' (2.21; cf. Joel 2.32 [LXX]). Both these statements point in the direction of a future mission to Gentiles, those presently 'far away' (2.39).[35]

The next two conversion stories signal a geographical advance beyond Jerusalem to the environs of Judea and Samaria. The cause for this missionary expansion is the persecution levelled against Stephen (6.9–8.1a), which results in the scattering of the church (8.1b-4). The geographical

33. Scholars who see in this verse a pattern for the church's mission in Acts include Weiss, Jackson and Lake, Dibelius, and Haenchen. For a recent challenge of this view, see Robert L. Brawley, *Luke–Acts and the Jews: Conflict, Apology, and Conciliation* (Atlanta: Scholars Press, 1987).

34. So F. F. Bruce, *The Book of Acts* (Grand Rapids: Eerdmans, rev. edn, 1988), p. 61: 'Luke sees in these words an adumbration of the worldwide Gentile mission, even if Peter could not have realized their full import when he quoted them on the day of Pentecost.' Hereafter, this text is cited as *The Book of Acts* (ET).

35. The context of the passage suggests that πᾶσιν τοῖς εἰς μακράν has Gentiles in view (cf. Eph. 2.13). See Jacob Jervell, *Luke and the People of God: A New Look at Luke–Acts* (Minneapolis: Augsburg, 1972), pp. 57-58.

correspondence to the missionary program of Acts 1.8 seems too close to be merely accidental.[36] The conversions of the Samaritans (8.5-25) and a eunuch from Ethiopia (8.26-40) narrated in this section of Acts provide apt illustrations, albeit in reverse order, of the widening of the church's geographical and ethnic boundaries. Both accounts involve persons whose status as 'Jews' is questionable. As the gospel spreads farther away from Jerusalem, the more concrete the mission to the Gentiles becomes.

The preaching of Philip to the ἔθνος of Samaria (cf. Acts 8.9) represents an intermediate stage in the church's mission, standing between the mission to Jews (Acts 1–7) and the mission to Gentiles (Acts 10–28). It is not altogether clear how the narrators of Luke and Acts intend the reader to understand the status of the Samaritans. Are they Jews or are they Gentiles? On the one hand, a distinction between Jews and Samaritans is clear from such passages as Lk. 17.18, which designates the Samaritan leper an ἀλλογενής, a term appearing only here in the New Testament. The usage of this term in the Septuagint often connotes 'non-Jew' or, at times, a Jewish proselyte.[37] It occurs in a temple inscription forbidding a 'foreigner' (ἀλλογενής) from entering the sanctuary.[38] The foreign status of Samaritans, of course, is assumed in the Parable of the Good Samaritan (Lk. 10.29-37), without which the story loses its contrastive force.[39]

On the other hand, Acts does not facilely identify Samaritans with Gentiles. Not only is ἀλλογενής a weaker term than ἀλλόφυλος, which describes the gentile Cornelius (Acts 10.28),[40] but Peter exhibits little of the reluctance to associate with Samaritans that he does with the household of Cornelius. Similarly, the circumcision party in Jerusalem simply does not exhibit the same concern over the inclusion of

36. In Acts 1.8 the Lukan Jesus directs his followers to bear witness 'in all Judea and Samaria'; in Acts 8.1b, the church is scattered throughout the regions of 'Judea and Samaria'.

37. Abraham, for example, circumcises every ἀλλογενής purchased from among the foreign nations (Gen. 17.27) while no ἀλλογενής was allowed to eat of the Passover (Exod. 12.43).

38. See the discussion in Philip Francis Esler, *Community and Gospel in Luke–Acts: The Social and Political Motivations of Lucan Theology* (Cambridge: Cambridge University Press, 1987), p. 149.

39. Noted by Black, 'The Conversion Stories in the Acts of the Apostles', p. 124.

40. So Jacob Jervell, *Luke and the People of God*, p. 131 n. 41.

Samaritan believers that they later exhibit over the inclusion of gentile believers.[41] Josephus shows just how ambiguous the Samaritans themselves could be on the question of their ethnic status.[42] The ambiguous nature of the evidence suggests that the Samaritans constitute for Luke a *tertium quid*, a group related to both Jews and Gentiles but not to be wholly identified with either.[43]

If Philip's preaching to the Samaritans represents a half-step in the direction of the evangelization of the Gentiles, his subsequent preaching to an Ethiopian eunuch (8.26-40) appears to complete the task. In baptizing a eunuch, Philip was baptizing one traditionally excluded from the assembly of Israel (Deut. 23.1; cf. Isa. 56.5), and thus most likely a Gentile.[44] His Jewish origin, however, cannot be entirely ruled out.[45] This very ambiguity suggests that the narrator does not regard him as the first 'official' Gentile to gain entry into the people of God: that distinction clearly belongs to the gentile Cornelius (Acts 15.14). The essentially private character of the eunuch's conversion, taking place on a 'desert road' extending from Jerusalem to Gaza (Acts 8.26),[46] carries

41. Black, 'The Conversion Stories in the Acts of the Apostles', pp. 128-29.

42. 'And when they [Samaritans] see the Jews in prosperity, they pretend that they are changed, and allied to them, and call them kinsmen, as though they were derived from Joseph, and had by that means an original alliance with them: but when they see them falling into low condition, they say they are in no way related to them, and that the Jews have no right to expect any kindness or marks of kindred for them, but they declare that they are sojourners, that come from other countries' (*Ant.* 9.291 [Whiston text]).

43. So Black, 'The Conversion Stories in the Acts of the Apostles', p. 129.

44. The hesitancy to regard the eunuch as a Gentile stems from Luke's identification of Cornelius and his household as the 'first' Gentile converts (Acts 15.14). So, for example, Wilson, *The Gentiles and the Gentile Mission in Luke–Acts*, p. 171.

45. In addition to Wilson above, see Johannes Munck, *The Acts of the Apostles: Introduction, Translation and Notes* (rev. William F. Albright and C.S. Mann; AB; New York: Doubleday, 1967), 78. More recently, John R.W. Stott argues that the eunuch is a Jew via birth or conversion, 'for the Jewish dispersion had penetrated at least into Egypt and probably beyond, and perhaps by now the promise to eunuchs of Isa. 56.3-4 had superseded the ban of Deut. 23.1' (*The Spirit, the Church, and the World: The Message of Acts* [Downers Grove: Intervarsity Press, 1990], p. 160).

46. This geographical notation affords a contrast with the 'household' character of Cornelius's conversion: the eunuch converts 'away from home'! On the possibility of αὕτη ἐστὶν ἔρημος at Acts 8.26 referring to the ancient ruins of Gaza, see

with it no 'public' consequences in the succeeding narrative as does the story of Cornelius, after which the church's mission to the Gentiles begins its rapid and systematic spread (11.19-21; 13.2).[47]

Nevertheless, there is much in this story that serves symbolically to portray a future mission to the Gentiles. The difficulty with which both the eunuch and Cornelius must approach baptism (κωλύω, Acts 8.36; 10.47; 11.17) forges an important connection between them. 'When Peter baptizes Cornelius', writes Tannehill, 'readers may well remember that Philip was earlier led to baptize a foreigner'.[48] In the case of the eunuch, the issue of foreign status is particularly acute, since the very designation of 'Ethiopian' ('ἰθίοψ) would envisage for Luke's readers one coming from the southernmost extremity of the earth.[49] It would also denote a person of dark skin, thus effectively breaking down the barriers of race.[50] Despite these powerful images of foreign status, it is doubtful that the eunuch represents a fulfillment of Acts 1.8c with its vision of a mission to the 'ends of the earth'. For Luke, this mission is clearly linked to the journeys of Paul who succeeds, at least in an initial way, in taking the gospel to the ἐσχάτου τῆς γῆς (13.47).[51] Linking the

Max Wilcox, *The Semitisms of Acts* (Oxford: Clarendon Press, 1965), p. 152.

47. 'The Ethiopian,' observes Tannehill, 'is not mentioned again, and there is no indication that the Jerusalem church learns of his conversion. There is no discussion in Jerusalem of the propriety of baptizing an Ethiopian eunuch as there is after the baptism of Cornelius... The scene is important for what it anticipates and symbolizes rather than for its consequences' (Tannehill, *The Narrative Unity of Luke–Acts*, II, pp. 107-108).

48. Tannehill, *The Narrative Unity of Luke–Acts*, p. 111. On the technical associations of κωλύω with baptism in the early church, see Oscar Cullmann, *Baptism in the New Testament* (trans. J.K.S. Reid; Chicago: Alec R. Allenson, 1950), pp. 71-80.

49. See Homer, *Odyssey* 1.23; Herodotus 3.114; Strabo, *Geography* 1.2.27. According to Gaventa, the difference between the Ethiopian eunuch and Cornelius is that one is proleptic and the other actual. 'If the inclusion of the eunuch symbolized the beginning of the gospel's movement to the end of the earth, the inclusion of Cornelius makes of that symbol an explicit fact' (*From Darkness to Light*, p. 124).

50. The dark skin of the Ethiopians was well-known in antiquity. See Philostratus, *Life of Apollonius* 6.2; Lucian, *adversus Indoctum* 28; Jer. 13.23. For a valuable survey of the available evidence, see Clarice J. Martin, 'A Chamberlain's Journey and the Challenge of Interpretation for Liberation', *Semeia* 47 (1989), pp. 105-135.

51. That Paul's mission at the close of Acts is left open-ended (28.28) suggests that the mission to the 'ends of the earth' is also left open-ended, fulfilling itself

eunuch's conversion to the fulfillment of Acts 1.8c also overlooks the way the story functions in the wider context of the Judean mission.[52]

The most explicit reference to a gentile mission prior to the evangelization of Cornelius appears in the story of the persecutor Saul (Acts 9.1-19a). Here the risen Jesus explicitly declares to Saul that he has been appointed 'to bring my name before Gentiles [ἐθνῶν] and kings and before the people of Israel' (Acts 9.15), a clear anticipation of his role in the second half of Acts (cf. 13.47). According to Tannehill, ἐθνῶν at 9.15 is emphatic, indicating 'a new development at this point in the narrative'.[53] By placing 'Gentiles' in the first position, the narrator effectively reverses the traditional order of Paul's missionary strategy in Acts, namely, to preach first to the Jews and then to the Gentiles.[54] It is the conversion of Cornelius and his household that later legitimates Paul's mission as one free from the constraints of circumcision and the law (Acts 15).

In the story of Saul's conversion, not only is the principal agent of the future gentile mission thus identified, but Saul's own role as the arch enemy of God signals the radical inclusion of outsiders into the community of faith. His role as the supreme persecutor of the church, which only intensifies as the story progresses (7.58; 8.1, 3; 9.1), confirms his status as one existing on the extreme periphery of Judaism.[55] Luke portrays Saul as a ravaging animal entering house after house in search of Christians (8.3).[56] The reference here to houses is ironic, anticipating not

whenever and wherever the gospel is proclaimed to new areas and peoples.

52. The geographical notations at the beginning and end of the Ethiopian story stress this connection (8.26, 40). Acts 8.40 pictures Philip continuing his evangelism of Judea until he comes to Caesarea, a city lying outside Judea in Lukan geography (Acts 12.19; 21.10).

53. Tannehill, *The Narrative Unity of Luke–Acts*, II, p. 119 n. 17.

54. The appearance of γάρ in 9.16 links Paul's witness to the motif of suffering (ὑποδείξω αὐτῷ ὅσα δεῖ αὐτὸν ὑπὲρ τοῦ ὀνόματος μου παθεῖν) and hence to situations of public defense (cf. Gerhard Lohfink, '"Meinen Namen zu tragen..." (Apg 9,15)', *BZ* 10 [1966], pp. 108-115). No doubt the reader is to think of those instances where Paul testifies before gentile rulers (Acts 24–25), kings (Acts 26), and the Sanhedrin (Acts 23). As this sequence of events reveals, the primacy of ἐθνῶν disrupts the natural narrative order.

55. Gaventa remarks that, from the standpoint of Luke, Saul is 'as far from the receptive Jews in Jerusalem (Acts 2.37-42) as he can be without being a Gentile' (*From Darkness to Light*, p. 67).

56. The Septuagint often employs λυμαίνομαι of beasts that ravage their prey (Dan. 6.22; Isa. 65.25; Ps. 79.14; Sir. 28.23).

only the sphere of his future missionary operations among the Gentiles (16.14-15, 31-34; 17.5; 18.7-8; 20.20) but the place of his own conversion at the hands of Ananias (9.10-12, 17-19a). In an action foreshadowing Peter's ministry to the household of Cornelius, Ananias enters (εἰσέρχομαι) the house of a certain Judas to fill Saul with the Holy Spirit (9.17). Upon being baptized, Saul 'took food' (λαβὼν τροφὴν), perhaps at the behest of his host (9.18-19a).[57] The result is that Saul regains his strength, leading directly to his powerful preaching in the synagogues (9.19b-22). An allusion to the Eucharist is perhaps present here.[58]

In the four conversion accounts presented above, one observes a noticeable progression in the church's outreach leading steadily up to the climactic events in the house of Cornelius. In these stories the missional impulse towards universal salvation grows steadily stronger, from Jews and Samaritans to an Ethiopian eunuch and arch enemy who himself converts in a house.[59] Thus, the note of an inclusive mission sounds with increasing clarity: the closer one moves to the proximate context of the Cornelius story, the louder and more distinctive the tones become. As Gaventa observes, 'The conversions of Samaritans, the Ethiopian eunuch, and the persecutor Saul provide the reader of Acts with a clear signal that the mission inaugurated at Pentecost does not belong to the Jews of Jerusalem or Judea...In this way Luke sets the stage for the narrative of Peter and Cornelius.'[60]

Proximate Context: Persecution by the Synagogue and the Positioning of Peter

The lack of any causal relation between the conversion of Cornelius in Acts 10.1–11.18 and the beginnings of the gentile mission at Antioch in 11.19-21 suggests that the former bears an intentional placement on the pages of Acts. The mission to the Gentiles at Antioch traces its causal

57. Stott asks, 'Did Ananias prepare and serve the meal, as well as baptize him?' (*The Spirit, the Church, and the World*, p. 176).

58. That Paul engages in such preaching immediately after taking food suggests that more than physical strength is in view. The verb used at 9.22 to describe Paul's strengthening (ἐνδυναμόω) is used primarily of religious and spiritual strength (W. Robertson Nicoll, (ed.), *The Expositor's Greek Testament*, II [New York: Hodder & Stoughton], p. 238).

59. See Robert F. O'Toole, *The Unity of Luke's Theology: An Analysis of Luke–Acts* (Wilmington: Michael Glazier, 1984), pp. 103-106.

60. Gaventa, *From Darkness to Light*, p. 107.

link to the scattering of the church arising in connection with the death of Stephen (cf. 8.1, 4; 11.19), not to the events transpiring in the house of Cornelius.[61] That one does not cause the other means that the narrator could well have placed the Cornelius episode elsewhere without disrupting the general narrative 'flow' in this section of Acts.[62] The rather awkward placement of Cornelius's conversion accentuates the importance of the story's proximate context, suggesting that the narrator had reasons for putting it where he did.

A careful analysis of the proximate context reveals that the persecution of Stephen essentially 'brackets' the story of Cornelius, being interrupted only by the introduction of Peter's wider Judean ministry (9.32-43). With the explicit reference to the 'scattering' of the church at 11.19, it is striking how the narrator of Acts intends the reader to recall the story of Stephen so soon after the events depicted in Acts 10.1–11.18. According to events described in Acts 6.9-14, certain members of the Synagogue of the Freedmen[63] stand up and argue with Stephen, ultimately conspiring against him when they fail to cope with his powerful wisdom. These actions initiate the conflict that not only results in Stephen's death but soon gives way to the fierce persecution against the church led by Saul.[64] As the prime instigator in the conflict,[65] the

61. Esler observes how 11.19, with its theme of scattering (οἱ μὲν οὖν διασπαρέντες), takes up immediately from 8.4 (οἱ μὲν οὖν διασπαρέντες), thus lacking any sign that 'the mission to the Gentiles in Antioch is a consequence of the conversion of a Roman centurion by Peter' (*Community and Gospel in Luke–Acts*, p. 96). The effect of this verbal linkage is to present the developments in Antioch as 'the continuation of the gospel's spread resulting from the scattering of believers by the persecution at the death of Stephen' (Tannehill, *The Narrative Unity of Luke–Acts*, II, p. 146).

62. The ambiguous temporal relation between Acts 10.1–11.18 and 11.19-21 further highlights the lack of any causal connection: 'Because the latter is caused by the scattering, an event placed some time before Peter's visit with Cornelius, it is possible to assume that the conversion of Cornelius and the spread of the gospel to Antioch were taking place in the same time period. In any case, the one did not cause the other' (Tannehill, *The Narrative Unity of Luke–Acts*, II, p. 147).

63. The synagogue was predominantly Greek-speaking in composition, as the reference to Cyrenians, Alexandrians, Cilicians, and Asians reveals (Acts 6.9). The source of Stephen's opposition is not so surprising when one considers the generally hostile stance of the Hellenistic synagogue towards the mission of Paul later in Acts.

64. In taking up the persecution instigated by the synagogue, Saul 'becomes the major representative of the attitude condemned by Stephen in 7.51-52' (Tannehill, *The Narrative Unity of Luke–Acts*, II, p. 114). Later in Acts, Paul recalls his

synagogue assumes the role of persecutor previously held by the temple and its authorities, who, despite repeated efforts, are ultimately unsuccessful in stilling the voices of Christian preachers (Acts 3–5; esp. 4.1-3; 5.17-18). That Luke indicts as many as five separate synagogues of the north African and Asian Diaspora as leading the charge against Stephen underscores the degree of the synagogue's culpable involvement, foreshadowing its essentially hostile posture towards God and God's messengers later in the Acts.[66]

The immediate result of the persecution of the synagogue is that the word of God grows, finding fertile soil in the regions of Samaria and Judea (Acts 8.1–9.31). The narrator interrupts this depiction of a gradually expanding mission, however, with his somewhat awkward introduction of Peter's Judean ministry at 9.32. The reason for this interruption becomes clear when one considers Peter's role as house evangelist in the next chapter of Acts. In moving Peter away from Jerusalem, where he last appears (Acts 5), to the coastal cities of Lydda and Joppa, the narrator puts Peter in closer proximity to Caesarea. Here Peter will be summoned to preach to the household of Cornelius, resulting in the conversion of the first Gentiles. Many cultures and races travelled the road that would eventually take Peter to the doorstep of Cornelius's house.[67] The reference to Peter's 'going through' (διερχόμενον) the regions of Judea at 9.32, the usual term for a missionary journey proper in Acts,[68] establishes an important travel motif in this section that explains Peter's proximity to Caesarea. Introducing Peter's larger Judean ministry at this particular juncture, then, has direct consequences for the story of Cornelius: Peter moves closer to Caesarea and to his encounter with a Roman centurion.

The significance of Peter's Judean ministry for the story of Cornelius is not solely geographical, however. In anticipation of his role as

persecutory activity in the synagogue (22.19; 26.11; cf. 9.2).

65. So Haenchen, *The Acts of the Apostles*, p. 271.

66. The precise number of synagogues involved in the dispute is uncertain. See Bruce, *The Book of Acts* (ET), p. 124.

67. J. Julius Scott, 'The Cornelius Incident in the Light of its Jewish Setting', *JETS* 34 (1991), p. 477. Scott points out that more rigorous Jews regarded the Jews of the coastal plain with a certain degree of suspicion by virtue of their frequent contact with Gentiles.

68. Noted by David J. Williams, *Acts* (NIBC; Peabody: Hendrickson, 1985, 1990), p. 154. See, for example, Acts 8.4, 40; 11.19; 13.6, 14; 14.24; 16.6; 18.23, 27; 19.1, 21; 20.2, 25.

household missionary, Peter heals the bedridden Aeneas (9.32-35; cf. κατακείμενον ἐπὶ κραβάττου, v. 33) and raises the beloved Dorcas in an upper room (9.36-42; cf. vv. 37, 39), both of which presuppose a domestic setting.[69] The latter story particularly prefigures Peter's ministry in the house of Cornelius. As in the Cornelius narrative, messengers summon Peter to the house of a person of notable deeds (9.38; 10.7, 17; 11.11, 13),[70] to which he responds in nearly identical terms: he 'arose and went with them' (9.39; 10.23b). Moreover, the conclusion of the story pictures Peter's staying many days (ἡμέρας ἱκανὰς μεῖναι) in the house of Simon the tanner (9.43), an occupation that rendered a Jew ritually unclean (cf. *m. Ket.* 7.10),[71] anticipating a similar scene at the close of Peter's mission to the gentile Cornelius (ἐπιμεῖναι ἡμέρας τινάς, 10.48). As a result, Peter is being prepared, both geographically and culturally, to perform his role as messenger to the house (10.5-6, 17-18).[72]

Pattern and Variation

In an insightful treatment of conversion in the New Testament, Gaventa draws attention to an aspect of the Cornelius story often overlooked by commentators, namely, 'the connection between the conversion of Cornelius and the issue of *hospitality*, the sharing of food and shelter between Jews and Gentiles'.[73] While this point is an extremely important

69. Κράβαττος is literally 'a poor man's bed' which finds its most natural setting in the household (see Elliott, 'Temple versus Household in Luke–Acts: A Contrast in Social Institutions', in Jerome H. Neyrey [ed.], *The Social World of Luke–Acts: Models for Interpretation* [Peabody: Hendrickson, 1991], p. 226). The 'upper room' where Dorcas is raised obviously presupposes a domestic structure of some kind (Acts 1.13; 20.28).

70. Both Dorcas and Cornelius are generous givers of alms and abound in good deeds (9.36; 10.2, 4).

71. According to Williams, Peter must overcome his personal scruples to stay with a 'suspect' Jew (*Acts*, p. 182). That Luke does not underscore Simon's unclean status is striking in light of Peter's initially scrupulous position in the story of Cornelius (Acts 10.14; 11.8).

72. 'Geographical locations,' observes Tannehill, 'are used to create links in narrative lines that will be broken by other material' (*The Narrative Unity of Luke–Acts*, II, p. 124). Thus, Cornelius's messengers eventually find Peter in a house at Joppa.

73. Gaventa, *From Darkness to Light*, p. 108 (emphasis hers). This motif is aided greatly by the presence of the foods vision (10.9-16), which Martin Dibelius regards as a Lukan composition. See his *Studies in the Acts of the Apostles*

one, it gains in potency when viewed against the larger pattern of the seventy-two messengers in the Gospel of Luke who enter into the houses of Gentiles, there offer their message of salvific peace, and accept a hospitable welcome in the house without regard for dietary restrictions (Lk. 10.5-7). The story of Cornelius is striking for the way it makes the spatial setting of the house a central component of its plot.[74]

Adding complexity to the conversion of Cornelius is its four-fold repetition on the pages of Acts (10.1-48; 11.1-18; 15.7-11,13-21), qualifying it as the most often repeated story in Acts.[75] While the first of these narrations (10.1-48) employs a narrator from outside or 'above' the text, the remaining three utilize narrators (characters) 'within' the text. The first has been termed the hyperdiegetic level, the second the intradiegetic.[76] In analyzing the pattern of the household mission below, it will be useful to analyze the story of Cornelius according to its respective narrative levels.

Hyperdiegetic Narration: The Original Account of the Conversion of Cornelius (10.1-48)

As one might expect, the original telling of the story of Cornelius is the occasion for the fullest explication of the household missionary pattern on the pages of Acts.[77] The pattern occupies a central position in the general plot structure of the story, which narrates Peter's journey to the house of Cornelius and his ultimate acceptance of hospitality from the

(ed. Heinrich Greeven; trans. Mary Ling; New York: Charles Scribner's Sons, 1956), pp. 111-13.

74. The house (οἶκος/οἰκία is either presupposed (10.2, 6, 17, 22, 30, 32; 11.11-12, 13-14) or expressly mentioned (10.9, 18, 20-21, 23, 25, 27-29, 33, 48; 11.3, 5) in nearly every scene.

75. The story of Cornelius is an example of 'repetitive narration', which 'reports repeatedly an event that happens once' (see Mark Allan Powell, *What is Narrative Criticism*? [Minneapolis: Fortress Press, 1990], p. 39). Scholars often fail to note how the speech of James (Acts 15.13-21) is also an exposition of the story of Cornelius.

76. On the various levels of narration available to an author, see Robert W. Funk, *The Poetics of Biblical Narrative* (Sonoma: Polebridge Press, 1988), pp. 30-34.

77. The account of Cornelius's conversion (10.1–11.18) divides neatly into seven scenes (10.1-8, 9-16, 17-23a, 23b-33, 34-43, 44-48; 11.1-18). See, for example, Krodel, *Acts*, p. 189 and Haenchen, *The Acts of the Apostles*, pp. 357-63. See the slight difference in Gaventa, *From Darkness to Light*, pp. 112-22. The last of these scenes (11.1-18) employs an intradiegetic narrator and is considered in the section below.

newly converted household. In this section I note the way this pattern is creatively integrated into the story of Cornelius, taking into account the new narrative situation posed by the book of Acts.

a. *Peter Enters the House of Cornelius.* The story begins by introducing Cornelius as 'a centurion of the Italian Cohort' (10.1), a designation that almost certainly establishes his status as a Gentile since Jews, from the time of Julius Caesar, were exempt from serving in the Roman army.[78] That Cornelius is a devout man who 'fears God with all his household' (10.2) makes him particularly noteworthy among the Gentiles, much like that of the centurion at Capernaum (Lk. 7.9). The issue of Cornelius's ethnicity provides the central conflict in the story, both initially between Peter and Cornelius (10.28) and, later, between Peter and his accusers at Jerusalem (11.3).[79] If Peter is to enter the house of Cornelius to perform his task as household evangelist, he must violate the 'social script' that effectively barred Jews from having social intercourse with Gentiles.[80]

To get Peter inside the house of Cornelius, the narrator creates a 'funneling effect' in the first half of the story.[81] The house functions in the first two scenes as the place of divine revelation, where both Peter and Cornelius receive visions eventually bringing the two unsuspecting parties together (10.1-8, 9-16).[82] The scenes are striking for their

78. Everett Ferguson, *Backgrounds of Early Christianity* (Grand Rapids: Eerdmans, 2nd edn, 1993), pp. 388-89; see *Ant.* 14.10.6, 12, 13. Black notes that 'Cornelius' occupation may serve primarily to underscore his identity as a Gentile' ('The Conversion Stories in the Acts of the Apostles', p. 156).

79. Luke employs three terms to highlight Cornelius's identity as a Gentile: ἔθνος (10.45; 11.1, 18; cf. 15.7, 14, 19), ἀλλόφυλος ('foreigner', 10.28), and ἀκροβυστία ('uncircumcision', 11.3).

80. Esler sets forth the literary and historical evidence for the Jewish ban on eating with Gentiles in *Community and Gospel in Luke–Acts*, pp. 76-86. Esler sums up his findings thus: 'The antipathy of Jews towards table-fellowship with Gentiles, in the full sense of sitting around a table with them and sharing the same food, wine and vessels, was an intrinsic feature of Jewish life for centuries before and after our period' (p. 84). Note how the centurion at Capernaum is keenly aware of the issue of 'space' (Lk. 7.6, 10). On the relation of social scripts to biblical narrative, see David B. Gowler, *Host, Guest, Enemy, Friend: Portraits of the Pharisees in Luke and Acts* (New York: Peter Lang, 1991).

81. On the use of funneling effect in the Gospel of Mark, see David Rhoads and Donald Michie, *Mark as Story: An Introduction to the Narrative of a Gospel* (Philadelphia: Fortress Press, 1982), p. 70.

82. The use of the 'double vision' technique also appears in the story of Ananias

respective use of the household setting. While praying in his house, Cornelius encounters an angel who instructs him to send for Peter, a Jew who is temporarily lodging in the house of Simon the tanner (10.3-8; cf. v. 30). Similarly, while Peter is praying on the housetop, he receives a vision from heaven instructing him to disregard the distinction between clean and unclean foods (10.9-16).[83] His emphatic response recorded at 10.14 ('I have never eaten anything that is profane or unclean!') reveals the kind of law-observant Jew Peter is at this juncture in the story.[84] Peter would never even entertain the thought of entering the house of an unclean Gentile! (cf. 10.28).

The next scene portrays the messengers sent by Cornelius arriving at the doorstep of Simon's house while Peter is still pondering the meaning of his vision (10.17-23a). Their refusal to enter the house until invited to do so (vv. 17-18,23a) highlights the problematic issue of space, this time from a gentile perspective.[85] While continuing to contemplate his vision, Peter receives explicit instructions by the Spirit to accompany the messengers to Cornelius's house 'without hesitating' (μηδὲν διακινόμενος, 10.20), a term capable of double meaning.[86] Once there, according to the messengers, Peter is to speak words for Cornelius to hear (ἀκοῦσαι ῥήματα, 10.22), resulting in the salvation of all his household (cf. 11.14). That the messengers describe Cornelius as a righteous man who 'fears God' (φοβούμενος τὸν θεόν) may be intended to encourage Peter's compliance by softening the impact of entering a

and Saul to bring two unsuspecting (and resistant) parties together (9.10-12). See Tannehill, *The Narrative Unity of Luke–Acts*, II, p. 116.

83. Peter sees the οὐρανός opened up and a great sheet containing all manner of foods descending to the earth (10.11). At the conclusion of the vision the sheet goes back up into the οὐρανός (10.16; cf. 11.5, 10). This literary *inclusio* stresses the divine origin of Peter's vision.

84. The emphatic πάντα at 10.12 indicates that both clean and unclean animals are included in the sheet, making understandable Peter's reaction (see Tyson, 'The Gentile Mission and the Authority of Scripture in Acts', p. 625). The μηδαμῶς in Peter's reaction is an intensifying compound negative: 'by no means!'

85. As Colin House observes, the Jewish concept of defilement 'prohibited unauthorized Gentile entry into Jewish homes' ('Defilement by Association: Some Insights from the Usage of ΚΟΙΝΟΣ/ΚΟΙΝΟΩ in Acts 10 and 11', *AUSS* 21 [1983], p. 144 n. 4).

86. In the middle voice, as here, the term basically means 'to doubt or hesitate' while in its active form it denotes the act of distinguishing. The shift to the active voice at 11.12 will be discussed later. See *BAGD*, see 'διακρίνω', p. 185. See also Richard I. Pervo, *Luke's Story of Paul* (Minneapolis: Fortress Press, 1990), p. 38.

Gentile's house.[87] Peter's subsequent offer of hospitality to the messengers of Cornelius (10.23a), however, shows that Peter's resistance to associating with Gentiles is now largely overcome. The story of Cornelius narrates two conversions, not one.[88]

The combination of the first three scenes prepares Peter for his climactic entry into Cornelius's house, which begins the process of realization when Peter accompanies the messengers to the city of Caesarea at the start of the fourth scene (10.23b). Luke now adds the theme of journey to the household mission. Peter's arrival in Caesarea soon brings him to the threshold of Cornelius's house:

> And on the following day he [Peter] entered [εἰσῆλθεν] Caesarea. Now Cornelius was expecting them, having called together his relatives and close friends (10.24).
>
> And when it came about that Peter entered [εἰσελθεῖν], Cornelius met him and worshiped him, falling at his feet (10.25).
>
> And as he was conversing with him [Cornelius], he [Peter] entered [εἰσῆλθεν] and discovered many people gathered together (10.27).

This three-fold appearance of εἰσέρχομαι not only accentuates the connection to the household protocol of the Seventy-two (Lk. 10.5a) but highlights the issue of space in the ensuing narrative; it is this act of entry that Peter's accusers in Jerusalem recall so vividly when they formulate their charge against him (11.3).

Peter's entry into Caesarea at 10.24 anticipates but does not fulfill the initial contact between Peter and Cornelius.[89] Tension in the story

87. 'In asking Peter to visit the house of a Gentile,' says Esler, 'the three men obviously thought they were likely to offend his Jewish sensibilities, for that is why they prefix their request with a statement of Cornelius' virtues... to make the notion of entering his house less shocking' (*Community and Gospel in Luke–Acts*, p. 94).

88. It is not entirely clear when Peter becomes convinced of the acceptability of Gentiles. Esler credits the change in Peter to the combined effect of the Spirit's directives and the arrival of Cornelius's messengers: 'Peter... now knows that, since the Spirit has directed him to the house of a Roman centurion, then God himself has abrogated the Jewish ban on the more intimate forms of fellowship between Jew and Gentile' (*Community and Gospel in Luke–Acts*, p. 94). The immediacy of Peter's realization, according to Esler, 'is implied in the text by the fact that he actually invites the men into the house where he is staying and gives them overnight lodging there' (p. 94).

89. As Funk observes, this verse functions 'to assemble two different groups of participants in proximity to each other' (*The Poetics of Biblical Narrative*, p. 151).

heightens when Cornelius, for his part, gathers all the extended members of his family into his house to await anxiously Peter's arrival. The mention of Caesarea is by no means insignificant to the narrative since, as the predominantly gentile capital of Judea, it was a city loathed by the Jews and thus a conspicuous site for the start of Christian missions.[90] As noted previously, Lukan geography consistently places Caesarea outside the boundaries of Judea.[91]

The second appearance of εἰσέρχομαι at 10.25 denotes Peter's entry proper into the house of Cornelius, effectively 'blurring the distinction between Jew and Gentile'.[92] The entry itself 'pre-focalizes' the scene, while the initial contact established between Peter and Cornelius 'focalizes' it.[93] Peter himself later recaptures the significance of this scene in quite succinct terms: 'we entered the man's house' (11.12). Entering the house of a Gentile, of course, was anathema to any self-respecting Jew. Even a moderately law-observant Jew, F.F. Bruce observes, 'would not willingly enter the dwelling of a Gentile, God-fearer though he might be'.[94] Cornelius's subsequent prostration at the feet of Peter (10.25b), an act that elicits Peter's strong rebuke (10.26), adds to the dramatic nature of the encounter (10.25-26).[95]

By having Peter first 'enter' Caesarea, Luke merges the city mission with that of the household (cf. Lk. 10.5-7, 8-12).

90. Scott, 'The Cornelius Incident in the Light of its Jewish Setting', p. 478. Kee observes that Caesarea 'symbolized and embodied for Jews in Palestine the cultural, economic and political dominance by a pagan power of the land that they considered to be theirs' (*Good News to the End of the Earth*, p. 51). As a Roman military official, Cornelius personally symbolizes that oppression.

91. Politically, of course, it was very much a part of Judea. See Acts 8.40; 12.19; 21.10.

92. Krodel, *Acts*, p. 193.

93. A pre-focalizer anticipates participant contact while a focalizer establishes it. See Funk's discussion (and examples) of pre-focalizers and focalizers in *The Poetics of Biblical Narrative*, pp. 100-15. According to Funk, 'the common form of the focalizer is simply the arrival or meeting of two or more participants' (p. 102).

94. Bruce, *The Book of Acts* (ET), p. 205. Marion L. Soards notes the ambiguous status of God-fearers: 'At times... they are highly regarded, but because they were uncircumcised, God-fearers were still considered to be unclean' ('The Historical and Cultural Setting of Luke–Acts', in Earl Richard [ed.], *New Views on Luke and Acts* [Collegeville: Michael Glazier Inc./The Liturgical Press, 1990], p. 40).

95. Cornelius's actions of falling (πίπτω) and worshiping (προσκυνέω) match those of John in his dramatic encounter with the angelic messenger in the book of Revelation (19.10; 22.8).

In his third and final act of entry at 10.27, Peter proceeds to meet the 'many people' (συνεληλυθότας πολλούς) gathered inside Cornelius's house. This use of a double focalizing technique is evident elsewhere in the Lukan corpus.[96] Here it gives Peter's actions a corporate focus since the entire household of Cornelius has gathered to hear the words of Peter. The significance of this corporate encounter will be examined in more detail below. Important for the moment is the justification Peter gives to explain his presence in the house of Cornelius: 'You yourselves know that it is unlawful for a Jew to associate with or to approach a foreigner; but God has shown me that I should not call any person [ἄνθρωπον] common or unclean' (10.28). The use of ἄνθρωπος here in connection with clean and unclean is significant: what earlier applies to foods now applies to people.[97] Peter's presence in the house of Cornelius is proof that Peter has undergone a process of conversion in the course of the story. He is now in position to preach salvific peace to the household. Cornelius himself sets the stage for this action by declaring to Peter in the final verse of the scene: 'So now all of us are here in the presence of God to listen to all that the Lord has commanded you to say' (10.33)

The first four scenes of the Cornelius story depict a series of world-shattering events designed to bring Peter into the house of Cornelius. As Peter enters this house, the reader does well to call to mind the kind of person targeted in the household mission of the Seventy-two. First, in entering the house of Cornelius, Peter enters the house of a Gentile. Peter, like the Seventy-two, disregards the social and ethnic boundaries separating Jews from Gentiles. As will soon become clear, one can hardly underestimate the significance of Peter's actions for the narrative of Acts as a whole. What is new to the pattern is the kind of Gentile Cornelius purports to be. As the recipient of a rather elaborate epithetical characterization (10.12, 22),[98] Cornelius assumes the status of a

96. See, for example, Lk. 17.12-13 (in Funk, *The Poetics of Biblical Narrative*, p. 106).

97. Tyson notes that the connection between unclean foods and unclean people is a close one in Luke's world. Since Lev. 11 regards anyone coming into contact with carcasses as unclean, it follows that 'anyone who does not observe the dietary regulations is unclean; unclean diet means unclean person' (Tyson, 'The Gentile Mission and the Authority of Scripture in Acts', p. 627).

98. Epithetical characterization involves 'telling' the reader directly about the traits of a given character, which usually requires less of a reader than 'showing' (see Powell, *What is Narrative Criticism*? pp. 52-53). Since the reader of Acts is twice

δίκαιος Gentile (10.22; cf. v. 35),[99] a description recalling a prior instance of household salvation well-known to the implied reader of Luke.[100] Excelling in both prayer and alms (10.2, 4), Cornelius is the consummate God-fearer (10.2, 22, 35), manifesting two of the three traditional components of Jewish praxis.[101] Despite this exalted status, however, Cornelius still belongs to ranks of the uncircumcision (ἀκροβυστία) and is therefore unclean (11.3).[102]

Although less apparent in some ways, Peter also enters the house of a socially and economically established householder. A Roman centurion occupied not only a position of prestige in the community but could expect to receive up to fifteen times the amount paid to an ordinary soldier.[103] The opportunities for economic enrichment in the Roman

informed of the righteous character of Cornelius (10.1-2, 22), Luke apparently does not want his audience to miss it.

99. This designation is used also of Jesus in Acts (3.14; 7.52; 22.14).

100. The similarities between Cornelius and Noah are striking. Like Cornelius, Noah is a δίκαιος 'Gentile' who receives special recognition by God (Gen. 6.9; 7.1; cf. Acts 10.4). Like Cornelius, Noah receives salvation along with his entire household (σὺ καὶ πᾶς ὁ οἶκός σου; Gen. 7.1; Acts 11.14), a feature with which he is often associated (Heb. 11.7; 1 Pet. 3.20). Moreover, both stories involve distinguishing between clean and unclean animals (Gen. 7.2-9; Acts 10.9-16). In light of Luke's familiarity with the Noah story (Lk. 17.26-27) and his strong affinity for Septuagintal language, he may intend a correspondence here, though more along the lines of scriptural echo than direct allusion. See the criteria set forth in Richard B. Hays, *Echoes of Scripture in the Letters of Paul* (New Haven: Yale University Press, 1989), pp. 29-32.

101. Only fasting is absent from the description of Cornelius's religious life. On the narratological portrayal of Cornelius as the consummate God-fearer, see Tyson, *Images of Judaism in Luke–Acts* (Columbia: University of South Carolina Press, 1992), pp. 37-38 and Creech, 'The Most Excellent Narratee', pp. 114-23.

102. See Soard's comment in footnote 94 above. Despite his righteous conduct, Cornelius is still regarded by Peter as an ἀλλόφυλος (10.28), a term that sometimes denotes a 'Philistine' in the Septuagint (Scott, 'The Cornelius Incident in the Light of its Jewish Setting', p. 479; cf. 1 Kgs 4.9; 7.11). What confirms Cornelius's acceptance for baptism is not his righteous character but the falling of the Holy Spirit upon his household (Tannehill, *The Narrative Unity of Luke–Acts*, II, p. 133). Thus, Haenchen's remark that the story is intended to show that 'the community does not accept just *any* Gentile, but only Gentiles of such piety that even a Jew must approve' (*The Acts of the Apostles*, pp. 357-58) appears wide of the mark.

103. So Bruce J. Malina and Richard L. Rohrbaugh, *Social-Science Commentary on the Synoptics Gospels* (Minneapolis: Fortress Press, 1992), p. 326. David Kennedy puts the centurion's pay at some sixteen times the basic legionary salary

military, notes B.S. Easton, were generally good, even for an honest person.[104] That Cornelius was capable of generous alms-giving, notable even to God (10.4), in addition to having many household servants and clients (10.7, 24), is indicative of his relative wealth on the pages of Acts. Like the centurion of Lk. 7.1-10, Cornelius appears as a generous benefactor of the Jewish community.

In view of Cornelius's economic position, it is noteworthy that his house is large enough to host not only the members of his immediate family but the 'many' friends and relatives who gather there to hear the message of Peter.[105] These individuals make up the church at Caesarea. The residence of Cornelius may well have become the center of Christian mission in that city, with additional families added to the faith (cf. 18.22). Thus, the physical structure of Cornelius's house performs an essential function in the story of Christian beginnings in Caesarea, though the narrator leaves most of the details to the informed imagination of the reader. Apart from its literary function, the double entry of Peter (10.25, 27) might suggest that the house was equipped with a gateway or pylon leading to a large central area (cf. 10.17).[106]

b. *Peter Preaches to the Household of Cornelius*. Once inside the house, Peter proclaims salvific peace to the household, which becomes the focus of the next scene (Acts 10.34-43). Attention now shifts from the house as an architectural location to 'house' as the recipient of salvation.

(David Noel Freedman, (ed.), *ABD* [New York: Doubleday, 1992], see 'Roman Army', V, p. 791). On the 'extratextual repertoire' of the implied reader of Luke–Acts, see John A. Darr, *On Character Building: The Reader and the Rhetoric of Characterization in Luke–Acts* (Louisville: Westminster Press/John Knox, 1992), pp. 22-23. According to Martin Hengel, a centurion belonged to the 'upper class' in Roman society (*Property and Riches in the Early Church: Aspects of a Social History of Early Christianity* [trans. John Bowden; Philadelphia: Fortress Press, 1974], p. 64).

104. B.S. Easton, *The Gospel According to St Luke* (Edinburgh, 1926), cited in I. Howard Marshall, *The Gospel of Luke: A Commentary on the Greek Text* (Grand Rapids: Eerdmans, 1978), p. 280. On the significance of Cornelius's social location for a reading of Luke, see Tannehill, '"Cornelius" and "Tabitha" Encounter Luke's Jesus', *Int* 48 (1994), pp. 347-56, who relies on Kennedy's assertion that a centurion possessed 'both considerable military and social status and wealth' (*ABD*, V, p. 791).

105. Including the six believers who accompany Peter from Joppa (11.12; cf. 10.23).

106. See Haenchen, *The Acts of the Apostles*, p. 350.

'And opening his mouth' (v. 34a), a phrase designed to introduce a weighty utterance,[107] is the narrator's way of stressing Peter's role as the proclaimer of this salvation (cf. 15.7).

In analyzing Peter's sermon, scholars have noted its stereotypical nature, contending that it is inappropriate to its present context.[108] At the same time, however, the emphasis on the 'facts' of Jesus' earthly career (vv. 37-41) makes the sermon particularly suitable for a gentile audience such as that gathered in the house of Cornelius.[109] The opening words of Peter (vv. 34b-35) are particularly descriptive of Cornelius, who exemplifies the kind of 'God-fearer' (ὁ φοβούμενος αὐτὸν) and 'doer of righteousness' (ἐργαζόμενος δικαιοσύνην) acceptable to God from every nation (cf. 10.2, 22).

Two features of Peter's sermon appear to echo the protocol of the household mission. The first is the specific mention of the εἰρήνη ('peace') of Jesus Christ (10.36; cf. Lk. 10.5b). Though God is the author of this peace, Peter is the one who offers it by reciting the story of Jesus to the household of Cornelius.[110] Second, Peter's reference to 'eating and drinking' at 10.41 not only recalls Jesus' post-resurrection eating activity with his disciples (Lk. 24.30, 41-43; Acts 1.4) but the table-fellowship practice of his earthly career which becomes part of the

107. Bruce, *The Acts of the Apostles: The Greek Text with Introduction and Commentary*, (Grand Rapids: Eerdmans, 3rd edn 1990), p. 260. Hereafter, this work is cited as *The Acts of the Apostles* (GT).

108. So Dibelius, who regards the opening phrase ('you know') as 'scarcely appropriate' to Cornelius, 'who, although he knows something of the Old Testament ...knows nothing about Jesus Christ' (*Studies in the Acts of the Apostles*, p. 111). The similarity of this sermon with others in Acts indicates that 'Luke wants to show his readers what Christian preaching is and ought to be' (p. 111).

109. C.H. Dodd sees the sermon as reflecting 'the form of kerygma used by the primitive church in its earliest approaches to a wider public' (*The Apostolic Preaching and Its Developments* [Grand Rapids: Baker Book House, 1980; reprint], p. 28). As such, it 'is quite intelligible in the situation presupposed that some account of the ministry of Jesus should have been called for when the gospel was taken to people who could not be acquainted, as the Jews of Judea were, with the main facts' (p. 28). For a recent defense of the appropriateness of Peter's speech, see Black, 'The Conversion Stories in the Acts of the Apostles', pp. 153-54.

110. The grammatical construction of this verse is notoriously difficult (see the standard commentaries for options). In my view, the words τὸν λόγον are best understood as an accusative of respect: 'With respect to the word which he sent to the sons of Israel, preaching peace through Jesus Christ, this one is Lord of all.' This reading keeps the focus on the universality of salvation, which is the point of 10.34.

charge to the Seventy-two (Lk. 10.7).[111] Peter himself will re-enact this table-fellowship practice by subsequently dining in the house of Cornelius (10.48; 11.3).

While the sermon begins with a focus on the person of Cornelius, by the sermon's end it is the household that has become the recipient of salvation. The destination of Peter's sermon clearly emerges at the start of the next scene: 'While Peter was still speaking, the Holy Spirit fell upon all those hearing the word' (10.44). The succinct way that this verse depicts the reception of the gospel by the household becomes characteristic of the later household conversion stories in Acts: a messenger speaks (λαλέω) and a household hears (ἀκούω) the salvific peace of the word (λόγος). The reference to 'all those hearing the word' (πάντας τοὺς ἀκούοντας τὸν λόγον) recalls, in the immediate context, the members of Cornelius's household who gather in his house 'to hear [ἀκοῦσαι] all the things being commanded to you [Peter] by the Lord' (10.33).[112] If Cornelius constitutes the original target of Peter's words (10.22), the household gradually becomes the primary hearer. For Luke, 'hearing' is the primary means of incorporation into the people of God (Lk. 8.19-21; 10.39; 11.27-28).[113]

A careful reading of the narrative up to this point allows one to identify the hearers of Acts 10.44 in more precise terms. 'Blood relatives' (συγγενεῖς, 10.24),[114] 'close friends' (ἀναγκαίους φίλους, 10.24),[115] domestic 'servants' (οἰκετῶν, 10.7)[116] and perhaps a devout soldier (10.7)[117] make up the οἶκος of Cornelius that converts at the preaching of Peter (10.2; 11.14). That Cornelius presides over a household of some

111. See under 'eating and drinking' in ch. 3 of this book. The theme of 'eating and drinking' thus links the two phases of Jesus' career—earthly and exalted.

112. The theme of hearing (ἀκούω) thus 'brackets' the sermon of Peter (10.33, 44).

113. See Maloney, *'All that God had Done with Them'*, p. 71.

114. The term συγγενής appears only here in Acts. It occurs in the Gospel of Luke, however, to denote blood relations (1.58; 2.44; 14.12; 21.16).

115. These friends were the *amici*, 'the trusted friends to whom intimacy was granted and from whom reliable support and devotion was expected' (Michael Green, *Evangelism in the Early Church* [Grand Rapids: Eerdmans, 1970], p. 209).

116. An οἰκέτης denoted a 'house servant' as opposed to a laborer who worked outside the house.

117. He is among those individuals who were in constant attendance upon Cornelius.

size is evident by the 'many' who gather in his house (10.27).[118] The first household conversion narrated in Acts is a household conversion indeed! The conversion of Cornelius's entire family, of course, does not come unexpectedly in the course of the story since Cornelius is initially described as one who feared God 'with all his household' (σὺν παντὶ τῷ οἴκῳ αὐτοῦ, 10.2), a use of epithetical characterization that anticipates a development later in the narrative.[119] The appearance of the 'οἶκος formula' both here and at 11.14 helps to mark the presence of a Lukan 'type-scene' found elsewhere in Acts (16.15; 16.31; 18.8).

The reception of the Holy Spirit by the household at Acts 10.44-48 becomes the occasion for the disappearance of Cornelius from the story and, ultimately, from the pages of Acts. When Peter and James later allude to the events of Acts 10, they speak of the conversion of a people, not an individual (15.7-11, 14).[120] The pervasive use of plural subjects and objects to describe the events immediately following Peter's sermon is illustrative of the way the narrator shifts the focus to the corporate sphere: the Holy Spirit falls not upon the individual Cornelius but upon 'all [πάντας] those hearing the word' (10.44). The circumcised believers from Joppa are seized with amazement when they see that 'the gift of the Holy Spirit had been poured out even on the Gentiles [τὰ ἔθνη], for they were hearing them [αὐτῶν] speaking in tongues and magnifying God' (vv. 45-46). Peter's decisive question is equally corporate in focus: 'Can anyone forbid water for baptizing these people [τούτους] who have received the Holy Spirit as we also have?' (10.47). Peter subsequently commands 'them' (αὐτοὺς) to be baptized in the name of Jesus Christ (10.48a). By story's end, the household, not Cornelius, becomes the primary actor: 'they' invite Peter to stay in the house for hospitable fellowship (cf. ἠρώτησαν, 10.48b). In this way, the household gradually supplants Cornelius as the primary focus of the narrative.

c. *Peter Stays in the House, Eating and Drinking.* At the close of the final scene in Acts 10, the newly converted household reciprocates Peter by offering him hospitality in the house of Cornelius: 'Then they asked

118. On the constitution of a typical Roman household, see Green, *Evangelism in the Early Church*, pp. 209-210.

119. Tannehill observes that such characterization 'may serve to "nail down" a characteristic that will contribute to a later development' (*The Narrative Unity of Luke–Acts*, II, p. 134).

120. As pointed out earlier, the name of Cornelius does not even appear in Acts 15!

him to stay on for some days' (10.48b).[121] This temporal notation, employing a compounded form of μένω drawn from the *Leitwörter* of the Seventy-two (Lk. 10.7), de-focalizes the scene,[122] leaving a lasting impression on the reader and preparing for the charge against Peter of eating in a Gentile's house (11.3).[123]

In view of the role that this charge will play in the ensuing narrative (see below), the importance of Peter's stay in the house of Cornelius far surpasses its brief mention at the close of Acts 10. Martin Dibelius observes how, by taking up residence in the house of Cornelius, Peter has 'entered upon a relationship with Cornelius which is so real as to entail sharing a common table with him'.[124] Like the Seventy-two before him who eat and drink whatever the household provides (Lk. 10.7), Peter partakes of table-fellowship with the household of Cornelius with the added assurance that God has removed the dietary restrictions separating Jews from Gentiles (Acts 10.9-16), giving concrete expression to his newly discovered truth that God makes no distinctions between them (Acts 10.34-35).

A close analysis of the charge at Acts 11.3 reveals its essentially two-

121. According to John B. Mathews, both the asking (ἐρωτάω) and the staying (ἐπιμένω) reflect technical terminology associated with the practice of hospitality in the early church ('Hospitality and the New Testament Church: An Historical and Exegetical Study' [ThD dissertation, Princeton Theological Seminary, 1964], p. 125). Literarily, 'staying' (μένω and compounds) is part of Luke's vocabulary for describing meal scenes (Arthur A. Just, Jr, *The Ongoing Feast: Table Fellowship and Eschatology at Emmaus* [Collegeville: The Liturgical Press, 1993], p. 222). The use of τότε suggests that the offer of hospitality comes as part of a reciprocal response to the baptism of the household.

122. In de-focalizing the scene, the narrator does not shift locale but expands the temporal duration. See Funk, *The Poetics of Biblical Narrative*, p. 122.

123. What Tannehill observes of the ending of Acts applies equally to other narrative endings: 'The final scene of a narrative is an opportunity to clarify central aspects of plot and characterization in the preceding story and to make a final, lasting impression on the reader' ('Rejection by Jews and Turning to Gentiles: The Pattern of Paul's Mission in Acts', in Joseph B. Tyson [ed.], *Luke–Acts and the Jewish People: Eight Critical Perspectives* [Minneapolis: Augsburg, 1988], pp. 92-93).

124. Dibelius, *Studies in the Acts of the Apostles*, p. 114. 'If Peter accepted the invitation to remain for some days with Cornelius in Caesarea,' says Tyson, 'then he would have also have eaten with him. At least, so much must be said in order to understand the question in 11.3' ('The Gentile Mission and the Authority of Scripture in Acts', p. 627). So also Larrimore C. Crockett, 'Luke 4.25-27 and Jewish-Gentile Relations in Luke–Acts', *JBL* 88 (1969), p. 180.

sided nature. The charge is not simply that Peter 'ate' (συνέφαγες) with uncircumcised men but that he 'entered' (εἰσῆλθες) the house of Cornelius in doing so. Tannehill perceptively notes what many commentators do not, namely, that '[B]oth eating and entry into the house are causes of objection in Acts 11.3.'[125]

The significance of these two related charges bears closer examination. The first charge on the lips of Peter's accusers centers on Peter's entry into the house of uncircumcised men.[126] The recurrence of εἰσέρχομαι here, obscured in many modern English translations,[127] distinctly recalls the three-fold entry motif back at 10.24-27. The accusers of Peter are keenly aware that in the course of converting a Roman centurion, Peter entered the house of a Gentile. The issue of 'space' thus stands at the foundation of their charge, permitting a glimpse into the Lukan conception of the gentile mission. For Luke, converting Gentiles means 'entering their homes, and accepting hospitality in those homes.'[128]

The second, related charge of 'eating' with Gentiles more directly corresponds to Peter's actions in Acts 10.48. Entry into the home of a Gentile was particularly loathsome for a Jew if it issued in table-fellowship.[129] By having Peter receive hospitality from the household of Cornelius, the Lukan narrator reveals his keen interest in 'the legitimation of complete fellowship between Jew and Gentile in the Christian

125. Tannehill, *The Narrative Unity of Luke–Acts*, II, p. 137 n. 19.

126. The Western text of 11.3 makes the connection to οἶκος explicit: 'you entered the house of uncircumcised men' (cf. NIV). If an explicit reference to οἶκος is lacking at 10.48 and 11.3, it is because it is simply assumed, as is the case historically: 'The setting for assembly was a given; it was presupposed and needed no elaborate discussion throughout the early Christian period' (Lloyd Michael White, 'Domus Ecclesiae—Domus Dei: Adaption and Development in the Setting for Early Christian Assembly' [PhD dissertation, Yale University, 1983], p. 2).

127. By not translating εἰσέρχομαι consistently with its prior usage at 10.24-27, many modern English translations leave readers unaware of the conscious connections between the two passages (e.g. NRSV).

128. Gaventa, *From Darkness to Light*, p. 120. She further observes that 'the inclusion of Gentiles and table-fellowship with Gentiles are inseparably linked' (p. 121).

129. Esler notes that it was but a 'short step' from the Levitical prohibitions on foods to a complete ban on table-fellowship, 'for a Jew could not safely eat any food supplied to him by a Gentile for fear that it had been stored or cooked in a vessel used for one of the forbidden foods and had thereby become ritually defiled' (*Community and Gospel in Luke–Acts*, p. 85).

community, not just the admission of the Gentiles to those communities'.[130] Moreover, it is more than likely, given Luke's interest in the symbolic power of food,[131] that the table-fellowship enjoyed by Peter and the newly converted household assumed a eucharistic character. It is scarcely conceivable that Luke did not intend the reader to see in this table-fellowship over the course of 'some days'[132] a reference to the Lord's Supper. Part of the paradigmatic significance of the Cornelius story, as Philip Francis Esler points out, 'is not simply the broad task of baptizing Gentiles, but also that of initiating Christian communities where Jews and Gentiles share common eucharistic meals'.[133]

As the scene of Peter's radical acceptance of Gentiles, the house of Cornelius assumes a certain 'sacred' status on the pages of Acts. It is in the house of Cornelius, the place where Peter 'enters' and 'eats', that God acts in a decisive way to remove the ethnic and social barriers between Jews and Gentiles. As Esler observes, 'The central issue in this narrative is not that the gospel has been preached to Gentiles, but the far more particular fact, of great ethnic and social significance, that Peter has lived and eaten with them'.[134] Household space that is originally common or profane (10.28) becomes, in the course of the story, the distinct locale for table-fellowship between Jews and Gentiles. As in the mission of the Seventy-two, the house is 'set apart' as the place of inclusive fellowship between the messenger and the newly converted

130. Esler, *Community and Gospel in Luke–Acts*, p. 96. According to Crockett, 'The fact of Jews and Gentiles living and eating together is the focal point of Luke's conviction that God's intention in the new age is to save both Jews and Gentiles and bring them into a productive mutual relationship' ('Luke 4.25-27 and Jewish–Gentile Relations in Luke–Acts', p. 181). Thus, Haenchen's point that Luke has substituted the 'lesser' charge of eating with Gentiles misses the point (*The Acts of the Apostles*, p. 359). As Gaventa points out, his view 'fails to see the pervasive thread of hospitality that runs throughout this narrative. It also overlooks the fact that the inclusion of Gentiles and table-fellowship with Gentiles are inseparably related. To balk at eating with Gentiles is to balk at receiving them into the community' (*From Darkness to Light*, p. 121).

131. See, Robert J. Karris, *Luke: Artist and Theologian* (New York: Paulist Press, 1985), pp. 47-78. Also John Navonne, 'The Lucan Banquet Community', *The Bible Today* 51 (1970), pp. 155-61.

132. The phrase ἡμέρας τινάς indicates an indefinite period of time, not the 'few days' of the NIV and NCV (cf. *Williams, Acts*, p. 196).

133. Esler, *Community and Gospel in Luke–Acts*, p. 96.

134. Esler, *Community and Gospel in Luke–Acts*, p. 93.

household (Lk. 10.7).[135] That a unique outpouring of the Holy Spirit transpires in the house of Cornelius as 'the final and irrefutable legitimation for the acceptance of the Gentiles into the community'[136] only adds to the emerging sacral status of the house,[137] a theme that will be taken up later in this study.

Intradiegetic Narration

A distinct feature of Lukan literary style, notes Henry J. Cadbury, is the tendency of the author to repeat the content of an original event on the lips of a later speaker.[138] Nowhere is this tendency more evident than in the story of Cornelius, which in a relatively short period of time becomes the basis of Peter's defense before his critics in Jerusalem (11.1-2) and, sometime later, will be classically recalled by Peter and James at the Jerusalem Council (15.7-11, 13-21).

a. *Peter's Defense Before His Jerusalem Accusers (11.1-18).* The seventh and final scene of the Cornelius story (11.1-18) is the occasion for Peter's defense before the circumcision party in Jerusalem (vv. 1-2), which accuses Peter of entering into the house of a Gentile and eating with uncircumcised men (v. 3). This accusation provides the important

135. The notion of sacred space in this study refers to the transformation of the house from simple domestic space to the place of Christian assembly, distinct from synagogue or temple. Historically, of course, one cannot speak of the complete 'sacralization' of the house until much later when it comes to have an exclusive liturgical function (cf. White, 'Domus Ecclesiae—Domus Dei'). Interestingly, White sees the beginning stages of this process occurring in the book of Acts, particularly in connection with the 'upper room' of the house (pp. 602-603).

136. Esler, 'Glossolalia and the Admission of Gentiles into the Early Christian Community', *BTB* 22 (1992), p. 136.

137. From a cultural anthropological perspective, the manifestation of a deity at a particular locale is foundational to its taking on a sacral character: 'Every sacred space', writes Mircea Eliade, 'implies a hierophany, an irruption of the sacred that results in detaching a territory from the surrounding cosmic milieu and making it qualitatively different' (Mircea Eliade, *The Sacred and the Profane: The Nature of Religion* [trans. Willard R. Task; New York: Harcourt, Brace and Company, 1959], p. 26).

138. After the 'Homeric manner', says Cadbury ('Four Features of Lukan Style', in Leander E. Keck and J. Louis Martin [ed.], *Studies in Luke–Acts: Essays Presented in Honor of Paul Schubert* [Nashville: Abingdon Press, 1966], p. 89). He cites Paul's conversion (Acts 9, 22, 26) and the letter of Claudius Lysias (Acts 23.26-30) as examples.

segue between the original events of Acts 10 and Peter's subsequent recounting of his experience at 11.4-18. The accusation, however, serves another purpose as well. It effectively links Peter's actions to the ministry of Jesus, who encountered similar criticism when he visited the house of Zacchaeus, a proto-typical Gentile: 'And when they saw this, they all began to complain, saying, "He has gone [εἰσῆλθεν] to lodge with a sinful man"' (Lk. 19.7; cf. 5.30). In entering the home of a Gentile and eating there, Peter has the actions of Jesus as authoritative precedent.[139]

The charge of 11.3 is determinative both for the nature and content of Peter's speech. The way in which this verse leads directly to Peter's narration of events at 11.4-18 suggests that any variations that occur in the course of the re-telling are best interpreted in light of the speech's apologetic character.[140] The charge thus becomes the 'interpretative principle' for understanding Peter's recounting of the story. What compels Peter to tell of his experiences in the house of Cornelius is not the general desire to inform but a specific, pointed charge. That charge centers around the sharing of food and shelter, not the baptism of a Gentile.[141]

In response to this charge, Peter begins to explain 'in orderly fashion' (καθεξῆς) the events transpiring in the house of Cornelius (11.4).[142] As Maloney astutely observes, 'Peter's defense does not consist in a logical or theological argument, but in a *narrative* of events.'[143] As the

139. On the significance of Zacchaeus as a story of household salvation, see ch. 3 of this book.

140. Translating the ὅτι clause at 11.3 in the form of a direct accusation increases the apologetic character of the account: 'So you have been visiting the uncircumcised and eating with them!' (NJB). So Maloney, *'All that God had Done with Them'*, p. 85 n. 10. On ὅτι as an interrogative ('Why did you enter...', NRSV), see C.F.D. Moule, *An Idiom Book of New Testament Greek* (Cambridge: Cambridge University Press, 1963), p. 132.

141. So Dibelius: 'It is not the centurion's belief which is being proved, but the apostle's right to enter the house of uncircumcised men—and then not in order to convert the uncircumcised to Christ, but in order to eat with them' (*Studies in the Acts of the Apostles*, pp. 118-19).

142. As Luke's orderly (καθεξῆς) narration of the Jesus story brings certainty to his reader/listener (1.3), so Peter's orderly (καθεξῆς) narration of events is designed to assure his audience of the propriety of his actions. For similar reasoning, see Luke T. Johnson, *Decision Making in the Church: A Biblical Model* (Philadelphia: Fortress Press, 1983), p. 76.

143. Maloney, *'All that God had Done with Them'*, p. 69, emphasis hers.

intradiegetic narrator, Peter naturally tells the story from his own experience of events. Since Peter initially shares the same perspective toward Gentiles and their houses as his accusers (10.14, 28), he hopes his first-person account of his own transformation will achieve a similar effect on them. Tannehill notes this aspect of the story well:

> The Jerusalem audience is like Peter, beginning with Peter's previous assumptions about the way a Jew should behave. A sequence of events led Peter to change his mind. Now his audience is being led through the same sequence of events so that they can appreciate and share Peter's new insight.[144]

The narrative begins not with the vision of Cornelius, as in Acts 10, but with Peter's vision of foods (11.5-10). In addition to reflecting Peter's own experience of events, the placement of the foods vision at the beginning of the narrative suggests that Peter is directly justifying his eating with Gentiles.[145] The vision of foods has convinced Peter of the propriety of accepting their hospitality.[146] Thus, the abrogation of the food laws becomes an explicit feature of the household mission.

While mentioning his praying in the city of Joppa (11.5), Peter omits any reference to his staying in the house of Simon the tanner, a rather surprising omission given the emphasis on Simon's house in Acts 10 as the scene of the original vision (10.6, 9, 17-23, 32; cf. 9.43). Simon's unclean vocation would immediately have raised the hackles of Peter's legalistic opponents. Peter also fails to mention his becoming hungry and desiring to eat (cf. 10.10), perhaps because he wishes to save his first explicit reference to eating until later in the vision. If Peter has enjoyed indiscriminate table-fellowship in the house of Cornelius, it is because *God* has told him it is now proper for him to kill and 'eat' (11.7).[147]

While praying in the city of Joppa, Peter reports that he saw a great object like a sheet being lowered 'from heaven' (ἐκ τοῦ οὐρανοῦ), stressing the divine origin of his vision.[148] That Peter describes the object

144. Tannehill, *The Narrative Unity of Luke–Acts*, II, p. 144.

145. So Dibelius, *Studies in the Acts of the Apostles*, p. 112.

146. Cf. David L. Tiede: 'The food vision apparently also convinced him [Peter] to accept their hospitality' ('Acts 11.1-18', *Int* 42 [1988], p. 177).

147. This verse contains Peter's first (and only) reference to 'eating', the substance of the charge levelled against him at 11.3.

148. As in Acts 10, the reference to οὐρανός forms a literary *inclusio* around Peter's report of the vision (11.5,10). The voice that Peter hears also comes down 'from heaven' (ἐκ τοῦ οὐρανοῦ, 11.9).

as coming 'right down to me' (11.5c) underscores the immediacy and reality of his experience. On the sheet, Peter says, were four types of animals—four-footed, beasts of prey, reptiles, and birds of the air (11.6). The expansion in the classification of animals from three to four (cf. 10.12) makes the indiscriminate command to kill and eat even more radical (11.7), accentuating Peter's response that he has never eaten anything unholy or unclean (11.8). That Peter's accusers in Jerusalem strongly share his view makes the declaration of the heavenly voice all the more relevant to the present situation: 'What God has cleansed, you must not call profane!' (11.9). The thrice repeated command of the heavenly voice adds to its certainty and strength (11.10).

Peter next narrates the arrival of Cornelius's messengers at the house of Simon without mentioning Simon by name (11.11). The addition of ἐξαυτῆς here ('at that very moment') connects the meaning of the vision to the events that would soon transpire in Cornelius's house. The explicit instructions of the Spirit ('the Spirit told me to go') at 11.12 add additional divine authority to the mission of Peter, who is to accompany Cornelius's messengers 'without discriminating' (μηδὲν διακρίναντα). This subtle shift to the active voice (cf. 10.20) indicates that Peter is now reflecting on his prior experience, which has taught him to consider no person common or unclean (10.28, 34-35).[149] The instructions of the Spirit also serve to contrast God's salvific intentions with the narrow viewpoint espoused by Peter's opponents in Jerusalem, who 'criticized' (διεκρίνοντο) Peter's actions (11.2).[150]

The vision of the foods, the timely (providential) arrival of Cornelius's messengers, and the explicit instructions of the Spirit prepare for Peter's climactic entry into the house of Cornelius, succinctly narrated at 11.12b: 'we entered the man's house'. This entry, the reader recalls, forms the basis of the complaint against Peter (11.3). At this point, however, Peter adds an important detail: the six Jewish believers accompanying him from Joppa (cf. 10.23b) entered the house with him, a point not

149. In the first account, the Spirit's instructions to Peter were to go 'without hesitating' or 'without doubting' (μηδὲν διακρινόμενος, 10.20).

150. Maloney observes that while διακρίνω is used in a different sense at 11.12, 'its echo certainly suggested to readers or listeners that Peter had cooperated with the order of the Spirit without argument (despite his resistance to the direction to "kill and eat" in his vision), and that it would be equally inappropriate for the listeners to his report to "make distinctions" or to continue to dispute the working of God's plan' (*'All that God had Done with Them'*, p. 75).

readily apparent at 10.24-27.[151] Not just Peter but an entire delegation of Jews are guilty of the charge of entering the house. Peter finds strength in numbers.[152] Apparently, the role of these six believers will be to provide, along with Peter, a unified Jewish witness to the working of God among the Gentiles.[153] The more precise reference to 'six', absent in the first account (cf. 10.23b), serves well in a polemical context by adding greater specificity (and therefore credibility) to the testimony of Peter.

Only after narrating his entry into the house does Peter report the initial vision given to Cornelius: 'And he [Cornelius] announced to us how he had seen the angel standing in his house and saying, "Send to Joppa and summon Simon, who is called Peter; he will speak words to you by which you will be saved, you and all your household"' (11.13-14). Peter reports these words precisely at the point where he, not the reader, would have heard them (cf. 10.30-32). The multiple layers of narration evident here—'Luke said that Peter said that Cornelius said that the angel said'—add reliability and authority to Peter's account.[154]

The report of the angel recounted at 11.14, including the characteristic 'οἶκος formula' ('you and all your household'), succinctly summarizes what the first account took fifteen verses to expound, namely, the salvation that comes to the household as a result of the preaching of Peter (10.34-48). Beginning here at 11.14, it will become the custom of the narrator of Acts to depict the salvation of households in the barest of terms, utilizing the same οἶκος formula (16.15; 16.31; 18.8). That this formula is now used to capture the larger experience of Cornelius's household portrayed earlier in ch. 10 suggests that it carries more pregnant meanings and associations than would otherwise meet the eye. The

151. Note the singular subjects in these verses. On the probable reading of εἰσῆλθεν at 10.24, see Bruce M. Metzger, *A Textual Commentary on the Greek New Testament*, corrected edn (New York: United Bible Societies, 1975), p. 374.

152. Maloney observes that 'they are all equally guilty of having "gone to uncircumcised men"' (*'All that God had Done with Them'*, p. 75).

153. 'If these six brethren now dispute Peter's account on other grounds, they run the risk of denying their own experience of God's power' (Johnson, *Decision Making in the Church*, p. 76). Similarly, Pervo sees their role as corroborating Peter's story to the Jerusalem church (*Luke's Story of Paul*, p. 39). Nowhere in the story, however, does the narrator expressly relate the function of the six Jewish believers.

154. This same phenomenon of multiple layers is observable in Acts 2 where it performs a similar function. See Mikeal C. Parsons, 'Christian Origins and Narrative Openings: The Sense of a Beginning in Acts 1–5', *RevExp* 87 [1990], pp. 408-409).

various persons who assemble to hear the words of Peter, for example, a theme more fully developed by the hyperdiegetic narrator in Acts 10, are now, upon reflection, simply termed the 'οἶκος'. This 'streamlining' of material is important in a speech designed to meet a specific charge and to perform a certain function.

In addition to its role as a summary device, the report of the angel expressly interprets the actions of Peter in salvific terms: 'He will speak words to you by which you will be saved [σωθήσῃ], you and all your household'. This use of σῴζω, the first such occurrence of soteriological language in the entire narrative, 'goes beyond previous indications of the purpose of sending for Peter'.[155] While providing a valid interpretation of what previously transpired in the house of Cornelius, the salvific terminology permits Peter a slight 'shift' in focus—from the specific issue of eating with Gentiles to the broader notion of saving Gentiles. In so doing, Peter makes table-fellowship an integral element of gentile salvation. If Peter is to speak the word of salvation to Gentiles, Peter must 'enter' the house of Cornelius, which implies that he may now 'eat' there as well.[156]

It is at this point in the narrative that Peter tells of the dramatic confirmation of the Spirit: 'And as I began to speak, the Holy Spirit fell upon them just as also upon us at the beginning' (11.15). By moving the Spirit's descent from the end of his message to the beginning (ἐν δὲ τῷ ἄρξασθαί με λαλεῖν; cf. 10.44), Peter invests the coming of the Spirit with an even more unexpected and decisive effect.[157] The parallel he draws between this outpouring and the original Pentecost in Acts 2 ('just as also upon us at the beginning') makes the case even more difficult for his accusers to refute: how can they accept the one and not the other? Peter's subsequent citation of the 'word of the Lord' regarding baptism with the Holy Spirit (11.16) is itself a citation of Jesus' words at Acts 1.5 (cf. Lk. 3.16), which becomes the 'key to the

155. Tannehill, *The Narrative Unity of Luke–Acts*, II, p. 144.

156. Notice how the twin issues of 'entering' and 'eating' are closely linked in the minds of Peter's accusers at 11.3. One should remember that the vision of Peter which declared the acceptability of Gentiles as *persons* (10.28) also declared the acceptability of *foods*. That Peter has just recited the vision of foods to justify his eating in the house of Cornelius (11.5-10) means that the statement of 11.18 recognizes the abrogation of the Jewish food laws. Black observes how 11.18 elevates Cornelius's conversion to a 'matter of principle' ('The Conversion Stories in the Acts of the Apostles', p. 149).

157. Haenchen, *The Acts of the Apostles*, p. 355.

interpretation of the original Pentecost event'.[158] In this way, Peter strengthens the connection between the two pneumatic outpourings.

Peter effectively turns the tables on his critics at the close of his defense by taking the role of the accuser: 'If, therefore, God gave to them the same gift that he gave us when we believed in the Lord Jesus Christ, who was I that I could hinder [κωλῦσαι] God?' (11.17). With this question Peter hopes that his accusers will come to the same understanding regarding the acceptance of Gentiles into the church as he has.[159] Significantly, Peter drops out any mention of his staying in the house of Cornelius for table-fellowship, preferring instead to leave it indirectly addressed. The strategy, it seems, proved effective for Peter: 'When they heard these things, they quieted down and glorified God, saying, "So then God has given even to the Gentiles the repentance leading to life"' (11.18). This silencing of Peter's critics means that they cease from criticizing Peter (11.3),[160] implying an acceptance of his ministry in the house of Cornelius.[161]

In recognizing the validity of gentile salvation as Peter narrates it, the Jerusalem community indirectly affirms Peter's right to enter into the house of a Gentile, preach the word of salvific peace, and remain in the house eating and drinking. At least from Peter's perspective, the 'what' of gentile salvation entails the 'how'. Thus, Gaventa observes how Luke uses the issue of hospitality in this account to show that 'the conversion of the first Gentile required the conversion of the church as well'.[162] The

158. Maloney, *'All that God had Done with Them'*, p. 76. She further says (p. 82): 'As Luke had prepared for the descent of the Holy Spirit on the apostles by preceding it with a word of promise from the Risen One (cf. Acts 2 with 1.5), here he also connects the descent of the Spirit on the gentiles with this same promise, depicting Peter as remembering it at this very hour (11.16).'

159. The reappearance of κωλύω here recalls the baptism of Cornelius and his household at 10.47.

160. See Johnson, *The Acts of the Apostles* (Collegeville: The Liturgical Press, 1992), p. 199.

161. Cf. Werner G. Kümmel: 'According to Acts 10.1–11.1-18, Peter had accomplished the first conversion of a pagan [?] through his preaching, and *by his report in Jerusalem he had achieved the sanction of the "apostles and brothers" there for engaging in table fellowship with the Gentiles*' (*Introduction to the New Testament*, rev. edn [trans. Howard C. Kee; Nashville: Abingdon Press, 1975]), p. 189, emphasis mine.

162. Gaventa, *From Darkness to Light*, p. 109. The story of Cornelius thus recounts three conversions: Peter, Cornelius, and now the Jerusalem church!

placement of 11.18 at the conclusion of the story 'means more than a general recognition that God, sometime and somehow, will enable Gentiles to find salvation. It means that a mission by Jews to Gentiles can begin because...God has removed the social barrier between Jews and Gentiles.'[163] That Peter's Jerusalem opponents are not entirely aware of the radical social ramifications of their decision, due largely to Peter's convincing narrative, is evident from the way that the issue of social intercourse re-surfaces in the 'decrees' of the later Jerusalem Council (15.20, 29; cf. 21.25).[164] This development, notes Richard I. Pervo, 'upsets and surprises the reader, who has been given to understand that the whole matter had been settled following the conversion of Cornelius'.[165]

b. *Peter and James Before the Jerusalem Council (15.7-11, 13-21).* Due perhaps to a pre-occupation with the well-known difficulties between Acts 15 and Galatians 2,[166] scholars do not always appreciate the tensions that Luke's portrayal of the Jerusalem Council presents within the text of Acts itself.[167] Both Acts 11 and 15 center on the problem of Jewish relations with the uncircumcised in the church (cf. 11.3; 15.1, 5), though each poses the issue somewhat differently. In Acts 11 the stress lies on the issue of table-fellowship, not conversion; in Acts 15 it is on the validity of gentile conversion apart from circumcision and the law. Yet, for Luke, the twin issues of conversion and table-fellowship are inseparable; it is simply not possible 'to fully accept someone with whom you are not willing to share in the intimacy of table-fellowship.'[168] Seen

163. Tannehill, *The Narrative Unity of Luke–Acts*, I, p. 136. The literary *inclusio* centered around the act of hearing (ἀκούω, 11.1,18) suggests that the Jerusalem community's response offers the appropriate closure to the issues raised in Acts 11. The ἄρα of 11.18 ('so then') is emphatic, introducing a conclusive statement (cf. H.E. Dana and Julius R. Mantey, *A Manual Grammar of the Greek New Testament* [New York: Macmillan, 1955], p. 242).

164. On the problems presented by the decrees in Acts, see M.A. Seifrid, 'Jesus and the Law in Acts', *JSNT* 30 (1987), pp. 39-57 (esp. pp. 41-44).

165. Pervo, *Luke's Story of Paul*, p. 51. This point is especially salient for Pervo's 'first-time' reader.

166. Most recently, Russell Lester, 'Galatians 2.1-10 and Acts: An Old Problem Revisited', in Keathley, *With Steadfast Purpose*, pp. 217-38.

167. An exception is Jack T. Sanders, *The Jews in Luke–Acts* (Philadelphia: Fortress Press, 1987), pp. 114-22.

168. John B. Polhill, *Acts* (NAC; Nashville: Broadman Press, 1992), p. 256. 'It

in this way, Acts 15 poses a practical (and radical) solution to the problem of table-fellowship with Gentiles: make them Jews.[169]

Peter's rehearsal of the Cornelius story before the Council at Jerusalem (15.7-11), as opposed to his prior narration in Jerusalem (11.5-17), is interesting for its lack of a distinctly apologetic starting point. Peter is not defending himself against the charge of eating with Gentiles in gentile houses as formerly (11.3) but applying the lesson of Cornelius to the debate surrounding the missionary work of Paul and Barnabas (15.3-4, 12), whose success among the Gentiles (cf. 13.1–14.28) has raised the question of the basis of gentile salvation in an acute form (15.1, 5). The new context is critical for understanding the absence of the household missionary pattern in Acts 15: Peter is no longer recounting a *personal* experience in the house of Cornelius but fashioning a *theological* argument to justify Paul's work among the Gentiles.[170] The recollection of 'the early days' (ἀφ' ἡμερῶν ἀρχαίων, 15.7) suggests that the Cornelius event now lies in the distant past.[171]

Peter begins his 'theologizing' of the Cornelius event by briefly alluding to his sermon in the house of Cornelius ('by my mouth', 15.7), omitting entirely the crucial events that led him there. In the ensuing narrative, Peter repeats some of the familiar themes of the prior Cornelius story but now with an eye toward their theological significance. As in Acts 10.44, the Gentiles of Cornelius's household 'hear the word of the gospel' (ἀκοῦσαι τὰ ἔθνη τὸν λόγον τοῦ εὐαγγελίου, 15.7), but now for the first time Peter stresses their response of faith (καὶ πιστεῦσαι), a theme appearing twice more in the course of the narrative (15.9, 11). The epitome of Peter's argument makes faith (not circumcision) salvifically operative: 'but through the grace of the Lord Jesus we believe [πιστεύομεν] so as to be saved, in the same

is salutary to remind ourselves,' writes G.H.C. Macgregor, 'that even today there are Christians, e.g., in a mixed white or colored community, who will freely admit the equality of their brethren "in Christ", and yet rigidly refuse social intercourse with them' (*The Acts of the Apostles* [IB; Nashville: Abingdon Press, 1954], p. 196).

169. As Esler notes, 'The question of table-fellowship between Jew and Gentile is not explicitly raised in Acts 15, but its presence is everywhere implied' (*Community and Gospel in Luke–Acts*, p. 98).

170. Noted by Tannehill, *The Narrative Unity of Luke–Acts*, II, p. 184.

171. Maloney sees a theological motive behind the use of the phrase, namely, to show that 'God's plan for the salvation of the gentiles is not something new, but has been "from of old"' (*'All that God had Done with Them'*, pp. 138-39).

manner as they' (15.11).[172] Whereas the gift of the Holy Spirit remains largely unchanged in its present context (15.8; cf. 10.44; 11.15), Peter now interprets the cleansing of the Gentiles (καθαρίσας), as well as God's refusal to make distinctions (οὐθὲν διέκρινεν), no longer in a ceremonial sense (foods) but in a moral one: God has cleansed their hearts by faith (15.9). In treating the Cornelius event this way, 'Peter is drawing emphatic theological conclusions from specific aspects of his past experience'.[173]

In the speech of James (15.13-21), the narration is one step removed, resulting in an even less personal narrative: 'Simeon has recounted how God first concerned himself to take from among the Gentiles a people for his name' (15.14). The emphatic presence of πρῶτον looks back upon the Cornelius event as the first 'official' instance of gentile conversion in Acts while λαὸν, a term found elsewhere in Luke for Israel, stresses the oneness of the people of God, composed of both Jews and Gentiles.[174] Seeing that Scripture itself justifies the inclusion of Gentiles among the people of God (15.15-18; cf. Amos 9.11-12, LXX),[175] James proposes that circumcision not be made a requirement for salvation (15.19) but that gentile believers abstain from four things—meat sacrificed to idols,[176] fornication, the meat of strangled animals, and blood (cf. v. 29; 21.25). With these 'decrees', James brings the issue of

172. The construction πιστεύομεν σωθῆναι should probably be understood as an infinitive of result ('we believe so as to be saved'). It then becomes Peter's answer to the question posed at the outset (15.1), confirming the Lukan Paul's position on the justification of the Gentiles (13.38-39).

173. Tannehill, *The Narrative Unity of Luke–Acts*. II, pp. 184-85.

174. Except for Acts 15.14 and 18.10, λαός always signifies Israel in the Lukan corpus (so Nils Dahl, 'A People for His Name', pp. 319-27). The lines of distinction, however, must not be drawn too sharply at 15.14. The awkward phrasing (ὁ θεὸς ἐπεσκέψατο λαβεῖν ἐξ ἐθνῶν λαὸν τῷ ὀνόματι αὐτοῦ) suggests that 'the author was wrestling a bit with his syntax in his effort to express, in this compact formulation, the astonishing fact that God was creating out of Israel and out of the ἔθνη a single λαός' (Maloney, *'All that God had Done with Them'*, p. 157).

175. This appeal to Scripture presents a stark contrast to the original story of Cornelius which adduces no scriptural support to justify the conversion of the Gentiles. See Tyson, 'The Gentile Mission and the Authority of Scripture in Acts', pp. 619-31.

176. The phrase τῶν ἀλισγημάτων (15.20) is later described as εἰδωλοθύτων (15.29), the usual term for eating meat sacrificed to idols (cf. 1 Cor. 8.1, 4, 7, 10; 10.19, 28; Rev. 2.14, 20).

table-fellowship to the fore,[177] compromising the freedom achieved by the household mission in the process. Whereas Peter formerly enters the home of Gentiles and eats their food, reflecting the abrogation of the dietary laws (10.9-16; 11.5-10; cf. Lk. 10.7), James mitigates this indiscriminate eating by imposing certain restrictions upon it. The tension between the two narratives has not escaped astute readers of Acts.[178]

How should one understand this tension on the pages of Acts? While, importantly, both Acts 11 and 15 allow for table-fellowship between Jews and Gentiles in the church, two factors tip Luke's hand in favor of the more radical precedent set by the household missionary pattern. First, it is clear that he presents James's decision in Acts 15 as a 'compromise' position with certain Jews of the sect of the Pharisees (15.5). The reappearance of the decrees at 21.25 suggests that 'James is proposing that Gentiles be asked to abstain from certain things especially offensive to a Jewish sense of cultic purity so that Jewish Christians may remain in the fellowship of the church without being forced to give up their way of life'.[179] Secondly, the places designated at 15.23 as the recipients of the decrees (Antioch, Syria, and Cilicia) preclude the decrees from having universal scope. Apart from 16.4, no evidence exists in Acts that Paul ever implements the decision of the Jerusalem Council.[180]

177. So most commentators (*contra* Sanders, *The Jews in Luke–Acts*, p. 120). Only fornication (πορνεία) does not pertain to table practice. Interestingly, the oldest extant manuscript witness (the Chester Beatty papyrus—P45) omits the reference to πορνεία, making the decrees exclusively centered on table practices.

178. Tyson ('The Gentile Mission and the Authority of Scripture in Acts', p. 628) calls the decrees of 15.20 'a notorious problem for those who think that the vision of Peter constitutes an annulment of the laws of kashrut'. He mentions two possible solutions. One is to see in James's admonitions a reference to ethical standards only (Western text). Another is to interpret the decrees as dealing with the ways animals are killed and prepared for eating. Such proposals, however, only underscore the tension that exists between these two narratives. See also Seifrid, 'Jesus and the Law in Acts', pp. 41-44.

179. Tannehill, *The Narrative Unity of Luke–Acts*, II, p. 191. This verse is discussed at greater length in ch. 6 of this book. According to Bruce, the decrees come in response to the 'weaker brethren' of Jewish birth, 'not all of whom could be expected immediately to acquire such an emancipated outlook on food-laws and the like as Peter and Paul' (*The Book of Acts* [ET], p. 311; this citation is from the first edition).

180. On the geographical limitation of the Jerusalem Council, see Brawley, *Luke–Acts and the Jews*, pp. 42-43 as well as Williams, *Acts*, pp. 260-61. According to the latter, the churches in southern Galatia receive the decrees (16.4) because they

These factors suggest that the stories of household conversion showcase Luke's true sentiments on the issue.[181]

Narrative Function

That the story of Cornelius performs a crucial function in the narrative of Acts is recognized by nearly all commentators. My task in this section is to construe that function in light of its literary pattern of household evangelism, one that directs Peter to enter the house of a Gentile, preach salvific peace to the household, and stay in the house for inclusive table-fellowship.

The function of the Cornelius story consists of three related aspects. First, by means of Peter's radical act of entry into the house of Cornelius, salvation is made available to the Gentiles. The mission to households, with its unique directive to enter indiscriminately into (gentile) houses with the message of salvific peace, becomes the crucial *modus operandi* of the expanding church. Peter's role as traveling missionary to the house of a Roman centurion at Caesarea occasions the first significant shift in the geography of Acts, away from the regions of Judea and Samaria, and to the households located at the 'ends of the earth' (Acts 1.8).[182] The paradigmatic position of the Cornelius story is evident from the way that the narrator delays reporting a systematic mission to the Gentiles (11.19-21) until *after* the climactic events transpiring in Cornelius's house. Thereafter, Paul is free to begin his work among the Gentiles (13.1–28.31).

The conversion of a Gentile, of course, does not come totally unexpectedly on the pages of Acts. The prior impulses in the direction of a full-fledged mission to Gentiles, beginning with Pentecost and continuing with the Samaritans, the Ethiopian eunuch, and Saul, anticipate and

constitute 'daughter churches' of Antioch. Strategically, no stories of household conversion appear in those regions earmarked by the Jerusalem decrees.

181. Esler points to the four instances in Acts that showcase table-fellowship between Jewish and gentile Christians (10.1–11.18; 16.11-15; 16.25-34; 18.1-11; in *Community and Gospel in Luke–Acts*, pp. 40-41). Without realizing it, Esler enumerates the four accounts of household conversion.

182. Elliott observes that 'this pericope marks the advance of the messianic movement to Caesarea, the seat of Roman power in the land, and, as a key transitional episode, sets the stage for the mission to the Gentiles beyond the limits of the Holy Land (11.19ff.)'. See his 'Household and Meals vs. Temple Purity Replication Patterns in Luke–Acts', p. 105.

locate their fulfillment in the conversion of Cornelius, the Gentile *par excellence*. What does come unexpectedly, however, is *the way* in which the Gentiles are incorporated into the people of God as equal and full partners with Jews. This second and related function again underscores the importance of the household pattern: by Peter's sharing of food and shelter with the household of Cornelius as *per* in the protocol of the Seventy-two, God effectively removes the barrier of table-fellowship between Jews and Gentiles, a fact underscored by the appearance of the food vision abrogating Jewish dietary concerns. Salvation of the Gentiles in Acts, therefore, consists not solely in freeing them from the constraints of circumcision and the law but in making them fellow members of the covenant community, sharing a common table with Jews.

The kind of radical table-fellowship envisioned in the house of Cornelius calls for the establishment of a new 'sacred space', the third related function of the story. As noted previously, the issue of 'space' figures prominently in the story of Cornelius (11.3), with the house becoming the scene of full eucharistic fellowship between messenger and household (cf. Lk. 10.7). Temple and synagogue, the traditional religious institutions of first-century Judaism, stand opposed to providing Gentiles equal participation in the people of God. Only the house/household, with its emphasis on kinship and solidarity, 'is capable of embodying socially and ideologically the structures, values, and goals of an inclusive gospel of universal salvation'.[183]

The global context of Acts permits a subtle yet perceptible contrast between house and temple as competing locales of divine presence.[184] The dramatic outpouring of the Holy Spirit in the house of Cornelius confirms Peter's radical activity there and constitutes a second 'Pentecost' with important parallels to Acts 2. Peter, the chief evangelist on both occasions, offers vivid testimony:

> Can anyone forbid water for baptizing these people who have received the Holy Spirit *as we also have*? (10.47)
>
> And as I began to speak, the Holy Spirit fell upon them just *as also upon us at the beginning* (11.15)
>
> And God, the knower of the heart, bore witness to them by giving them the Holy Spirit, *just as also he did to us* (15.8)

183. Elliott, 'Temple versus Household in Luke–Acts', p. 213.

184. The following offers an extended discussion of the way in which the house is contrasted with both temple and synagogue in the global and proximate contexts of the Cornelius story.

This three-fold comparison clearly invites the reader to interpret the conversion of Cornelius in light of the original Pentecost event. As Maloney observes: 'In all these cases the reference is clearly to the event depicted by Luke as the first Pentecost of the Christian community in Acts 2.1-4.'[185]

Significantly, the setting for this original Pentecost event is not the temple, where the disciples appear at the close of the Luke's Gospel (24.53), but the οἶκος, where the entire community gathers to await the promise of the Holy Spirit: 'And suddenly from heaven there came a sound like a rushing violent wind, and it filled the entire house where they were sitting' (Acts 2.2; cf. 1.4-5).[186] Both the Gentiles of Cornelius's household and the Jewish believers of Pentecost experience the filling of the Holy Spirit in a house.[187] The expression, 'filled the entire house' (ἐπλήρωσεν ὅλον τὸν οἶκον), clearly echoes 1 Kgs 8.10-11,[188] which describes the glory[189] of the Lord filling the temple of

185. Maloney, *'All that God had Done with Them'*, p. 76. Of the correspondences between Cornelius and Pentecost, Maloney says: 'There is not the slightest ambiguity: the gift of the Holy Spirit to the gentiles at Caesarea is described as being exactly the same as what happened to the members of the original Jerusalem community "at the beginning"' (p. 76).

186. The 'house' of 2.2 is probably to be identified with the 'upper room' of 1.13, a 'sacred' locale in Acts (White, 'Domus Ecclesiae—Domus Dei', pp. 602-603).

187. Elliott, 'Household and Meals vs. Temple Purity Replication Patterns in Luke–Acts', p. 105. The narrator's use of the house setting for the original Pentecost introduces obvious tensions at various points in the story. Krodel, for example, observes that 'Luke does not bother to tell us how all 120 members of the community could find space in that house' (*Acts*, p. 74). Moreover, nowhere does the narrator ever expressly shift the scene away from the house, leaving one to wonder how the multitude could 'come together' in the house where the disciples were speaking with other tongues (2.6). This emphasis on the house gives the Pentecost conversion a distinctly 'household' character: the community gathers in the house where it attracts a multitude of hearers (2.2), Peter directs his message of salvation to 'all the house' of Israel (2.36), and the believing community regularly celebrates the Eucharist in the house (2.46).

188. The text (3 Kgdms 8.10-11) reads: 'And it came about that as the priests went out of the holy place, that the cloud filled the house [ἔπλησε τὸν οἶκον]. And the priests could not stand to minister from the presence of the cloud, because the glory of the Lord filled the house [ἔπλησε…τὸν οἶκον]' (cf. Ezek. 43.4, 6; cf. 10.4-5, 18). The use of πίμπλημι here rather than the Lukan πληρόω is not significant in light of the virtually identical meaning of the two terms.

189. God's 'glory' was post-biblically expressed as God's *shekinah*, which represented the 'nearest Jewish equivalent to the Holy Spirit' (J.D. Douglas, ed., *NBD*

Solomon. This 'filling' largely accounted for the temple's sacred character.[190] The shift of the divine presence away from the temple to the house thus intimates a transference of sacred space: 'The *oikos* and not the *naos* is henceforth the locus of God's presence and benediction.'[191]

This gradual replacement of the temple is foreshadowed at the close of Acts 2 when the house alone becomes the setting for a distinctive Christian worship. While the Pentecost converts keep up their attendance at the temple, they reserve the 'breaking of the bread' for the house (2.46).[192] In the remaining chapters of Acts, the temple functions only as 'the scene and subject of conflict' (3.1–4.22; 5.17-42; 21.26-30).[193] The one exception to this rule—Paul's reception of his Gentile commission in the temple (22.17-21)—only serves to drive him farther away from it.[194] The most explicit challenge to the temple as a sacred institution occurs in the speech of Stephen (7.46-50), who, in denying that the Most High dwells in temples 'made with hands' (χειροποιήτοις), equates the temple of Solomon with pagan idol houses (7.48; cf. 17.24).[195] This speech, notes Elliott, represents 'a turning point

[Wheaton: Tyndale House Publishers, 2nd edn, 1982], see 'Shekinah', by R.A. Stewart).

190. Esler notes that 'a belief in Yahweh's albeit mysterious presence in the Temple was the whole reason for the worship carried on there, in both prayer and sacrifice' (*Community and Gospel in Luke–Acts*, p. 153).

191. Elliott, *Home for the Homeless: A Sociological Exegesis of 1 Peter* (Philadelphia: Fortress Press, 1981), p. 199.

192. See Naymond H. Keathley, 'The Temple in Luke and Acts: Implications for the Synoptic Problem and Proto-Luke', in *With Steadfast Purpose*, p. 95. 'Breaking bread' is Luke's customary phrase for the Eucharist (Lk. 24.29-30, 35; Acts 2.42; 20.7, 11; 27.35). Translating κατ' οἶκον in its non-distributive sense at Acts 2.46 ('in the house'), a usage found elsewhere in the New Testament (1 Cor. 16.19; Col. 4.15; Phlm 2), heightens the rhetorical contrast between house and temple as respective spheres of religious activity.

193. Elliott, 'Temple versus Household in Luke–Acts', pp. 216-17. Elliott observes that in the remainder of Luke's account 'the temple plays no positive role as a place of Christian assembly or symbol of Christian identity' (p. 217).

194. Noted by Francis D. Weinert, 'The Meaning of the Temple in Luke–Acts', *BTB* 11 (1981), p. 88. Despite this observation, Weinert argues for a wholly positive stance towards the temple in the Lukan writings.

195. The term χειροποίητος regularly appears in the Septuagint to denote an idol or idol house, the product of human hands (e.g., Lev. 26.30; Wis. 14.8). Esler calls Acts 7.48 'the shoal upon which all attempts to argue for a totally favorable attitude to the Temple in Luke–Acts must inevitably founder' (*Community and Gospel in*

between the earliest phase of the church's life and its connection with the temple (Acts 1.1–8.1a) and its full-scale mission to the households of the diaspora (8.1b–28.31)'.[196]

If the global connection between the two Pentecost narratives contrasts the institutions of house and temple,[197] the proximate context of the Cornelius story juxtaposes the house with the institution of the synagogue. The way in which the synagogue persecution 'brackets' the story of Cornelius suggests that the Lukan narrator intends a subtle, yet perceptible, contrast between the receptive οἶκος and the recalcitrant synagogue, especially in light of the explicit reappearance of this theme in the Lukan presentation of the Pauline mission. In city after city, Paul turns to the household after encountering stiff opposition in the synagogues. The initial acceptance/final rejection motif typifying Jewish response on the pages of Acts is probably a Lukan creation.[198] In a telling incident at Corinth, Paul departs from the synagogue of the Jews and takes up residence with a respected God-fearer, whose house is located 'next door to the synagogue' (Acts 18.7). That Paul proceeds to convert the president of the synagogue while based in the house of a Gentile only adds to the symbolic irony present in the account.[199]

This picture of the house and synagogue as competing institutions on the pages of Acts is present in the Cornelius story in another way as well. As the paradigmatic God-fearer on the pages of Acts, Cornelius represents a potential, if not actual, member of the synagogue

Luke–Acts, p. 134). Notice the context of pagan idolatry in the use of the term at Acts 17.24.

196. Elliott, 'Temple versus Household in Luke–Acts', p. 216.

197. Certain other 'replacement' motifs also appear within the story of Cornelius itself. Cornelius is praying at the 'ninth hour' (10.3), the hour of the *tamid* (evening) sacrifice in the temple. The prayers and alms of Cornelius which ascend as 'a memorial [μνημόσυνον] before God' (10.4), an expression that denotes the fragrance of sacrifice rising up before Yahweh (Lev. 2.2, 9; 6.15), suggest that 'Cornelius' prayers and alms in his home are equivalent to or a replacement of the "clean" sacrifices at the Temple' (Elliott, 'Household and Meals vs. Temple Purity Replication Patterns in Luke–Acts', p. 106). Elliott sees a further contrast in this direction with the instructions to Peter to 'sacrifice [θῦσον] and eat' in the house of Simon (10.13; 11.7) rather than in the temple at Jerusalem (p. 106).

198. See Tyson, 'The Jewish Public in Luke–Acts', pp. 577-83. For Tyson, the incident in the Nazareth synagogue (Lk. 4.16-30) provides the literary pattern that will be worked out in the rest of the Gospel and in Acts.

199. The significance of this scene must await the discussion of the next chapter.

community.[200] His conversion, therefore, represents the winning of one on the margins of Jewish life to the new faith.[201] That Cornelius served as an influential patron of the Jewish community at Caesarea (Acts 10.2), perhaps after the manner of the centurion at Capernaum who built for the Jews their synagogue (Lk. 7.5), previews an important event appearing elsewhere in Acts. Acts 17, for instance, reports how certain synagogue Jews at Thessalonica became 'jealous' over the loss of a great multitude of God-fearers and leading women, who subsequently established themselves in a house (vv. 4-5). As Esler observes, the prominent feature of the nearly twenty conversion accounts in the book of Acts 'is that Luke portrays Christian evangelism as having been successful almost entirely among Jews and God-fearers attending synagogues where the Gospel was first preached'.[202]

The legitimation of table-fellowship between Jews and Gentiles established by the pattern of the household mission results in the emergence of a new religious space distinct from temple and synagogue. This development, of course, comes as no surprise to the attentive listener to the Lukan Jesus, who predicted the destruction of the temple (Lk. 13.34-35)[203] and warned his followers to expect persecution from the synagogue (Lk. 21.12). Thus, in sending his messengers into houses with the message of peace, Jesus anticipates the development of a new center of religious life for his community that would promote the unhindered expression of radical inclusiveness (Lk. 10.5-7). In Acts, the hospitality of households, exemplified in the story of Cornelius, makes possible 'the Christian worship, common meals, and courage-sustaining fellowship of the group'.[204]

200. Esler surmises that Cornelius was a member of the synagogue community (*Community and Gospel in Luke–Acts*, p. 37). In Acts, God-fearers are often associated with the synagogue (13.43; 17.4, 17; 18.7; cf. Lk. 7.1-10).

201. Gerhard Friedrich, (ed.), *TDNT*, trans. Geoffrey W. Bromiley, IX (Grand Rapids: Eerdmans, 1974), see 'φοβέω', by Horst Balz, p. 213.

202. Esler, *Community and Gospel in Luke–Acts*, p. 38.

203. Keathley notices how this first negative treatment of the temple in Luke is 'to be more fully developed later in the Lukan writings' ('The Temple in Luke and Acts', p. 85).

204. Floyd V. Filson, 'The Significance of the Early House Churches', *JBL* 58 (1939), p. 109.

Conclusion

While scholars have long recognized the corporate character of Cornelius's conversion on the pages of Acts, rarely have they made it the distinct focus of their interpretation. This chapter, in contrast, has proposed reading the Cornelius story against the backdrop of the Gospel of Luke: by entering into Cornelius's house, speaking words of salvific peace to the household, and staying in the house to eat and drink with Gentiles, Peter fulfills the dominical program of evangelizing households given to the Seventy-two (10.5-7). While a number of new elements appear throughout the course of the narrative, most notably Peter's vision of unclean foods, this pattern constitutes the essential 'plot' of the story, leading to the charge that Peter ate with Gentiles in a Gentile's house.

As the fullest expression of the household missionary pattern on the pages of Acts, the Cornelius episode establishes certain precedents and contributes certain themes that receive varying degrees of repetition on the pages of Acts. The stories of Lydia, the Roman jailer, and Crispus are noteworthy for the way that they, too, entail the conversion of entire households to the Christian faith. It now remains to consider the ways in which each of these stories contributes to the on-going theme of the salvation of the house.

Chapter 5

THE HOUSEHOLD CONVERSIONS OF LYDIA, THE ROMAN JAILER AND CRISPUS

Introduction

Alongside the story of Cornelius, the three remaining instances of household conversion in Acts seemingly pale in significance. They are less protracted in character and their meaning and function in Acts have proven more difficult to define. When viewed against the pattern of the mission to households, however, the conversions of Lydia (16.11-15), the Roman jailer (16.25-34), and Crispus (18.1-11) assume a greater degree of importance than previously recognized.

That the remaining stories follow in the wake of Peter's radical encounter with the household of Cornelius is itself one of their distinguishing features and a critical ingredient for their interpretation. Each employs the characteristic 'οἶκος formula', signifying that the original experience of household salvation is in some way repeating itself on the pages of Acts.[1] This phenomenon illustrates an important aspect of Luke's literary method, as Richard I. Pervo observes: 'One of Luke's primary artistic gifts is the capacity to spring imagination by a word or a phrase rather than by elaborate or protracted exposition. Through this economy the author can suggest an entire scene or circumstance with a few words.'[2] Pervo goes on to say that 'by the paucity of circumstantial detail Luke allows and invites readers to create their own scenes and fill in incidents'.[3] In the story of Cornelius, however, the first and fullest expression of the pattern of the Seventy-two in Acts, the reader has a paradigmatic scene by which to judge the other accounts.

1. See Acts 16.15; 16.31; 18.8. On the importance of this formula as a rhetorical marker, see ch. 4, pp. 87-89.

2. Richard I. Pervo, *Luke's Story of Paul* (Minneapolis: Fortress Press, 1990), p. 13.

3. Pervo, *Luke's Story of Paul*, p. 13.

The Conversion of Lydia and her Household (16.11-15)

The brevity of the Lydia story makes its significance easy to overlook (Acts 16.11-15). In a recent study of the conversion stories in Acts, Robert Allen Black notes the difficulty in finding 'any remarks in the literature of scholarship concerning the function of this story in Luke–Acts'.[4] On those rare occasions when Lydia does succeed in attracting some scholarly attention, her story usually appears only in connection with a larger issue, such as the doctrine of infant baptism[5] or Luke's treatment of women.[6] Yet, as the 'most illustrious convert of Philippi',[7] Lydia demands study in her own right and from a perspective that is distinctively Lukan. As a female head of house, who converts with her entire household, Lydia belongs to that distinct class of conversions in Acts properly termed 'household conversion'.[8]

4. Robert Allen Black, 'The Conversion Stories in the Acts of the Apostles: A Study of Their Forms and Functions' (PhD dissertation, Emory University, 1985), p. 167.

5. For the relevant literature, see ch. 1, pp. 4-5. More recently, R.S. Cherry, 'Acts 16.14f.', *ExpTim* 75 (1964), p. 114; J.W. Scott, 'Dynamic Equivalence and Some Theological Problems in the NIV', *WTJ* 48 (1986), pp. 351-61.

6. So, for example, Rosalie Beck, 'The Women of Acts: Foremothers of the Christian Church', in Naymond H. Keathley (ed.), *With Steadfast Purpose: Essays on Acts in Honor of Henry Jackson Flanders, Jr*, (Waco: Baylor University, 1990), pp. 279-307; Susanne Heine, *Women and Early Christianity: Are the Feminist Scholars Right?* (trans. John Bowden; London: SCM Press, 1987), pp. 83-86; Jacob Jervell, 'The Daughters of Abraham: Women in Acts', ch. 9 in *The Unknown Paul: Essays on Luke–Acts and Early Christian History* (Minneapolis: Augsburg Publishing House, 1984), pp. 146-57; William E. Tanner, *Jews, Jesus and Women in the Apostolic Age* (Mesquite: Ide House, 1984), pp. 71-73. An exception, in addition to Black's work above, is Rosalie Ryan, 'Lydia, A Dealer in Purple Goods', *The Bible Today* 22 (1984), pp. 285-89. For an interesting historical treatment, see Charles L. Cohen, 'Two Biblical Models of Conversion: An Example of Puritan Hermeneutics', *CH* 58 (1989), pp. 182-91.

7. So Robert F. O'Toole, *The Unity of Luke's Theology: An Analysis of Luke–Acts* (Wilmington: Michael Glazier, 1984), p. 124.

8. Donald Wayne Riddle observes that 'Lydia is one in whose case an entire household accepted Paul's message' ('Early Christian Hospitality: A Factor in the Gospel Transmission', *JBL* 57 [1938], pp. 152-53).

Narrative Context

The conversion of Lydia and her household occurs during the course of Paul's inaugural mission to Europe (Acts 15.36–18.22). Paul, who receives his commission from the risen Lord while traveling the road to Damascus (Acts 9.1-19), now takes over the task of household evangelizing from Peter.[9] In the three remaining accounts of household conversion, Paul, not Peter, appears in the role as household evangelist.[10] It is Paul's first mission to Europe that is important as an interpretative framework for the Lydia story, providing both its global and proximate context.

a. *Global Context: The Jerusalem Decrees and the Conversion of Upper Class Women.* In the narrative sequence of Acts, Paul's second missionary journey, the journey to Europe, follows the conclusion of the Council at Jerusalem (Acts 15.36).[11] There the leaders of the church settle upon a series of decrees which, while freeing the believing Gentiles from the obligations of circumcision, nevertheless require a modification in their table-fellowship practice with Jews (15.20, 29). The relevance of the Jerusalem Council for this journey is two-fold. First, it sets the stage for the replacement of Barnabas as a traveling companion to Paul. Though Barnabas accompanies Paul on his first missionary journey (13.1–14.28) and is present with him at the Council (15.2-4, 12), he subsequently separates from Paul over the issue of John Mark (15.37-39).[12] Paul finds an able replacement in the person of Silas (15.40-41), a leader in the Jerusalem congregation and a bearer of its letter to the Gentiles (15.22). The selection of Silas is noteworthy because of the role he soon

9. On Peter-Paul parallels in Acts generally, see Susan Marie Praeder, 'Jesus-Paul, Peter-Paul, and Jesus-Peter Parallelisms in Luke–Acts: A History of Reader Response', in *SBLSP*, Kent Harold Richards (ed. Chico, CA: Scholars Press, 1984), pp. 23-39.

10. Unlike Peter, Paul functions in his role with the help of others, most notably Silas, who figures most prominently in the conversion of the jailer.

11. The period of time denoted by μετὰ δέ τινας ἡμέρας in this verse is indeterminate, recalling its earlier appearance at Acts 10.48.

12. Luke portrays Barnabas's separation (15.36-39) in an essentially negative light. By siding with a deserter (τὸν ἀποστάντα ἀπ' αὐτῶν, v. 38), Barnabas shares in the 'apostasy' of John Mark (so Luke T. Johnson, *The Acts of the Apostles* [Collegeville: The Liturgical Press, 1992], p. 288). That Barnabas and Mark proceed to Cyprus (v. 39), Barnabas's place of origin (4.36), suggests that Barnabas 'has, simply, taken his relative/friend, and gone home' (p. 288).

plays as a fellow speaker of salvation to the households of Lydia and the jailer of Philippi.[13] It is doubtful, however, that Silas's Jerusalem provenance carries any symbolic import in this section of Acts.[14]

Second, as Paul and Silas proceed on their mission, they deliver the decrees decided on by the Jerusalem church (16.4) to the churches of southern Galatia (16.4),[15] thus extending the original purview of the Council.[16] Most likely David J. Williams is correct in seeing these congregations as 'daughter churches' of Antioch and thus as appropriate recipients of the decrees (cf. Acts 13.1-3).[17] The tension between the decision of the Council and the story of Lydia will be explored later in this chapter. Already at Acts 16.4 the decrees are a source of some tension, following on the heels of Paul's decision to circumcise Timothy, who now becomes the third member of the missionary party to the house (16.1-3).[18] The inclusion of Timothy is no incidental detail for

13. Note ἐλαλοῦμεν at Acts 16.13 and ἐλάλησαν at Acts 16.32 (cf. 16.31). His role in the conversion of Crispus is conceived somewhat differently by the narrator (18.5).

14. Robert C. Tannehill sees the partnership of Silas, one of the 'leading men' of Jerusalem (15.22), as an attempt to portray a 'unity of purpose' between Jerusalem and Antioch in this section of Acts (*The Narrative Unity of Luke–Acts*, II [Philadelphia: Fortress Press, 1986], p. 196). This interpretation, however, appears doubtful for three reasons: 1. Silas's Jerusalem provenance is nowhere stressed in the succeeding narrative (e.g., 15.40); 2. Silas becomes Paul's companion only as a kind of afterthought, the result of Barnabas's 'apostasy' (15.36-41; see footnote 12 above; 3. the missionary party soon expands to include Timothy (16.1-3), whose ethnic origin is a matter of confusion in Acts.

15. The reference to τὰ δόγματα at Acts 16.4 recalls the appearance of the verb δοκέω (from which δόγμα is derived) to describe the decision of the Council (Acts 15.22, 25, 28).

16. 'The delivery of these [decrees] beyond Cilicia', notes Johnson, 'had not been part of their original charge' (*The Acts of the Apostles*, p. 284). The Romans administered Syria and Cilicia (cf. Acts 15.23) under the one province of Syro-Cilicia, with Antioch as its capital city.

17. David J. Williams, *Acts* (NIBC; Peabody: Hendrickson, 1985, 1990), pp. 260-61. Geographical considerations, according to Williams, prevent Paul from publishing the decrees farther afield (p. 261). Williams makes this point in connection with the historical Paul but his insight remains valid for an interpretation of Acts.

18. It appears that the narrator regards Timothy as a Jew, since the circumcision of a Gentile so soon after the Council would introduce unbearable tensions in the narrative. Timothy's descent from a Jewish mother (16.1), however, raises the question of whether the matrilineal principle existed in the first century (see Shaye J.D. Cohen, 'Was Timothy Jewish? Patristic Exegesis, Rabbinic Law, and Matrilineal

Luke, providing a partial answer to the Lord's request to send additional laborers into the harvest, the harvest of house and city (Lk. 10.2).

After coming to Philippi, the scene of Lydia's conversion, Paul and his companions proceed on to the cities of Thessalonica, Berea, Athens, and Corinth. Each belongs to Paul's European itinerary and thus to the global context of the Lydia story. At Thessalonica (Acts 17.1-9), a large number of 'god-fearing Greeks' and 'leading women' of the synagogue convert at the preaching of Paul, arousing the jealousy of 'the Jews' (v. 4).[19] The same experience occurs at Berea (Acts 17.10-15) where, in response to the preaching of Paul and Silas in the synagogue, a large number of 'prominent Greek women' believe in the Lord (v. 12). At Athens (Acts 17.16-34), Paul converts a certain Dionysius, a member of the Areopagus, along with a woman named Damaris (v. 34). Both are influential because both are named.[20] The final scene in Corinth (Acts 18.1-17) has Paul meeting up with Aquila and Priscilla (v. 2), a couple who shared the same trade as Paul (v. 3). That Priscilla was the more influential of the two is evident by the way her name appears before her husband's later in the chapter (18.18, 26).[21]

As the above paragraph reveals, the conversion of prominent (gentile) women is a distinctive mark of Paul's mission to Europe.[22] While this phenomenon is perhaps explicable from solely a geographical perspective,[23] it reflects an emphasis in this section of the narrative of Acts as

Descent', *JBL* 105 [1986], pp. 251-68). Cohen traces this principle to the first quarter of the second century. Christopher Bryan argues, however, that it was already present in Luke's day ('A Further Look at Acts 16.1-3', *JBL* 107 [1988], p. 294).

19. According to Abraham J. Malherbe, Luke attributes Jewish opposition at Thessalonica to 'the social factor of competition for converts of high status' (*Paul and the Thessalonians: The Philosophic Tradition of Pastoral Care* [Philadelphia: Fortress Press, 1987], p. 17). The decisive role that the house of Jason plays in the narrative (17.5-9) will be discussed later in this chapter in connection with the conversion of Crispus.

20. On the identification of Damaris, F.F. Bruce considers it possible, though unlikely, that she was a God-fearer who heard Paul in the synagogue (*The Book of Acts*, rev. edn (Grand Rapids: Eerdmans, 1988), pp. 343-44. Hereafter, this work is cited as *The Book of Acts* (ET).

21. Her position at Acts 18.26 suggests that she is the chief instructor of Apollos, a man 'mighty in the Scriptures' (18.24; see Beck, 'The Women of Acts', p. 297). She also appears first at Rom. 16.3 and 2 Tim. 4.19 (cf. 1 Cor. 16.19).

22. Only Priscilla is expressly identified as a Jew (Acts 18.2). See Tanner, *Jews, Jesus and Woman in the Apostolic Age*, p. 73.

23. 'It is noticeable that in the three Macedonian towns, Philippi, Thessalonica,

well.[24] The conversion of Lydia thus fits well into this global context provided by Luke. As a gentile God-fearer (σεβομένη τὸν θεόν) with a profitable trade and large retinue, she is one of those prominent women who responds positively to Paul and his message (16.14-15). Her economic position allows her to open her home to Paul and to his associates, an invitation that Paul finds hard to resist.[25] She offers a striking contrast to those 'prominent' and 'devout' women of Pisidian Antioch who team up with certain leading men to oppose Paul during the course of his first missionary journey (Acts 13.50).[26]

b. *Proximate Context: Divine Intervention and Geographical Expansion*. If divine intervention marks key points in the story of Cornelius,[27] it is no less pivotal to the conversion of Lydia. The proximate context of the story particularly stresses the role of deity in directing Paul to his encounter with Lydia (16.6-10). Twice in this brief travel section the narrator notes the overturning of Paul's plans by supernatural means.[28] In the first case, Paul, Silas, and Timothy are 'forbidden by the Holy Spirit to speak the word in Asia' as they pass through the regions of Phrygia and Galatia (16.6).[29] The second portrays them

and Berea,' writes Williams, 'women are mentioned especially as influenced by the gospel' (*Acts*, p. 284). On the considerable freedoms enjoyed by women of Macedonia, see W.D. Thomas, 'The Place of Women in the Church at Philippi', *ExpTim* 83 (1971-72), pp. 117-20.

24. The editors of the Western text appear deliberately to downplay the prominence of women in this section of Acts (see Beck, 'The Women of Acts', p. 283).

25. 'Lydia...comes across in Acts as capable of managing others and as having that particular talent of making it hard for others to refuse what she insists upon' (Francis X. Malinowski, 'The Brave Women of Philippi', *BTB* 15 [1985], p. 60).

26. Despite this negative role here, the 'normal response of God-fearing prominent women is positive in Acts, and their activity in spreading the gospel is vital' (Beck, 'The Women of Acts', p. 300).

27. See, for example, Ernst Haenchen, *The Acts of the Apostles: A Commentary* (trans. Bernard Noble and Gerald Shinn; Philadelphia: The Westminster Press, 1971), p. 362. Divine initiative is mediated via ecstatic visions (10.1-8, 9-16), the direct intervention of the Spirit (10.19-20), and the pouring out of the Holy Spirit on the household of Cornelius (10.44-46).

28. O'Toole notes how travel motifs 'permeate the whole of Luke–Acts. Travel becomes significant because Jesus and his disciples travel to achieve God's salvific will or make it available to all' (*The Unity of Luke's Theology*, p. 72).

29. Thus, an ironic note is introduced when the first convert in Europe is an Asiatic (16.14)! The presence of λαλέω at both 16.6 and 16.13-14 heightens the contrast.

seeking to go into Bithynia, only 'the Spirit of Jesus did not allow them' (16.7). The first instance recalls a similar intervention of the Spirit in the story of Cornelius (10.19-20, 44) while the second identifies Jesus as the real director of the mission.[30] The theme of divine intervention links this travel section to the conversion of Lydia, who has her heart opened by the risen Lord (ὁ κύριος) in response to the things spoken by Paul (16.14).[31]

While at Troas, Paul encounters in a night vision a man of Macedonia requesting assistance: 'Cross over and help us!' (16.9-10).[32] The narrator couches this appeal in the language of prayer drawn from the Greek Old Testament.[33] While the exact nature of Paul's experience remains obscure,[34] the vision serves in the present context to steer the mission away from Asia to Europe, a mission that commences with the conversion of Lydia and her household. As a result, the missionary party[35] perceives God's call to evangelize the regions of Macedonia (16.10b). Thus, what Ernst Haenchen observes of the prior divine interventions applies here equally as well: 'Not by human calculation and planning was the Pauline mission brought to Troas and then to Macedonia, but by the mysteriously intervening *providentia specialissima* of God.'[36] The result

30. Jesus appears as a participant in the story earlier at Acts 7.56 and 9.4.

31. John R.W. Stott observes that 'although the message was Paul's, the saving initiative was God's' (*The Spirit, the Church and the World: The Message of Acts* [Downers Grove: Intervarsity Press, 1990], p. 263).

32. The use of a vision (ὅραμα) to mark an advance in the story's plot recalls a similar function in the story of Cornelius where a vision serves to bring Cornelius and Peter together (10.3, 17, 19; 11.5). Paul's vision 'at night' anticipates a similar vision in the story of Crispus (Acts 18.9; cf. 23.11). Attempts to identify the ἀνήρ who appeals to Paul for help have ranged from Alexander the Great to the author of Acts! Such guesswork, of course, is quite beside the point.

33. 'The use of the verb βοηθεῖν ("help/assist")', notes Johnson, 'is deeply evocative of biblical prayer, which uses this language for the help from God that is salvation' (*The Acts of the Apostles*, p. 286). Some of the passages he cites include Exod. 18.4; Ps. 36.40; 39.13; 43.26; 61.8; 78.9; Isa. 41.10, 14; 49.8.

34. That Paul receives his vision 'at night' suggests that he experienced a dream. If such is the case, Paul's vision is similar to a dream of Apollonius of Tyana in which a woman appears to him with a request to visit her before he leaves for Rome, which he interprets of the necessity to visit Crete (Philostratus, *Life of Apollonius* 4.34).

35. The vision of the man from Macedonia becomes the occasion for the first 'we' section of Acts, beginning at 16.10 (ἐζητήσαμεν).

36. Haenchen, *The Acts of the Apostles*, pp. 484-85. Haenchen sees in this

of Paul's vision is that the gospel in Acts expands its geographical boundaries, furthering its march to the 'end of the earth' (Acts 1.8).[37] As the first convert on European soil, Lydia represents a most significant step in that expansion.

Pattern and Variation

The conversion of Lydia is striking for the way it both departs from and adheres to the pattern of household evangelizing. It is only *after* Lydia hears Paul at a place of prayer (Acts 16.13-15a) that she invites the messengers to 'enter into my house and stay' (εἰσελθόντες εἰς τὸν οἶκόν μου μένετε, Acts 16.15b), affecting not just the poetic sequence of the story but its referential action as well.[38] Nevertheless, the pattern quickly resumes with Lydia's invitation to hospitality. The verbatim repetition of standard household *Leitwörter*, coupled with the salvation of the personified οἶκος (Acts 16.15a), expressly recalls the household protocol of the Seventy-two (Lk. 10.5-7).[39]

a. *The Pattern Broken.* After a brief sea voyage to the coast of Europe, Paul and the missionary party arrive in the city of Philippi (16.11-12). The narrator marks the arrival of the gospel in Europe by noting the status of Philippi as a leading city of the district of Macedonia and a Roman colony, facts that underscore the importance of the mission's

initiative a reminder of the story of Cornelius: 'By the way in which Luke developed it, it was made clear to the reader that the turning of the Christian mission to the Gentiles did not originate in any human desire but solely in the divine resolution. Here we have another important turning point in the history of the Christian mission. Only this time it is not a new group of men but a new area which is opened up for the Christian mission' (p. 485).

37. 'The direct religious experience,' says Charles H. Talbert, 'enables the fulfillment of the command of the risen Jesus in Acts 1.8' (*Acts* [KPG; Atlanta: John Knox, 1984], p. 69).

38. Poetic sequence refers in this context to the order of events as it appears in the narrative itself; the referential action refers to the chronological or 'logical' order of events that must be reconstructed by the reader. See Norman R. Petersen, *Rediscovering Paul: Philemon and the Sociology of Paul's Narrative World* (Philadelphia: Fortress Press, 1985), pp. 43-53.

39. Richard J. Dillon likewise sees the story of Lydia as reflecting the dominical program of converting households (*From Eye-Witness to Ministers of the Word: Tradition and Composition in Luke 24* [AnBib; Rome: Biblical Institute Press, 1978], pp. 190-92).

new geographical sphere. After staying in the city for some days,[40] Paul eventually finds his way to a riverside and begins speaking to a group of women assembled for prayer on the day of the Sabbath (16.13).

Among the women gathered to hear Paul preach is 'a woman named Lydia' (τις γυνὴ ὀνόματι Λυδία, 16.14a), a phrase that may denote a proper name or simply a place of origin ('the Lydian woman').[41] Judging from the characteristics ascribed to her at 16.14,[42] she represents the typical target of the household mission. First, as a seller of purple fabric, an item of luxury in both Luke's social and symbolic worlds,[43] Lydia almost certainly was a person of some means;[44] Thyatira, her home town, was the center of the purple-dye industry in the ancient world.[45] That she was capable of hosting several guests in her home,[46] in addition to members of her own household traveling with her

40. Once again, the phrase ἡμέρας τινάς (16.12) marks an indefinite period of time (cf. Acts 10.48; 15.36).

41. Thyatira, Lydia's home city, was located in the ancient kingdom of Lydia, eventually subsumed by the Roman province of Asia (see Pliny the Elder, *Natural History* 5.10).

42. Like Cornelius, Lydia is the focus of a rather elaborate characterization.

43. The most coveted color in the ancient world, purple was the color of royalty, worn by kings of Assyria and Babylonia and adopted by Alexander the Great (see Ryan, 'Lydia, A Dealer in Purple Goods', pp. 287-88; cf. Mk 15.17, 20; Jn 19.2, 5; Rev. 17.4; 18.12). In the story of the rich man and Lazarus, purple symbolizes wealth. The rich man, Luke says, 'dressed in purple and fine linen' (Lk. 16.19).

44. Wayne A. Meeks, *The First Urban Christians: The Social World of the Apostle Paul* (New Haven: Yale University Press, 1983), p. 62. Ryan notes that, unlike weavers, purple merchants were highly regarded and often accrued much wealth ('Lydia, A Dealer in Purple Goods', p. 288).

45. Noted as early as Homer (*Iliad* 4.141-42). Textile production, in general, constituted an important industry in the Roman Empire: 'The need of clothing the army and civilians, weaving canvas for sailing ships, as well as the demand for the fine fabrics from the aristocrats, kept textile workshops at full production. Often the workshop employed over a hundred slaves, and the operation was at times taken over by the imperial government' (Ryan, 'Lydia, A Dealer in Purple Goods', p. 287).

46. The missionary party at this juncture included Paul, Silas, Timothy, and perhaps the author of Acts, the 'we' of 16.10. John B. Polhill observes: 'Lydia's invitation to the four missionaries to stay in her home in itself indicates that she had considerable substance, such as guest rooms and servants to accommodate them adequately' (*Acts* [NAC; Nashville: Broadman Press, 1992], p. 349). So also Marion L. Soards, 'The Historical and Cultural Setting of Luke–Acts', in Earl Richard (ed.), *New Views on Luke and Acts* (Collegeville: Michael Glazier/The Liturgical Press, 1990), p. 44.

(16.15b, 40),[47] reinforces the impression of Lydia as a person of social mobility and economic substance. Second, in identifying Lydia as a σεβομένη τὸν θεόν, an expression used of Gentiles who adhere to the Jewish synagogue, Luke places her in that category known as 'God-fearers'.[48] As a gentile adherent of the synagogue who converts with her entire household, Lydia recalls the prior conversion of Cornelius, the God-fearer *par excellence.* This time, however, it is a *female* householder that converts.[49]

The above considerations are quite consistent with the kind of householder targeted by the household mission. Lydia is both a Gentile and a person of some means. The divergence in the account centers on the place where Lydia hears the saving message: 'And on the day of the Sabbath we went outside the gate to a riverside, where, according to custom, there was a place of prayer; after sitting down we began speaking to the women who had gathered there' (16.13). Here the household messengers speak[50] their message in a 'place of prayer' (προσευχή), not in a house (οἶκος, οἰκία) envisioned by the mission of the Seventy-two (Lk. 10.5). It is possible that προσευχή denotes a domestic structure of some kind, in which case the variation exists solely on a rhetorical level.[51] In Hellenistic Jewish literature, however, the term is virtually

47. Whether Lydia's household included small children/infants is a matter of much debate, lying at the center of the paedo-baptist controversy. Unlike the other three household conversion accounts (10.43-44; [15.7]; 16.34; 18.8), the narrator nowhere ascribes the act of believing to Lydia's household. Only Lydia as such believes (16.14-15). See Cherry, 'Acts 16.14-15', p. 114. For a more recent treatment of the problem, see Scott, 'Dynamic Equivalence and Some Theological Problems in the NIV', pp. 351-61.

48. This phrase denotes Gentiles 'who accepted the ethical monotheism of Judaism and attended the synagogue, but who did not obligate themselves to keep the whole Jewish law' (BAGD, see 'σέβω', p. 746). In Acts 17.4, 17 and 18.7, σέβω denotes Gentiles closely associated with the synagogue (cf. 13.50). For a different understanding of this term, see Max Wilcox ('The God-Fearers in Acts—A Reconsideration', *JSNT* 13 [1981], pp. 102-22) who questions the pervasive equation of σεβόμενοι τὸν θεόν with 'God-fearers'.

49. The significance of Lydia's role as a female head of house will be noted below.

50. The verb λαλέω, prominent in other accounts of household conversion (11.14-15; 16.32; 18.9), appears at both 16.13 and 14 to describe Paul's message to the women. Jervell notes that 16.13 is the only such instance in Acts of Paul speaking to or with women (*The Unknown Paul*, p. 151).

51. The reference to 'sitting down' (καθίσαντες) could imply a formal seating

synonymous with συναγωγή[52] and it is perhaps best to see this connection here.[53]

In addition to the strong Hellenistic evidence, certain features in the story itself favor the identification of the 'place of prayer' with a synagogue. First, the identification explains Luke's curious reference to a riverside (ποταμός) since synagogues, as Josephus attests, were often constructed by a river or body of water.[54] Second, it best fits Lydia's

arrangement and thus a structure of some kind. I. Howard Marshall surmises that προσευχή denotes a house where the women gathered to pray (*The Acts of the Apostles: An Introduction and Commentary* [TNTC; Grand Rapids: Eerdmans, 1980], p. 267). Only at Acts 16.13 and 16 does Luke use the term προσευχή to denote a physical location (cf. οἶκος προσευχῆς, Lk. 19.46).

52. Both Philo and Josephus use the term as a virtual equivalent for 'synagogue' (see *Flaccus* 45, 47–49; *Against Apion* 2.10; *Antiquities* 14.258). See the additional evidence in Emil Schürer, *The History of the Jewish People in the Age of Jesus Christ (175 bc—ad 135)*, II (rev. Geza Vermes, Fergus Millar, and Matthew Black; Edinburgh: T. & T. Clark, 1979), p. 439 n. 61. In one passage Josephus speaks of προσευχή in Tiberias as 'a large edifice', one 'capable of receiving a great number of people' (*The Life of Flavius Josephus* 277; cf. 280, 293). While the Septuagint regularly employs προσευχή in the customary sense of 'prayer', an exception appears at 3 Macc. 7.20 where it most likely refers to a synagogue.

53. Schürer assumes the identification of προσευχή and συναγωγή at Acts 16.13 and 16 based on an extensive survey of Hellenistic Jewish literature (*The History of the Jewish People in the Age of Jesus Christ*, pp. 439-47, esp. pp. 444-45). The two terms likely derive from differing geographical spheres. Προσευχή is the only term found in synagogue inscriptions in Egypt dating from the third to first centuries. Συναγωγή, on the other hand, appears to reflect Palestinian usage (George A. Buttrick, (ed.), *IDB* [New York: Abingdon Press, 1962], see 'Synagogue', by I. Sonne, p. 477).

54. He mentions a decree of Halicarnassus permitting Jews to 'build places of prayer [προσευχὰς] near the sea, in accordance with their native custom' (*Ant.* 14.258 [Loeb]; see also, the Tebtunis Papyri I. 86.17, 29; cf. Ezra 8.15, 21; Ps. 137.1). 'The preference was to build synagogues outside the cities in the neighborhood of rivers or by the sea-shore', notes Schürer, 'so that all could perform the necessary ablutions before taking part in worship' (*The History of the Jewish People in the Age of Jesus Christ*, pp. 440-41). In the Lydia story, it was 'usual' or 'customary' (ἐνομίζετο) to find a προσευχή by the riverside (cf. NJB, Moffatt), a reading that is preferable to the Alexandrian ἐνομίζομεν ('we were supposing') which is badly corrupted (so Bruce, *The Book of Acts*, p. 310). Bruce M. Metzger terms the textual problems associated with this verse 'well-nigh baffling' (*A Textual Commentary on the Greek New Testament*, corrected edn [New York: United Bible Societies, 1975], p. 447).

status as a σεβομένη τὸν θεόν[55] as well as the temporal reference to the day of the Sabbath (τῇ τε ἡμέρᾳ τῶν σαββάτων). Paul's custom in Acts is to seek out a synagogue on the Sabbath as a venue for his preaching.[56] These considerations lead John B. Mathews to identify the προσευχή of Acts 16.13 (v. 16) with a συναγωγή.[57] Thus, while this identification is not without its problems,[58] Lydia appears to convert in a synagogue of the Jews, albeit a highly irregular one.

This emphasis on προσευχή as the place of hearing necessitates a break in the previous household pattern. An aberrant synagogue located on the banks of a river, not the preferred domestic space of the house, becomes the locale for Paul's decisive speaking (λαλέω) of the word (16.13-14). Unlike the mission of the Seventy-two, the mission to Europe begins outside the pale of both house and city (cf. ἔξω τῆς πύλης, v. 13). On this occasion Lydia 'was listening' (ἤκουεν) to the things spoken by Paul, responding positively when the risen Lord opens her heart.[59] While the two *Leitwörter* of speaking (λαλέω) and hearing

55. God-fearers, as noted above, were regular attenders at the synagogue services. In Acts, σεβόμενοι are closely associated with the synagogue (13.43; 16.14; 17.4, 17; 18.7).

56. See Acts 13.5, 14, 44; 14.1; 17.1-2, 10, 17; 18.4, 19; 19.8. According to Schürer, προσευχή at Acts 16.13 and 16 'is obviously the ordinary place of Sabbath meeting at which Paul also preached' (*The History of the Jewish People in the Age of Jesus Christ*, p. 445).

57. John B. Mathews, 'Hospitality and the New Testament Church: An Historical and Exegetical Study' (ThD dissertation, Princeton Theological Seminary, 1964), p. 205 n. 1. See also Johannes Munck, *The Acts of the Apostles: Introduction, Translation and Notes* (rev. William F. Albright and C.S. Mann; New York: Doubleday, 1967), p. 161, who interprets προσευχή as 'probably synonymous with a synagogue'. In a more recent sifting of the evidence, James A. Crampsey writes: 'Whether in fact it [προσευχή] means a synagogue in 16.13, as it does frequently elsewhere, cannot be completely settled, though the evidence is strongly in favor of the identification' ('The Conversion of Cornelius [Acts 10.1–11.18]: Societal Apologetic and Ecclesial Tension' [PhD dissertation, Vanderbilt University, 1982], p. 81).

58. Ten male Jews were normally required for the establishment of a synagogue (Pirke Aboth 3.7). Thus, the exclusive mention of women at 16.13 remains 'puzzling' (Jervell, *The Unknown Paul*, p. 151). One possible solution is that Jews were expelled from Philippi at the same time Claudius expelled Jews from Rome (cf. Acts 18.2), although it is difficult to know to what extent imperial decrees were carried out among the colonies.

59. The paradigm for Lydia is Mary, who was also 'listening' (ἤκουεν) to the word of Jesus (Lk. 10.39). The imperfects in both cases are iterative, stressing the continuous act of listening.

(ἀκούω) recall a key exchange between messenger and household in the story of Cornelius (10.44), in the case of Lydia Paul speaks only to a group of women that had assembled; moreover, only Lydia, not her household, expressly 'listens' to the word of salvation. The type-scene is not simply aborted; it never really begins.[60]

It is surprising, then, that the narrator includes the household in the salvation of Lydia. Both Lydia and her household receive baptism to signal their acceptance of the messianic faith (ὡς δὲ ἐβαπτίσθη καὶ ὁ οἶκος αὐτῆς, 16.15a). Here the story of Lydia goes beyond the story of Cornelius in mentioning the actual baptism of the household (cf. 10.48). Of greater rhetorical import, however, is the reappearance of the characteristic 'οἶκος formula' (καὶ ὁ οἶκος αὐτῆς), qualifying the conversion of Lydia as a story of household conversion.[61]

b. *The Pattern Resumed.* That the household receives baptism along with Lydia is the telling sign that the story belongs to the dominical program of evangelizing households. Her character strength effectively restores the pattern on the pages of Acts: 'She exhorted us saying, "If you have judged me faithful to the Lord, enter [εἰσελθόντες] into my house and stay [μένετε]"' (16.15b). Entering (εἰσέρχομαι) and staying (μένω) in households is part and parcel of the mission of the Seventy-two (Lk. 10.5-7).[62] Just as the household of Cornelius invited Peter to stay in the house for table-fellowship (10.48), so Lydia exhorts the wayfaring messengers to accept the hospitality of her house. In so doing, she becomes the first to play host to Paul since the inception of his mission in Acts 13.[63] 'Once the heart is opened, the home is open too.'[64]

Paul's delayed entry into the house focuses particular attention on the

60. On the aborting of type-scenes in biblical narrative, see Robert Alter, *The Art of Biblical Narrative* (New York: Basic Books, 1981), pp. 60-62.

61. The Western text adds πᾶς before ὁ οἶκος, bringing the phrase into alignment with Acts 10.2; 11.14; [16.33-34]; 18.8 (ὅλος).

62. Halvor Moxnes ('Patron-Client Relations and the New Community in Luke–Acts', in Jerome H. Neyrey (ed.), *The Social World of Luke–Acts: Models for Interpretation* (Peabody: Hendrickson, 1991), p. 262, sees the pattern of reciprocity in the story of Lydia as reflecting the mission of the Seventy(-two).

63. Noted by Tannehill, *The Narrative Unity of Luke–Acts*, II, p. 196. Previous references to hosts in Acts include Simon the tanner (9.43), Cornelius (10.48) and Mary, the mother of John Mark (12.12).

64. Stott, *The Spirit, the Church, and the World*, p. 263.

third element in the household missionary pattern. Like the house that becomes the center of the new believing community (Lk. 10.7), the house of Lydia becomes 'the cradle of the Christian community in Philippi'.[65] As such, it serves two important functions in the life of the Philippian church. First, it provides the place of table-fellowship between messengers and the newly converted household. If the pattern of the Seventy-two holds true, Paul and his associates 'stay' in the house of Lydia, eating and drinking what the household provides (cf. Lk. 10.7). As a word belonging to the table-fellowship matrix in the Gospel of Luke, μένω implies a fellowship meal.[66] Peter's stay in the house of Cornelius certainly involved table-fellowship with Gentiles (10.48), though his eating activity does not become explicit until his opponents bring charges against him in Jerusalem (11.3). Like Mary before her, Lydia's 'listening' is followed in due course by the celebration of a meal (Lk. 10.38-42).[67]

As in the story of Cornelius, the meals celebrated in the house of Lydia no doubt involved the Eucharist. An important verbal clue appears in the way the narrator presents Lydia's appeal to the wayfaring missionaries to accept the hospitality of her home: 'she urged [παρεβιάσατο] us' (16.15c). Significantly, this term occurs only here and at Lk. 24.29 where the disciples of Emmaus 'urged' (παρεβιάσαντο) Jesus to stay with them in their house at the close of a day's journey. Jesus subsequently 'entered' (εἰσῆλθεν) their house in order 'to stay' (τοῦ μεῖναι) with them, enjoying a meal that soon issues in the celebration of Eucharist (24.30).[68] Like Lydia, the two disciples of Emmaus have their eyes opened by the risen Lord, though in the course of celebrating the sacred meal (24.31; see also vv. 32, 45). The fascinating

65. Heine, *Women and Early Christianity*, p. 84.

66. Arthur A. Just, Jr, *The Ongoing Feast: Table Fellowship and Eschatology at Emmaus* (Collegeville: The Liturgical Press, 1993), p. 222. See, for example, Lk. 1.56; 9.4; 10.7; 19.5; 24.29(2×). As Just observes: 'To spend the night at someone's house necessarily implies that a meal would be eaten' (p. 188). On the eating associations of the term, see also Mathews, 'Hospitality and the New Testament Church', pp. 172, 180.

67. E. Jane Via, 'Women, the Discipleship of Service, and the Early Christian Ritual Meal in the Gospel of Luke', *Saint Luke Journal of Theology* 29 (1985), pp. 55-56. For Via, the meal in the house of Mary and Martha possesses symbolic images of the Eucharist.

68. On the relation of the Emmaus meal to the Eucharist, see Just, *The Ongoing Feast*, pp. 236-53.

parallels between this account and the story of Lydia suggest that Paul's eating in the house of Lydia was similarly eucharistic in nature.

Second, the house of Lydia is the place where the community gathers to hear the word of God. When Paul and Silas are later released from prison, they return to the house of Lydia to exhort the 'brothers' (ἀδελφοὺς) who gather there (16.40), a term that is certainly inclusive of women.[69] The house itself was a location traditionally identified with women.[70] The presence of ἀδελφοί in the house of Lydia indicates that the exhortation given on this occasion was particularly religious in nature. The term marking this exhortation (παρακαλέω) appears elsewhere in Acts to denote proclamation, particularly to a Christian audience (11.23; 14.22; 15.32; 20.1-2, 12).[71] The house thus becomes the unique 'space' for Christian gathering and proclamation of the word.[72] The departure of Paul and Silas from the house of Lydia is a departure from the congregation.[73] As the place of both word and sacrament, the house of Lydia shifts in the course of the story from the simple domestic space of the household to the 'sacred' space of the newly formed people of God.

Narrative Function

Attempts to discover the significance of the story of Lydia have not met with a great deal of interest in current Lukan research. The observation of Black bears repeating: 'It is hard to find any remarks in the literature of scholarship concerning the function of this story in Luke–Acts.'[74] Interpreting the Lydia story against the pattern of the mission to households, however, yields additional insights into the way this story functions on the pages of Acts.

First, the story of Lydia, with its notable break in the household

69. Here is an example where the text itself demands inclusive gender translation (NRSV: 'brothers and sisters') of a masculine term. The 'brothers' certainly included Lydia! Cf. Jervell, *The Unknown Paul*, p. 151.

70. See Beck, 'The Women of Acts', pp. 287, 294-95.

71. The story of Lydia also employs a non-religious sense of the term (16.9, 15, 39). According to Otto Schmitz, παρακαλέω has a distinctively prophetic sense at Acts 16.40 (*TDNT*, V; see 'παρακαλέω/παράκλησις', Otto Schmitz, p. 796).

72. Bruce observes that the related expression λόγος παρακλήσεως was a technical term for a sermon delivered in synagogue (*The Book of Acts* [ET], p. 252). Cf. Acts 13.15; Heb. 13.22.

73. Haenchen, *The Acts of the Apostles*, p. 499.

74. Black, 'The Conversion Stories in the Acts of the Apostles', p. 167.

missionary pattern, emphasizes the importance of the οἶκος over the προσευχή as the new space for the people of God. If Paul and Silas continue to seek converts at the 'place of prayer', which seems likely (16.16a), the contrast becomes all the more striking: they preach the word in the synagogue but meet with the disciples in the house (16.40). By the story's end, the house has supplanted the synagogue as the center of the messianic community at Philippi. This break in the pattern permits a closer comparison between the house and the synagogue than previously in the story of Cornelius, which relies chiefly on narrative 'bracketing' to make a similar point.

The qualifications that make Lydia an ideal candidate of the household mission serve to further the contrast between house and synagogue. As a God-fearer loosely connected to the synagogue, her conversion represents the winning of one on the margins of Judaism to the messianic community centered in the house. As a Gentile of some status and economic means, she represents the type of convert that creates jealousy on the part of 'the Jews'. By offering her house to Paul, she uses her resources to advance the mission, resulting in the separation of the community from the synagogue. As the first convert on European soil, Lydia provides a proper example of the use of wealth[75] by foreshadowing the conversion of other prominent women, such as the women of Thessalonica (17.4), Berea (17.12), and Athens (17.34) who, presumably, are willing to use whatever material resources are at their disposal to advance the mission.[76] At Corinth, for example, Priscilla, along with her husband Aquila, offers her home as lodging for Paul as he preaches in the synagogue (18.1-4). Thus, Lydia proves to be 'the first of a series of such patronesses whom Paul acquired as he moved from city to city'.[77]

75. According to O'Toole, Lydia demonstrates 'a right attitude toward wealth' (*The Unity of Luke's Theology*, p. 125).

76. That Luke is deliberate in showing Lydia as an example of wealth is apparent from the next scene involving the exploitation of the slave-girl (16.16-23). As Johnson observes: 'Lydia and the owners of the slave-girl provide the same set of examples: the wealthy but devout Lydia expresses her openness to the message by opening her house; the avaricious owners symbolize their rejection of the apostles by dragging them to court because of losing "their hope for a profit"' (*The Acts of the Apostles*, p. 298). Luke is fond of contrasting positive and negative examples of wealth; for example, Barnabas and Ananias/Sapphira (Acts 4.36–5.11).

77. E.A. Judge sees the Lydia episode as the 'turning point' in Paul's decision to accept the patronage of eminent personages. He sees this change of tactics as the

If, then, the narrator intends a subtle contrast between the house and synagogue in the story of Lydia, why does he use the term προσευχή which only obscures an explicit reference to the synagogue? In Acts, συναγωγή, not προσευχή, regularly denotes the meeting houses of Jews in the Diaspora.[78] The answer may lie in the way prayer appears at key moments in the progress of salvation history.[79] Prayer accompanies the spread of the gospel at critical junctures in Acts, from Jerusalem (1.14, 24), to Samaria (8.14-15), and to the ends of the earth (10.4, 9, 30-31; 11.5). Paul, who becomes the primary agent of the gentile mission while praying in the temple (22.17; cf. 9.11), begins his initial journey with Barnabas only after prayer is offered on their behalf by the church at Antioch (13.3). Thus, as Stephen S. Smalley observes, prayer 'is not introduced simply as an aspect of piety or a didactic comment upon it, but rather to underline critical moments in the unfolding of the *Heilsgeschichte*'.[80] It is, of course, an important prelude to the mission of the Seventy-two (Lk. 10.2).

In light of the strategic role accorded to prayer by the narrator of Acts, the reappearance of προσευχή in the Lydia story should not strike the reader as strange. The mission to Europe, as Winfried Elliger regards it, is the decisive step in the mission to the 'end of the earth' (Acts 1.8).[81] The subsequent journey of Paul to Europe (18.23–21.14)

beginnings of 'Paul the Sophist' ('The Early Christians as a Scholastic Community: Part II', *JRH* 1 [1960–61], p. 128). Tannehill, too, notes how the events of Acts 16.14-15 'show an interest in the key role of a patroness of the community and hostess for the missionaries in the founding of a church' (*The Narrative Unity of Luke–Acts*, II, p. 196).

78. Acts 13.5, 14; 14.1; 17.1, 10, 17; 18.4, 7, 19, 26; 19.8. See Schürer, *The History of the Jews in the Age of Jesus Christ*, p. 440. Other terms denoting the synagogue in antiquity (e.g. προσευκτήριον, εὐχεῖον, σαββατεῖον) do not appear in Acts.

79. The theme of prayer, as noted above, is already intimated in the use of βοηθέω at 16.9. See footnote 33.

80. Stephen S. Smalley, 'Spirit, Kingdom and Prayer in Luke–Acts', *NovT* 15 (1973), p. 61. See also Allison A. Trites, 'The Prayer Motif in Luke–Acts', in Charles H. Talbert (ed.), *Perspectives on Luke–Acts* (Edinburgh: T. & T. Clark, 1978), pp. 179-81, 84-86. O'Toole sees the reference to prayer in the Lydia story as belonging to Luke's general theme of God's salvific will for the nations (*The Unity of Luke's Theology*, p. 72).

81. Winfried Elliger, *Paulus in Greichenland* (Stuttgart: Verlag Katholisches Bibelwerk, 1978), p. 26. Elliger sees the mission into Europe as the decisive turning to Gentiles, the result of the Jerusalem Council's decision to turn to the non-Jew

breaks no new geographical ground.[82] Thus, in response to the prayerful request of the Macedonian man, and while the women gather together to pray, Paul finds his first convert on European soil in the person of Lydia.[83] Like Cornelius before her, Lydia's prayers receive an answer with the coming of the messenger to the house (cf. 10.2, 4, 30-31). Προσευχή, then, performs a dual function in the story of Lydia, providing not only the setting for her conversion but re-introducing the theme of prayer at a critical geographical juncture in Acts.[84]

A second function of Lydia's conversion in Acts stems from the positioning of the account in the aftermath of the Jerusalem Council. This placement causes the story to comment on both the theological and practical actions of the Council. First, as a gentile woman who responds to the preaching of Paul, Lydia expands an issue that originally centered on men. In commenting on Acts 15, Linda M. Maloney observes: 'No commentator seems as yet to have made the observation that the center of this controversy is the admission of gentile *men* (not simply "gentiles") into the Christian community' (15.1, 5).[85] By placing the story of Lydia in such close proximity to the Jerusalem Council, the narrator extends the community's decision to include gentile women as well. In this way Lydia functions as a kind of female 'Cornelius', who is accepted by the Lord for hearing the word of God and heeding it (cf. Lk. 11.27-28).

A second way that the story of Lydia comments on the actions of the Council centers on the practical issue of dealing with Gentiles. The

(pp. 27-28). For a modification of Elliger's position, see Black, 'The Conversion Stories in the Acts of the Apostles', p. 205 n. 172.

82. The second journey to Europe covers no new ground and lacks the note of divine initiative (18.23) that clearly marks the first journey to Europe (16.6-10). Even the journey to Rome lacks a strong note of divine initiative, coming as a result of Paul's appealing to Caesar (25.11). Clearly, the first European journey is the decisive one.

83. Beck observes how women throughout Acts engage in an active prayer ministry, from the earliest Pentecost believers (2.42) to Mary (12.12) and the women of Philippi (16.13-14). See 'The Women of Acts', p. 305.

84. Here is an example where variation in a literary pattern 'makes possible the introduction of new information' (McMahan, 'Meals as Type-Scenes in the Gospel of Luke', p. 61).

85. Linda M. Maloney, *'All that God had Done with Them': The Narration of the Works of God in the Early Christian Community as Described in the Acts of the Apostles* (New York: Peter Lang, 1991), p. 91 n. 33.

resumption of the household missionary pattern results in the messengers's entering and eating with Gentiles in a Gentile's house, just like Peter previously entered and ate with Gentiles in the house of Cornelius. By offering her house as a place of hospitality, Lydia becomes the first host to Paul since his mission began in Acts 13 and, more importantly, the first since the decision of the Jerusalem Council in Acts 15. The story thus offers the first real test to see what kind of ministry the Lukan Paul will have among the Gentiles. Accepting Lydia's hospitality effectively marks a new direction for Paul, 'for never before had he used a gentile home as a base'.[86] The way in which Lydia implores the missionary party to accept lodging in her house underscores the apparent novelty of the event.[87]

The account of Paul's stay in the house of Lydia offers no real evidence that Paul or the missionary party conformed their eating habits in accordance with the Jerusalem decrees. The language of hospitality invoked on this occasion (μένω) clearly echoes the mission of the Seventy-two, suggesting that Paul and his associates were free to eat 'whatever they set before you' (Lk. 10.7). Moreover, the precedent set earlier in the house of Cornelius emphasized the complete freedom of table-fellowship between Jews and Gentiles and the abrogation of distinguishing food concerns (10.1–11.18); that approach seems to have been followed in the house of Lydia as well. As will be noted in ch. 6 of this book, Luke reserves the fullest expression of Jew–Gentile commensality for stories of household conversion.

While Paul and Silas earlier appear as being faithful to the decrees of the Jerusalem Council, delivering them to the churches of southern Galatia (16.4), the expansion of the gospel into Europe appears to alleviate the missionary party of the responsibility of carrying the decrees any farther afield. This study has already noted the limited geographical range of the Council's decision (15.23).[88] The emphasis on divine intervention at Acts 16.6-10 not only underscores the new geographical

86. Pervo, *Luke's Story of Paul*, p. 56. 'The Lord who had opened her heart', observes Pervo, 'also opened his. The barriers between Jew and gentile, female and male, are beginning to dissolve.'

87. Judge, 'The Early Christians as a Scholastic Community: Part II', p. 128. According to Philip Francis Esler, the missionaries are hesitant to accept Lydia's hospitality because she is a Gentile (*Community and Gospel in Luke–Acts: The Social and Political Motivations of Lucan Theology* [Cambridge: Cambridge University Press, 1987], p. 101).

88. See ch. 4, p. 128-29.

sphere of the European mission but legitimates Paul's table-fellowship practice in the house of the first European convert. As divine direction leads Peter to his stay in the house of Cornelius, so divine direction leads Paul to his stay in the house of Lydia. In both instances, radical table-fellowship is the by-product of a mission directed by the Lord of the house.

The Conversion of the Roman Jailer and his Household (16.25-34)

In some ways the story of the jailer at Philippi stands as the most unique household conversion on the pages of Acts. On the one hand, it contains the most emphatic and prolific use of the 'οἶκος formula', itself subject to multiple variation:

> And they said, 'Believe in the Lord Jesus, and you will be saved, you and your household' (σὺ καὶ ὁ οἶκός σου) (16.31).
>
> And they spoke to him the word of the Lord together with all the people in his house (σὺν πᾶσιν τοῖς ἐν τῇ οἰκίᾳ) (16.32).
>
> ...and immediately he himself was baptized, and all his household (οἱ αὐτοῦ πάντες) (16.33).
>
> ...and after bringing them into his house, he set food before them, and he rejoiced with all his household (πανοικεὶ) because he had believed in God (16.34).

Four times in a short span Luke emphasizes that the jailer's family was complete.[89]

On the other hand, the motifs of entering (εἰσέρχομαι) and staying (μένω) in a house, belonging to the *Leitwörter* of the Seventy-two and reiterated in the stories of Cornelius and Lydia, are strangely absent in this account, though the use of similar and/or synonymous expressions resonates with images drawn from the household mission.[90] These initial observations suggest that the story of the Roman jailer is the most varied among the four accounts of household conversion.

89. Noted by Joachim Jeremias, *The Origins of Infant Baptism: A Further Reply to Kurt Aland*, trans. Dorothea M. Barton (Naperville: Allenson, 1963), p. 15.

90. According to Alter, the occasional avoidance of repetitive *Leitwörter* 'whether through substitution of a synonym or of a wholly divergent word or phrase for the anticipated recurrence, may also be particularly revealing' (*The Art of Biblical Narrative*, p. 180).

Narrative Context

Establishing the global and proximate parameters of the story of the jailer is a more difficult task than in the stories of Cornelius and Lydia. Globally, the conversion of a Roman civic official recalls the story of Sergius Paulus, a proconsul of Cyprus who 'believed' in the Lord (Acts 13.6-12). It is not clear, however, whether ἐπίστευσεν at 13.12 signifies a true conversion to the Christian faith.[91] Moreover, the story really illustrates the triumph of Christianity over magic and bears little resemblance to the conversion of the jailer at Philippi.[92] In terms of the household motif, a better link is to the conversion of Cornelius, as will be demonstrated below.

The proximate context is also somewhat difficult to determine. The story unfolds in three distinct scenes: 1. the exorcism of a 'python spirit' from a slave girl who brought her masters much profit, resulting in the eventual imprisonment of Paul and Silas (16.16-24); 2. the occurrence of an earthquake preparing for a salvific encounter with the jailer (16.25-34); and 3. the release of Paul and Silas from prison and their subsequent departure from the city (16.35-40).

For the purposes of this study, it seems best to treat the second scene as constituting the story of the jailer proper, with the first and third scenes belonging to its proximate context. Two reasons suggest this course of action. First, the salvation of the household belongs only to the second scene; the sequence of instruction, baptism, and common meal occurs without any recourse to what comes before or after. Second, the events of 16.25-34 can be easily extracted from the text without any disruption between the first and third scenes, suggesting that these verses form a kind of interlude with their own inherent plot structure.[93]

91. 'Sergius Paulus "believed"', notes Frank Stagg, 'but it is not said that he was or was not converted. He may simply have believed that the missionaries were men of God and true prophets' (*The Book of Acts: The Early Struggle for an Unhindered Gospel* [Nashville: Broadman Press, 1955], p. 139).

92. Black sees two themes at work: the superiority of Christianity over magic and the opposition of non-Christian Jews to the conversion of the Gentiles ('The Conversion Stories in the Acts of the Apostles', p. 161). Neither of these themes belongs to the household conversion proper in Acts 16.25-34. For a more recent treatment, see Susan R. Garrett, *The Demise of the Devil: Magic and the Demonic in Luke's Writings* (Minneapolis: Fortress Press, 1989), pp. 79-87.

93. In the first and third scenes, for example, Paul and Silas are still in prison, despite their release by the prison guard at 16.30!

a. *Global Context: The Conversion of Roman Soldiers.* Unlike Zacchaeus, Cornelius, Lydia, and Crispus, the Roman jailer remains nameless throughout the account in which he appears. Despite attempts in the manuscript tradition to identify this figure more precisely,[94] he appears simply as a δεσμοφύλαξ (a 'prison guard', 16.23; cf. v. 27), a designation he retains even after he becomes personal host to Paul and Silas (16.36). That he remains nameless is a noteworthy variation for Luke, who normally manifests keen interest in the names of his characters's hosts.[95] Furthermore, the jailer receives no epithetical characterization from Luke, a striking departure from the previous accounts of household salvation.[96]

The lack of detail surrounding the jailer, however, does not mean that one can know nothing of his essential character. His occupation as a prison guard contains its own inherent characterization that is helpful for locating the story's global connections. As part of the Roman civil service, the jailer is a distinctly Roman character, representing the 'establishment' of Roman society and culture. The city of Philippi, of which he is in some way representative, was a distinctly Roman city and figures prominently in the course of the story ('these men are troubling our city', 16.20). Having come under Roman control in 168 BCE, Philippi later became the scene of the decisive victory of Antony and Octavian (later Augustus) over the forces of Brutus and Cassius in 42 BCE, becoming a Roman colony. As such, Philippi utilized Roman law and modeled its constitution after the municipal constitution of Rome.[97] Though Acts mentions other cities known to have been Roman colonies,[98] only Philippi receives the designation κολωνία as such (16.12). The details of the city's administration provided by the Lukan

94. On attempts to give the jailer a name, see Kirsopp Lake and Henry J. Cadbury, *The Beginnings of Christianity: Part I. The Acts of the Apostles*, IV (Grand Rapids: Baker Book House, 1979, reprint), p. 199. Two miniscules identify the jailer with Stephanas, whose household Paul personally baptized at Corinth (1 Cor. 1.16; 16.15).

95. So Bruce, *The Book of Acts* (ET), p. 200. See Acts 9.11, 43; 10.48 (cf. v. 1); 16.14; 18.3, 7; 21.8, 16.

96. Zacchaeus is described as being a chief tax collector, wealthy, and small in stature (Lk. 19.2-3) while the stories of Cornelius and Lydia are particularly rich in epithetical characterization (Acts 10.1-2, 22; 16.14).

97. Bruce, *The Book of Acts* (ET), p. 309.

98. For example: Antioch of Pisidia, Lystra, Troas, Iconium, and Corinth.

narrator offer an authentic picture of life in a Roman colony and add to the Roman flavor of the account.[99]

As the warden of a prison, the jailer most likely came from the ranks of the Roman military establishment.[100] From the time of Julius Caesar, soldiers often settled Roman colonies as a reward for faithful service and to insure loyalty to Rome.[101] The jailer's quick recourse to suicide at the prospect of allowing his prisoners to escape (16.27) reveals a soldier's sense of duty and discipline, a practice followed elsewhere by soldiers in Acts (12.19; cf. 27.42).[102] Thus, the conversion of a Roman soldier/jailer recalls the earlier conversion of another military man—the centurion Cornelius, who also receives salvation along with his entire household. As a centurion, Cornelius was a Roman citizen; as a commander of a cohort from Italy, his Roman credentials receive further accentuation on the pages of Acts (10.1). The conversions of Cornelius and the jailer reveal an interest in the salvation of soldiers present elsewhere in the Lukan writings (Lk. 3.14; 7.1-10; 23.47; Acts 10.7; 27.31).

b. *Proximate Context: Imprisonment and Release.* The two scenes bracketing the conversion of the jailer focus on the imprisonment and release of the wayfaring messengers. The first scene (16.16-24) begins with Paul and Silas's returning to the 'place of prayer' and thus to the original place of Lydia's conversion (16.16a). The Lukan narrator recalls the household conversion of Lydia even as he prepares for the

99. The administration of Philippi was entrusted to two στρατηγοί (= Latin *praetors*) who figure prominently in the narrative (16.20, 22, 35-36, 38). They utilized the services of certain ῥαβδοῦχοι (16.35, 38) or 'police-attendants' whose rods symbolized the magistrates' authority to carry out corporal and capital punishment (cf. 16.22).

100. Bruce suggests that he was a retired Roman soldier (*The Book of Acts*, p. 315). Philippi itself bore the marks of a 'military town'. It was the place where Octavian settled a number of his retired veterans after his defeat of Antony and Cleopatra at the Battle of Actium in 31 BCE.

101. The practice of establishing colonies was carried on by Caesar's adopted son Octavian (Augustus) who once boasted that he had settled colonies of soldiers in Africa, Sicily, Macedonia, both Spains, Achaea, Asia, Syria, Gallia Narbonesis, and Pisidia (*res gestae* 5.28).

102. 'Possibly his attempted suicide,' says Stagg, 'was simply in keeping with a code of honor which as a military man he would observe voluntarily' (*The Book of Acts*, p. 172). In the prison escape story recorded at Acts 12.1-19, soldiers function as guardians of the prison (12.4, 10, 19).

conversion of the jailer and his household. Depicting Paul's exorcism of a slave-girl who brought her masters much profit by fortunetelling (16.16b-18), the scene is important for the way it sets in motion the events that ultimately lead to the imprisonment of Paul and Silas and to their dramatic encounter with the jailer of Philippi.

The charge for which Paul and Silas are subsequently imprisoned appears on the lips of the girl's owners at 16.20-21: 'These men are disrupting our city, being Jews [Ἰουδαῖοι ὑπάρχοντες], and are advocating customs that are not lawful for us to receive nor to do, being Romans [Ῥωμαίοις οὖσιν].' Since exorcism was not a legally punishable offense in the eyes of Roman law, the accusers foment public opposition against Paul and Silas by appealing to their un-Romanlike practices or 'customs' (ἔθη). Precisely what customs are in view is difficult to say.[103] Some commentators think the charge against Paul and Silas pertains to illegal Jewish proselytizing,[104] but A.N. Sherwin-White has observed that such an injunction did not come into force until the mid-second century, at the earliest.[105] The thesis of Daniel R. Schwartz that Paul and Silas are accused of promoting a new religious sect is unlikely, given the lack of a clear distinction between Judaism and Christianity in the minds of the accusers.[106]

Interestingly, the prideful reference to Ῥωμαῖοι in the above charge appears later in the third scene when Paul and Silas obtain their release from prison (16.35-40). There Paul claims that the treatment they received was unbecoming to 'Romans' and demands personal escort out of the prison (16.37-38). The reference is usually taken in a distinctly political sense: for the first time in Acts, Paul invokes his prerogative as

103. Haenchen remarks that the ἔθη that the Romans find unacceptable 'cannot be more closely defined' (*The Acts of the Apostles*, p. 496). According to A.N. Sherwin-White, 'It is not because of the depravity of the practices introduced by Paul, but because of their un-Roman character, that the magistrates are urged to intervene' (*Roman Society and Roman Law in the New Testament* [Grand Rapids: Baker, 1978, reprint], p. 80).

104. See, for example, Haenchen, *The Acts of the Apostles*, p. 496 n. 5.

105. Sherwin-White, *Roman Society and Roman Law in the New Testament*, pp. 81-82.

106. The accusers simply refer to Paul and Silas as 'Jews' (16.20). The view advanced by Schwartz understands the participle ὑπάρχοντες at 16.20 as concessive ('*although* these men are Jews...') with the implication that Paul and Silas are advocating something Jews themselves would consider unlawful ('The Accusation and the Accusers at Philippi', *Bib* 65 [1984], pp. 357-63).

a Roman citizen (cf. 22.25-29).[107] This appeal to Roman citizenship, however, raises a tension in the narrative long recognized by scholars: why does Paul delay his announcement until *after* his beating and subsequent imprisonment, especially when he appeals to his Roman citizenship elsewhere to avoid harsh treatment by the Roman military establishment (22.25)? Hans Conzelmann recognizes the tension but attributes it to Luke's apologetic purposes.[108]

Pattern and Variation

Unlike the story of Cornelius, nothing in the preceding narrative prepares for the eventual occurrence of a household conversion. Nothing exists to suggest that Paul and Silas were aware of the personal circumstances of the jailer or that he even had a household. In light of the singular nature of the jailer's question at 16.30 ('what must *I* do to be saved?'), the inclusion of the household is striking indeed: all those 'in the house' hear the word of the Lord (16.32), receive baptism with the head of house (16.33), and rejoice in the context of a common meal (16.34). This series of salvific stages resonates with echoes of the household missionary pattern, fulfilling the prior words of Paul to the jailer: 'Believe in the Lord Jesus, and you will be saved, you and your household' (16.31). In the story of the jailer, the faith of one becomes the faith of all.

a. *Speaking the Word in the House.* The evangelization of the jailer's household comes about as the result of an earthquake that loosens the chains of the prisoners and brings the jailer to the brink of suicide (16.25-28). Unlike the two prior instances of miraculous prison release in Acts (cf. 5.17-23; 12.1-19), however, no prisoners at Philippi escape, a fact that the jailer soon confirms (16.29). Such an unusual occurrence prompts the jailer to seek out the deeper implications of the event, asking Paul and Silas: 'Sirs, what must I do to be saved?' (16.30). The purpose of the earthquake is not to achieve release for Paul and Silas but to create a saving encounter with the jailer and his household, which the

107. The NRSV, NIV, NCV, NJB, NAB and REB translate Ῥωμαῖοι at 16.37-38 as 'Roman citizens'. Only the NASB preserves the more ambiguous 'Romans'.

108. Hans Conzelmann, *Acts of the Apostles* (trans. James Limburg, A. Thomas Kraabel, and Donald H. Juel; ed. Eldon Jay Epp with Christopher A. Matthews; Philadelphia: Fortress Press, 1987), p. 133.

jailer himself recognizes.[109] Once again, divine providence is at work in a story of household conversion. It is in the house of the Roman jailer, not within the walls of the prison, where Paul and Silas speak the salvific word: 'They spoke to him the word of the Lord together with all who were in his house' (16.32). This shift in settings, suggested by the notation at 16.30 ('he brought them outside'), is significant in a story that focuses on prison release. Interestingly, nowhere does the narrator specify that Paul and Silas enter (εἰσέρχομαι) the house of the jailer; Luke varies the pattern by placing the messengers already within the confines of the home, thus presupposing household entry.[110] The entry motif simply does not perform the same critical role as it does in the story of Cornelius; any reluctance to enter the home of a Gentile on the part of the household messengers virtually disappears in the story of the jailer.

It is possible that the initial entry of the household messengers does not occur until 16.34 when the jailer brings Paul and Silas into his house and sets food before them. In this case, πᾶσιν τοῖς ἐν τῇ οἰκίᾳ αὐτοῦ at 16.32 denotes simply the members of the jailer's household apart from any architectural connotations, leaving the place of the missionary proclamation unspecified.[111] In light of Lukan usage elsewhere, however, this interpretation appears doubtful. Nowhere in Luke or Acts does οἰκία stand for the personified house, only a house in an architectural sense.[112] Whereas both οἶκος and οἰκία occur interchangeably in Acts as terms of architectural location, only the former stands for the 'family' as such.[113] Moreover, the most natural place for the household to gather

109. Black ('The Conversion Stories in the Acts of the Apostles', p. 171) remarks: 'God's hand in creating this opportunity is clearly visible in the miracle of the earthquake (as the jailer realized).'

110. If the location of the jail was in the basement of the jailer's house (see BAGD, see 'ἀνάγω', p. 53), this feature would explain the omission of the entry motif. For the expression οἶκος φυλακῆς, see *Barn.* 14.7 (Isa. 42.7).

111. Haenchen, for example, is uncertain as to where the baptismal instruction of the jailer and his household took place (*The Acts of the Apostles*, p. 498).

112. This usage reflects the distinction in Attic law between οἶκος (the entire estate) and οἰκία (the house itself). John H. Elliott includes Acts 16.32 as an example of how physical houses functioned as the place for the origination and development of Christian mission (*A Home for the Homeless: A Social-Scientific Criticism of 1 Peter, its Situation and Strategy* [Minneapolis: Augsburg–Fortress Press, 1990], p. 188 n. 111).

113. Cf. BAGD, see 'οἰκία', p. 557.

was in the house of the jailer.[114] The only other occurrence of πᾶσιν τοῖς ἐν τῇ οἰκίᾳ in the New Testament (Mt. 5.15) clearly refers to an architectural dwelling.[115] Modern English translations appear unified in rendering οἰκία as 'house' at Acts 16.32.[116]

By omitting any express reference to entry, the narrator immediately focuses on the preaching of Paul and Silas in the house of the Roman jailer. 'They spoke the word of the Lord' (ἐλάλησαν τὸν λόγον τοῦ κυρίου) recalls how Peter spoke the word in the house of Cornelius (10.44). That Cornelius's household hears the word of salvific peace (τοὺς ἀκούοντας, 10.44b) implies that the jailer's does as well. As in the story of Cornelius, all the members of the family gather in the house to hear the word of the Lord. In Acts, speaking and listening comprise the basic exchange between messenger and household.

What was the content of the proclamation on this particular occasion? Unfortunately, no sermon accompanies the event in the jailer's house. Paul and Silas simply speak the 'word of the Lord'. That this word at least included a reference to the salvific peace of the household, however, is suggested by the appearance of the *pax* motif at 16.36, where the jailer bids Paul and Silas to 'go in peace' (πορεύεσθε ἐν εἰρήνῃ) after receiving orders to release them. This reference may afford a clue as to what was spoken on this occasion since this distinctively Jewish expression is scarcely conceivable on the lips of a Roman pagan with no connection to the synagogue.[117] Perhaps the messengers emphasized the 'peace' of Jesus Christ in breaking down the barriers between Jew and Gentile, particularly given the anti-Jewish sentiments of the city (Acts 16.20-21; cf. 10.36; Eph. 2.14-15, 17). The common meal soon to take place in the jailer's house thus provides concrete evidence of the newly established commensality between Jew and Gentile (16.34).[118]

114. Williams surmises that the house where the jailer and his household received baptismal instruction stood next door to the prison (*Acts*, p. 290).

115. See BAGD, see 'οἰκία', p. 557.

116. See, for example, the NRSV, NASB, NIV, NCV, NAB, REB. Only the NJB renders the term 'household' in this verse.

117. 'Go in peace' was a common Hebrew greeting (see Mk 5.34; Lk. 2.29; 7.50; 8.48; Jn 14.27; Acts 15.33). 'It was the jailer himself', comments Marshall, 'who bade the missionaries depart in peace, taking up the Jewish form of greeting which had become part of Christian usage' (*The Acts of the Apostles*, p. 274).

118. Polhill observes that 'the jailer treated Paul and Silas in a most unusual fashion for prisoners. He took them into his house and fed them at his own table' (*Acts*, p. 356).

b. *Salvation of the Household.* After hearing the word of Paul and Silas, the jailer proceeds to wash their wounds (16.33a).[119] Coming immediately prior to baptism, this act serves as a prelude to a more significant cleansing: 'and immediately he himself was baptized, and all his household' (16.33b). As John Chrysostom observes of the jailer: 'He washed and was washed; he washed them from their stripes, and he himself was washed from his sins.'[120] In Acts, baptism marks the acceptance of salvation by the household.[121] The different household terminology employed by the narrator in this verse (οἱ αὐτοῦ πάντες) is itself a variation of the traditional 'οἶκος formula' appearing earlier at 16.31. The entire sequence of 16.32-34 is rich with variations of household language.[122]

The actual location where the baptism occurs is ambiguous. Luke only says that the jailer 'took' Paul and Silas that very hour of the night (16.33a). Does this reference to taking suggest a shift to another location or simply describe movement within the house? Zahn supposed the latter, thinking that the baptism took place inside another room in the jailer's house;[123] more recently, Polhill supposes that the baptism occurred in the courtyard where the household water supply would be located.[124] Apart from the baptism of the Ethiopian eunuch, which occurs alongside a desert road (8.26, 38), Acts manifests little interest in the actual places of baptism. More critical for Luke is the act of solidarity expressed in the baptism of the household; as a result of the jailer's faith in God, an entire household is won to faith in the Lord Jesus.

c. *Sharing a Meal in the House.* After receiving baptism along with his entire household, the jailer brings Paul and Silas into the house to celebrate a common meal.[125] The house, which formerly functioned as the

119. 'Once the household has assembled', notes Pervo, 'they share their message and receive in turn treatment for their injuries' (*Luke's Story of Paul*, p. 58).

120. John Chrysostom, *Homily on the Acts of the Apostles*, 36.2.

121. Acts 10.48; 16.15a; 18.8. Only the stories of Lydia and the jailer, however, expressly narrate the baptism of the household.

122. See p. 157 above.

123. As with the baptism of Saul, Zahn supposed that the baptism of the jailer and his household took place in an adjoining bathroom (noted in Haenchen, *The Acts of the Apostles*, p. 498 n. 1).

124. Polhill, *Acts*, p. 356.

125. If Paul and Silas speak in the house as 16.32 suggests, 16.34 actually describes a re-entry into the house. Esler explains this tension in terms of an

place of missionary proclamation, now becomes the scene of table-fellowship for the new people of God. That the house is large enough to host the missionary party in apparent relative comfort, in addition to housing all the members of the jailer's family, is one indication of the jailer's socio-economic status on the pages of Acts.[126] Like the communities established in the homes of Lydia and Cornelius, the newly formed church meets in the home of the newly converted head of house.

Indications exist to suggest that the meal celebrated in the jailer's house was eucharistic in nature. As Demetrius R. Dumm rightly emphasizes, the allusions to food in this passage are 'so unexpected and unusual that they can scarcely be dismissed as normal narrative details'.[127] The first is the 'hour of the night' (16.33) during which the meal took place—well past midnight (cf. 16.25)! The lateness of the hour suggests that the food served on this occasion was more than a meal; it was, in fact, a celebration of salvation (Lk. 10.7).[128] A second clue is the phrase Luke uses to describe the meal scene proper; literally, the jailer 'set a table' (παρέθηκεν τράπεζαν) before Paul and Silas (cf. Lk. 10.8; 11.6; 1 Cor. 10.27).[129] When applied figuratively, τράπεζα ('table') denotes a meal or food.[130] The image of the table, however, is striking given its prior appearance in the Gospel of Luke:

> Nevertheless, look, the hand of the one betraying me is with me on the table [ἐπὶ τῆς τραπέζης] (22.21).
>
> ...in order that you might eat and drink at my table [ἐπὶ τῆς τραπέζης] in my kingdom...(22.30).

'artificial plot sequence' that 'avoids having Paul enter into table-fellowship with an outright pagan' (*Community and Gospel in Luke–Acts*, p. 101). The term ἀνάγω at 16.34 may carry more the sense of 'bring back' or 'return'. See the examples listed in LSJ, see 'ἀνάγω', p. 102.

126. Meeks, *The First Urban Christians*, p. 64. As a civil servant, the jailer belonged to the sturdy 'middle class' of Roman society.

127. Demetrius R. Dumm, 'Luke 24.44-49 and Hospitality', in Daniel Durken (ed.), *Sin, Salvation, and the Spirit* (Collegeville: The Liturgical Press, 1979), p. 232.

128. Cf. Tannehill, *The Narrative Unity of Luke–Acts*, II, p. 200.

129. This expression appears as early as Homer (*Iliad* 24.476; *Odyssey* 5.196; 7.174-5; 17.333). The identical phrase occurs in Herodotus 6.139 and *Ant.* 6.338. As part of their inclusive mission, the Seventy-two are to eat 'the things set before you' (τὰ παρατιθέμενα, Lk. 10.8)!

130. See, for example, Acts 6.2; 1 Cor. 10.21; *Did.* 11.9.

Of the four Gospels, only Luke contains a reference to the τράπεζα at the institution of the Lord's Supper.[131] The 'table' around which Jesus and his disciples gather to eat anticipates that 'table' around which they will gather at the Messianic Banquet. Every meal in Luke and Acts is a proleptic celebration of the coming kingdom of God, including that of the jailer and his household.[132]

A third indication is the note of festivity that attends the shared meal: the jailer 'rejoiced greatly' (ἠγαλλιάσατο) as a result of believing in God (16.34b). This term distinctly recalls the experience of the early Jerusalem believers who took their meals with gladness of heart (ἀγαλλίασις) while breaking bread from house to house (2.46).[133] The rarity of this verb and its cognate noun in the Lukan writings makes such a connection all the more striking. Thus, while none of the three factors above can by themselves establish the presence of the Eucharist in the house of the Roman jailer, together they argue for the presence of sacramental overtones in the meal scene at 16.34. As Pervo remarks, 'This is not explicitly described as a eucharist, but the allusions are plain. Every meal in Luke–Acts has dimensions that intimate the eucharist.'[134]

Narrative Function

Though to a lesser degree than the story of Cornelius, the conversion of the Roman jailer stands as a landmark event in the book of Acts. First, Paul's preaching in the house of the jailer results in the conversion of the first true pagans to the Christian faith.[135] Stagg observes of the jailer:

131. According to Just, Luke's usage of τράπεζα at 22.21 stamps the Last Supper with a distinctively table-fellowship character. Both Matthew (26.23) and Mark (14.20) prefer the term 'dish' (τρύβλιον). See Just, *The Ongoing Feast*, p. 245. Paul uses the expression τραπέζης κυρίου ('table of the Lord') to denote the Lord's Supper at 1 Cor. 10.21.

132. B.P. Robinson, 'The Place of the Emmaus Story in Luke–Acts', *NTS* 30 (1984), p. 486. Just sees the Emmaus meal as the proto-typical meal of the new age (*The Ongoing Feast*, p. 249-50).

133. 'Breaking bread' is a technical phrase in Acts to denote the Eucharist (2.42; 20.7; 27.35). In the story of Emmaus, Jesus breaks bread as part of the dominical program to the household (Lk. 24.30, 35). See ch. 3, pp. 78-79.

134. Pervo, *Luke's Story of Paul*, p. 58.

135. Black remarks that there 'were probably pagan converts in the regions of Asia Minor that Luke passes over quickly in Acts 15.41–16.10 but he does not mention them' ('The Conversion Stories in the Acts of the Apostles', p. 172). The term 'pagan' in this study carries no pejorative overtones but simply describes Gentiles with no connection to the synagogue.

'This is the first clear case of a Gentile's conversion out of paganism and apart from Jewish influence.'[136] As a staunch member of the Roman pagan establishment, the jailer represents a fourth group of converts in Acts in addition to Jews, Samaritans and god-fearing Gentiles.[137] By means of this story, the gospel continues its march to the 'end of the earth' (Acts 1.8).

The jailer thus stands alongside Cornelius as one of the two most significant gentile converts in Acts. Both come from the ranks of the Roman military and both convert as part of the dominical program of evangelizing households. Unlike Cornelius, however, the consummate 'God-fearer', the jailer bears little or no connection to the Jewish synagogue. The absence of any meaningful connection to the synagogue in the global or proximate context of the jailer story lends emphasis to the wholly pagan character of the account at Philippi, which accords well with the anti-Jewish sentiment of the city.[138]

The admission of an outright pagan into the church gives added importance to the question put to the missionaries by the jailer: 'What must I do to be saved?' (16.30). When viewed after the Jerusalem Council, convened to decide the basis of Gentile salvation, the question takes on a further nuance: 'What must a pagan do to be saved?'[139] The answer provided by the household missionaries—'believe [πίστευσον] in the Lord Jesus and you will be saved [σωθήσῃ]' (16.31)—echoes the words of Peter expressed earlier at the Council: 'through the grace of the Lord Jesus we believe [πιστεύομεν] so as to be saved [σωθῆναι]' (15.11).[140] The almost identical answers make faith, not circumcision, the basis of Gentile (and pagan) salvation. Thus, in some ways, the conversion of the jailer stands as a test case of the decision rendered by the apostles and elders at Jerusalem.[141]

136. Frank Stagg, *The Book of Acts*, p. 172. Stagg thus regards 16.25-34 as 'one of the key passages of the whole book of Acts'.

137. Stagg, *The Book of Acts*, p. 107.

138. Philippi was, as Francis X. Malinowski observes, 'a town openly hostile to Jews' ('The Brave Women of Philippi', *BTB* 15 [1985], p. 60). The events at Philippi offer a rare instance of Roman officials openly hostile to Christian missionaries.

139. Cf. Stagg, *The Book of Acts*, p. 172.

140. On the translation of Acts 15.11, see ch. 4, p. 127 n. 172.

141. So Black, 'The Conversion Stories of the Acts of the Apostles', p. 172. Black believes that the positioning of the jailer story so soon after the Jerusalem Council lends credence to this view (p. 173).

A second function of the story relates closely to the first: if Paul and Silas convert a household of pagan Gentiles, they subsequently eat with a household of pagan Gentiles. The conversion of the jailer thus expands the purview of table-fellowship in Acts. If Peter's objectors could find fault with his eating with a righteous and god-fearing Gentile, what would they have said to Paul's eating in the house of an idolatrous pagan?

This radicalization of the table-fellowship theme is observable within Acts 16 itself. That the narrator 'sandwiches' the story of the jailer between two references to Lydia and her household (16.11-15, 40) suggests that he intends a close correspondence between them.[142] When viewed in close proximity to each other, the two stories provide a notable progression in the table-fellowship motif. First, whereas Paul formerly eats in the house of a god-fearing Gentile, he now eats in the house of an outright pagan. Lydia, like Cornelius before her, belonged to a class of Gentiles closely aligned with Judaism. Thus, if Lydia and her household become Paul's first (gentile) hosts, the jailer and his household become his first pagan hosts.

Secondly, the story of the jailer contains an explicit meal scene that is lacking in the story of Lydia: the jailer 'set a table' before them (16.34). This expression makes explicit what was only implicit in the story of Lydia, namely, Paul's stay in the house for the purpose of 'table-fellowship'. As in the story of Lydia, there is no indication that Paul and Silas enforced the decrees of the Jerusalem Council in the house of the Roman jailer (15.20, 29). Both stories maintain the principle of freedom from Jewish dietary concerns established in the house of Cornelius. In the jailer story, however, this point becomes unmistakably clear: the unusual circumstances surrounding the jailer's conversion would hardly have allowed him the time to offer the Jewish emissaries ritually prepared food! Rather, the events transpiring in the house of the jailer offer a fitting example of messengers eating what the household members provide (Lk. 10.7).

Thirdly, by means of rich table imagery and clear textual associations,

142. On the close correspondence between two type-scenes, Alter remarks: 'Occasionally, a type-scene will be deployed in conjunction with a pointed use of narrative analogy by setting two occurrences of the same type-scene in close sequence' (*The Art of Biblical Narrative*, p. 181). The narrative transitions from Lydia to the jailer (16.16a) and from the jailer to Lydia (16.40) further encourage comparison between them.

the meal in the house of the jailer comes closer to an explicit identification with the Eucharist and hence to a meal that is religious in character. The festive events taking place in his home clearly stem from the jailer's faith in God.[143] As with the mission of the seventy-two emissaries, a meal becomes the particular expression of universal salvation (Lk. 10.7).

Once recognized, the radical table actions of Paul and Silas in the house of the jailer help to alleviate one of the long-recognized tensions in the story, namely, the delay of Paul and Silas in announcing their status as Ῥωμαῖοι (16.35-39), a revelation that could have spared them a severe flogging and a night's stay in jail. The placement of this announcement *after* the scene in the jailer's house suggests a more subtle understanding of Ῥωμαῖος on the part of the Lukan narrator; Paul and Silas show themselves to be Romans by staying in a Roman house and eating Roman food. They are not simply Romans politically, they are Romans culturally as well.[144] Thus, the events of 16.32-34 offer a fitting answer to the charge that landed them in prison in the first place: 'These men are troubling our city, being Jews, and they are announcing customs that are not lawful for us to receive or do, being Romans' (16.20-21). The actions of Paul and Silas in the house of the Roman jailer show this charge to be false; they do in fact behave like Romans, not like Jews! The 'customs' (ἔθη) which they are accused of bringing to Philippi almost certainly included the Jewish food laws since these were part and parcel of the Jewish faith and one of its most distinguishing features.[145]

Though rarely recognized as such, the conversion of the Roman jailer stands as a radical act on the pages of Acts. It not only entails preaching to an outright pagan but a flagrant disregard of Jewish dietary concerns. The result is that Paul and Silas compromise their position as Jews by living like Romans. The role of deity in the account largely confirms this

143. The adverb πανοικεὶ at 16.34b, only here in the New Testament, may modify either ἠγαλλιάσατο ('he rejoiced greatly with all his household because he believed in God') or πεπιστευκὼς ('he rejoiced greatly because he believed in God with all his household'). In either case, the actions clearly stem from the jailer's faith in God.

144. In making this connection I do not wish to deny the obvious political associations of Ῥωμαῖοι at 16.37 and 38; the primarily cultural use of the term at 16.21, however, does permit one to perceive deeper cultural implications as well.

145. Except at 25.16 where Roman customs are in view, ἔθος always pertains to Jewish legal matters in Acts (6.14; 15.1; 16.21; 21.21; 26.3).

radical table-fellowship of Paul and Silas. After all, it was a timely earthquake that created the circumstances leading directly to the conversion of the jailer and his household in the first place. Thus, as in the stories of Cornelius and Lydia, divine initiative and providence guides the course of the household mission at pivotal points, affirming its radical vision of universal salvation.

The Conversion of Crispus and his Household (18.1-11)

Luke reserves his final story of household conversion for Crispus, the president of the synagogue at Corinth (Acts 18.1-11). The appearance of the characteristic 'οἶκος formula' at 18.8 (Crispus believed 'with all his household') qualifies Crispus to stand alongside Cornelius, Lydia, and the jailer as the fourth recipient of household salvation in Acts. Though the account has commanded little attention on the part of Lukan scholarship, its subtle use of symbolism and irony makes it perhaps the most intriguing of the four. As the fourth and final account of household conversion, it assumes an importance rarely recognized in Lukan scholarship.

Narrative Context

Like Lydia and the jailer, the conversion of Crispus occurs during the course of Paul's inaugural European mission. This conversion, as Gerd Theissen notes, 'was of great significance for the founding of the community in Corinth'.[146] Though focusing on different individuals and their households, both Paul's letters and Acts testify to the importance of household conversion for the beginnings of the church at Corinth.[147]

a. *Global Context: House versus Synagogue.* Perhaps the most striking element of the story of Crispus is the contrast it presents between the house and the synagogue. After encountering stiff opposition from the Jews, Paul enters the residence of Titius Justus, whose house was 'next door to the synagogue' (18.7b). Esler notes the 'comic feature' of this action, though he regards it as unintentional by Luke.[148]

146. Gerd Theissen, *The Social Setting of Pauline Christianity: Essays on Corinth* (ed. and trans. John H. Schutz; Philadelphia: Fortress Press, 1982), p. 73.

147. Paul identifies the 'household of Stephanas' as the first-fruits at Corinth (1 Cor. 16.15; cf. 1.16).

148. Esler, *Community and Gospel in Luke–Acts*, p. 40.

The juxtaposition of the house and synagogue as two competing institutions on the pages of Acts occurs both before and after the story of Crispus, though not with the same degree of dramatic and symbolic flair. Hints of a future tension first appear in the inaugural mission to the Gentiles, whose unified acceptance of the gospel in the house of Cornelius presents a stark contrast to the hostile actions of the Hellenistic synagogue, leading to the stoning of Stephen and the scattering of the church. While the Cornelius event depends primarily on contextual factors to establish its connection with the synagogue, the conversion of Lydia includes a subtle contrast of the house and synagogue within the story itself. Lydia, the first convert in Europe, gives heed to Paul's message at a 'place of prayer' (= synagogue) but subsequently offers her house as the center of the new Christian community, the place of word and sacrament (Acts 16.13-15, 40). The shift, however, is only partially negative: the Lukan narrator departs from his normal way of speaking about the synagogue and gives no hint of synagogue recalcitrance.

The contrast between house and synagogue sharpens as the mission to Europe progresses. After leaving Philippi, Paul travels to Thessalonica where, according to his custom, he begins preaching in the synagogue (συναγωγή, Acts 17.1-3). His success there among the God-fearing Greeks and prominent women (17.4) creates jealousy on the part of 'the Jews', who lead an attack upon the house (οἰκία) of a certain Jason (17.5). According to Abraham J. Malherbe, Luke's stereotypical presentation of Paul's mission elsewhere in Acts suggests that 'we should understand Jason's house as having been the base for Paul's work among the Gentiles *after* his separation from the synagogue, as Titius Justus' house would be in Corinth (cf. Acts 18.6-7)'.[149] The scene thus witnesses a strategic shift away from the synagogue to the house as the new sphere of religious activity. That 'brothers and sisters' (ἀδελφοὺς)

149. Abraham J. Malherbe, *Paul and the Thessalonians: The Philosophic Tradition of Pastoral Care* (Philadelphia: Fortress Press, 1987), pp. 13-14, emphasis mine. Malherbe writes: 'The compressed account in Acts 17.1-9 should be examined in the light of other accounts in Acts where Paul's founding of churches is described. Generally, a sequence of events is visualized in which Paul is rejected by the synagogue, turns to Gentiles, and (because of his success with them) brings about Jewish opposition (13.46-50; 18.5-17; cf. 16.12-40; 19.8-41), which modify the pattern. Most important to Luke are the beginning and end of the sequence, and he passes over the intervening events in Thessalonica... But the sudden appearance of Jason suggests that Luke wants the reader to understand that a similar sequence of events has occurred' (p. 14 n. 34).

are present in the house of Jason suggests that it has become the distinct locale of Christian assembly at Thessalonica and the center of Paul's missionary activity (17.6).[150]

Another change of location, similar to the one at Corinth, occurs during Paul's visit to Ephesus in the course of the third missionary journey (Acts 19.8-10). Paul enters the synagogue and begins 'reasoning' (διαλεγόμενος) with the Jews (19.8), recalling his prior preaching style in the synagogues of Europe (cf. 17.2, 17; 18.4, 19). His preaching soon results in the hardening of the Jews, who begin publicly to speak evil of the Way (19.9). Paul's response to this recalcitrance is similar to the scene at Corinth: he withdraws from the synagogue and sets up headquarters elsewhere, this time in the school of Tyrannus (19.10). Here the σχολή of Tyrannus functions in the same manner as the οἰκία of Titius Justus at Corinth.[151] That Paul 'separated the disciples' from the synagogue (19.9) suggests a sense of permanency to the arrangement: 'Christian disciples are becoming a separate religious community.'[152]

b. *Proximate Context: Paul's Speech before the Areopagus and the Decision of Gallio.* Like the account of the jailer, the conversion of Crispus appears as part of a larger narrative complex. Acts 18 contains four distinct scenes depicting the beginning of the church at Corinth: 1. Paul's coming to Corinth and taking up residence with Aquila and Priscilla (vv. 1-4); 2. Paul's preaching and subsequent separation from the synagogue (vv. 5-8); 3. Paul's vision and decision to remain at Corinth (vv. 9-11); 4. Gallio's decision not to interfere (vv. 12-17).[153]

150. Is the church meeting in the house of Jason the product of a household conversion? As a likely Gentile and person of some means (who can afford to post bond for Paul—17.9), Jason certainly meets the requirements of the household mission. The absence of the 'οἶκος formula', however, disqualifies it from the type-scene matrix.

151. Bruce notes that the lecture hall of Tyrannus 'served the purpose in Ephesus that the house of Justus did in Corinth' (*The Acts of the Apostles* [GT], p. 408). Conzelmann similarly notes: 'The breaking away of the congregation to become an independent group has its counterpart in 18.6' (*Acts of the Apostles*, p. 163). That Paul's ministry at Ephesus also involved an extensive use of household space is clear from Acts 20.20.

152. Tannehill, 'Rejection by Jews and Turning to Gentiles: The Pattern of Paul's Mission in Acts', in Joseph B. Tyson (ed.), *Luke–Acts and the Jewish People: Eight Critical Perspectives* (Minneapolis: Augsburg, 1988), p. 91.

153. So Krodel, *Acts,* p. 341.

While the conversion of Crispus belongs only to the second of these scenes, his rather abrupt appearance in the narrative makes his story difficult to extricate from the first and third scenes. That Crispus is the only convert expressly mentioned by Luke among the 'many' Corinthians who believed Paul's message (v. 9) suggests that he represents the example *par excellence* of the gospel's wider success at Corinth.[154] Only the fourth and final scene, the decision of Gallio, would appear to stand apart from the rest. The summary statement at Acts 18.11 sets this episode off as a new rhetorical unit, though it certainly relates to what has gone before.[155]

For the purposes of this study, therefore, the Gallio episode will be treated as part of the proximate context of the Crispus story. The refusal of Gallio, the proconsul of Achaia, to render a judgment against Paul represents a significant milestone in Acts and for early Christianity in general, namely, that 'Christianity is an inner-Jewish affair in which Rome does not meddle'.[156] Gallio's decision to extend the protection of Roman law to the nascent faith may well have served as legal precedent for other Roman judges to follow.[157]

More pertinent to this study, however, is the specific charge brought against Paul by his Jewish opponents: 'This man is persuading people to worship God contrary to the law' (18.13). While some scholars take νόμος ('law') here to refer to Roman law,[158] it is clear from Gallio's reference to 'your own law' (νόμου τοῦ καθ' ὑμᾶς, 18.15) that he interpreted it of the Jewish law.[159] If Roman law were in view, Gallio could not have dismissed the case so easily. As such, the complaint forms part of the 'Jewish case' against Paul in Acts contending that he

154. Thus, the 'story' of Crispus is an integral part of Christian beginnings at Corinth. With respect to Acts 18.1-17 as a whole, Haenchen observes that Luke 'has constructed our passage with a very carefully calculated gradation of events' (*The Acts of the Apostles*, pp. 537-38).

155. The decision of Gallio provides concrete demonstration of God's promise to Paul at 18.10 that 'no one will attack you or harm you'. According to Haenchen, 18.12-17 'forms the high point of the Corinthian stories and for that very reason had to be moved by the author to the end' (*The Acts of the Apostles*, p. 541).

156. Haenchen, *The Acts of the Apostles*, p. 541.

157. Bruce, *The Book of Acts* (ET), p. 354.

158. So, for example, Krodel, *Acts*, p. 347; Williams, *Acts*, p. 318.

159. Haenchen admits that 'Gallio's answer seems to imply that νόμος here means the Jewish law' (*The Acts of the Apostles*, p. 536). See also Esler, *Community and Gospel in Luke–Acts*, p. 126.

has forsaken the law of Moses and has taught the people to do so as well (cf. 21.21, 28; 24.5-6). Whatever took place in the house of Titius Justus, it led to the suspicion that Paul violated Jewish customs and behavior.

Prior to these events at Corinth, Paul travels to Athens where, according to his custom, he begins preaching in a synagogue of the Jews (17.16-17a). Unlike earlier at Thessalonica and Berea, however, Paul also begins preaching in the marketplace (ἀγορά) where he appears daily in the guise of a Cynic philosopher (17.17b).[160] While there, Paul encounters certain Epicurean and Stoic philosophers (17.18), leading directly to his defense before the Areopagus (17.19-31). The scene is interesting for the way it depicts Paul preaching in a strictly non-Jewish environment, to people with little or no connection to Judaism.[161] That the narrator shifts attention away from the synagogue to 'gentile space' anticipates the more decisive break with Jewish space that transpires in the story of Crispus. Upon leaving the synagogue, Paul declares: 'from now on I will go to the Gentiles' (18.6). While Paul meets a mixed response among the Gentiles at Athens (17.32-34), the heavily gentile (pagan) character of the scene is surely significant as an anticipation of Paul's turning to the Gentiles. The placement of the Areopagus speech just before this decisive event is strategic, reflecting a growing concern with gentile space in this section of Acts.

Pattern and Variation

The conversion of a synagogue president (ἀρχισυνάγωγος) stands as a novel event on the pages of Acts. The only prior mention of ἀρχισυνάγωγοι is at 13.15 where they invite Paul and Barnabas to speak in the synagogue at Pisidian Antioch during the course of the first missionary journey. The Gospel of Luke contains two instances where Jesus encounters a synagogue president, one positive and the other negative (8.49; 13.14). The first is particularly relevant to the story of Crispus since the healing of Jairus's daughter occurs as part of the dominical program to the house.[162] As Jesus brings salvation to the household of Jairus, so now an emissary of Jesus brings salvation to the household of Crispus.

160. Cynics were known in antiquity for their 'open-air' style of discourse (Epictetus, *Discourses* 3.22.26-30; Dio Chrysostom, *Oration* 32.9).

161. See Esler, *Community and Gospel in Luke–Acts*, p. 41. Other instances occur at Lystra (14.8-18), Philippi (16.32-34), and Ephesus (19.8-10).

162. See ch. 3, pp. 59-62.

a. *Paul Enters the House of Titius Justus.* Upon arriving in Corinth, Paul encounters a Jewish couple named Aquila and Priscilla in whose home he takes up residence (18.1-3). While staying there, Paul begins 'reasoning' (διελέγετο) in the synagogue every Sabbath (18.4), recalling his identical practice in the synagogues of Thessalonica (17.2) and Athens (17.17). When Silas and Timothy soon arrive from Macedonia (cf. 17.14), Paul ceases plying his trade of tent-making and devotes himself full-time to the preaching of the word (λόγος), though it is unclear how their arrival enables Paul to do so (18.5).[163] As in the synagogues of Macedonia, the Jews soon react negatively to Paul by resisting and blaspheming his message (18.6a). Paul's symbolic protest of shaking the dust from his clothes (18.6b) recalls the protocol given to the Seventy-two, who wipe the dust off their feet in response to a city's rejection (Lk. 10.11). This rejection by the Corinthian Jews significantly changes the scope of Paul's ministry: from now on he will 'go to the Gentiles' (18.6c).

A change in the direction of Paul's mission, however, necessitates a change in the geographical sphere as well: 'And crossing over from there, he entered [εἰσῆλθεν] into the house of a certain man named Titius Justus, a worshiper of God, whose house was next door to the synagogue' (18.7). Rejection by the synagogue results directly in Paul's entry into the house of a notable Gentile.[164] Little is known about Titius Justus, even the correct spelling of his name.[165] Like Lydia, he appears as a 'worshiper of God' (σεβομένου τὸν θεόν), which suggests that he is a gentile God-fearer associated with the synagogue (cf. 16.14). That his house is large enough to host the 'many' (πολλοὶ) Corinthians who heard Paul there (18.8; cf. λαός πολὺς, 18.10) further suggests a

163. According to William S. Kurz, this verse is an example of a 'narrative gap' that the reader must fill in (*Reading Luke–Acts: Dynamics of Biblical Narrative* [Louisville: Westminster Press/John Knox, 1993], p. 96). According to 2 Cor. 11.8 and Philippians 4.15, Silas and Timothy bring a gift from Macedonia.

164. On whether this action entailed leaving his quarters with Aquila and Priscilla, see below.

165. The manuscript tradition is quite diverse. Bruce thinks it probable that 'Titius Justus' is the correct form—'a Roman *nomen* and *cognomen* suggesting that he was a Roman citizen, perhaps a member of one of the Roman families settled in Corinth at the time when Julius Caesar made it a Roman colony' (Bruce, *The Book of Acts* [ET], p. 350). Edgar J. Goodspeed identifies him with the Gaius (his *praenomen*) of Rom. 16.23 and 1 Cor. 1.14. See 'Gaius Titius Justus', *JBL* 69 (1950), pp. 382-83.

relatively high socio-economic position on the pages of Acts.[166] Like other gentile householders before him, he places his house at the missionary's disposal, providing an example of the proper use of wealth.[167]

In entering the house of Titius Justus, however, does Paul take leave of his prior residence with Aquila and Priscilla? The antecedent of ἐκεῖθεν ('from there') at 18.7 is ambiguous, since the context supports a reference to both the house (v. 3) and the synagogue (v. 4). Theissen and Esler answer affirmatively, reflecting the viewpoint of the Western editors of Acts.[168] Esler, for example, says: 'In moving in with Titius Justus, Paul must leave the house of Aquila and his wife, although there is nothing in the text...to suggest that they had failed him in any way.'[169] Thus, for Esler, Paul's 'going to the Gentiles' means 'the deliberately public establishment of table-fellowship between Jews and Gentiles'.[170] Bruce, however, believes this view betrays a misunderstanding of Luke's intent: 'Paul did not remove his private lodgings from Aquila's house to that of Titius Justus, but made Titius Justus' house his teaching base instead of the synagogue.'[171]

Actually, the debate need not be drawn so starkly. That Paul shifts his venue of preaching is clear from the opposition he encounters in 18.6; in light of the resistance and blasphemy of the Jews, the synagogue hardly

166. According to Theissen, 'this location would allow Paul to discourse all day without interruption and to have his own private room' (*The Social Setting of Pauline Christianity*, p. 90). If Titius Justus is the Gaius of Rom. 16.23 and 1 Cor. 1.14 (see footnote 165 above), his house appears to have been exceptionally large, hosting the 'whole church' (1 Cor. 14.23).

167. If Paul departs from Aquila and Priscilla to take up residence in the house of Titius Justus (see below), this action would further bear on the social status of Titius Justus: 'It can only be assumed that it was not inferior to that of Aquila and Priscilla, as Paul would hardly have made claims on anyone who would have found it a greater burden than they had' (Theissen, *The Social Setting of Pauline Christianity*, p. 91).

168. Theissen, *The Social Setting of Pauline Christianity*, p. 90; Esler, *Community and Gospel in Luke–Acts*, p. 40. The Western text emends ἐκεῖθεν to read ἀπὸ 'Ακύλα.

169. *Esler, Community and Gospel in Luke–Acts*, p. 40.

170. Esler, *Community and Gospel in Luke–Acts*, p. 40 (see also p. 100). David P. Moessner also sees a reference to the house as a center of meal fellowship at 18.7 (*Lord of the Banquet: The Literary and Theological Significance of the Lukan Travel Narrative* [Minneapolis: Fortress Press, 1989], p. 251 n. 331).

171. Bruce, *The Book of Acts* (ET), p. 349.

remains a viable location for effective evangelization.[172] At the same time, Paul prefaces his actions with the rather curious affirmation that he is 'clean' (καθαρὸς) to go to the Gentiles. The term is in the emphatic position (καθαρὸς ἐγὼ), reflecting its importance as a justification for entering the house of Titius Justus.[173] While the term may serve in this context as a moral defense (cf. 20.26), the highly distinctive cultic sense of the cognate verb (καθαρίζω) in the original story of Cornelius (10.15; 11.9) carries the further implication that Paul is free, as was Peter, to enter and eat in the house of a Gentile without incurring ritual defilement.[174] The paradigmatic nature of the Cornelius account lends weight to perceiving such a meaning here.[175] Thus, while ἐκεῖθεν most naturally refers in the immediate context to Paul's withdrawal from the synagogue, it does not necessarily exclude the additional act of taking up residence in the house of Titius Justus. Such is an additional example of a 'narrative gap' present in this section of Acts.[176]

b. *Paul Preaches to the Household.* The change of spatial settings bears immediate results for Paul: 'And Crispus, the president of the synagogue, believed in the Lord with all his household, and many of the Corinthians, when they heard, were believing and being baptized' (18.8). Here the preaching of Paul in the house of Titius Justus appears only in the starkest and most indirect of terms, yet in ways that are highly reminiscent of Peter's experience in the house of Cornelius. Like Cornelius,

172. Metzger further adds that 'it is unlikely that opposition of the Jews in the synagogue would have caused Paul to change his residence from the home of Aquila, with whom Paul continued to have good relations' (*A Textual Commentary on the Greek New Testament*, p. 462).

173. The other two declarations of 'going to the Gentiles' in Acts contain no reference to ritual purity (13.46; 28.28). It obviously performs a special function in the story of Crispus.

174. According to Esler, the Lukan Paul 'is affirming that he is ritually pure in moving into the house of a Gentile and, it is implied, will remain so thereafter' (*Community and Gospel in Luke–Acts*, p. 100). On the importance of ritual purity and household entry, see ch. 2 of this book, pp. 41-42. Later, when Peter narrates the Cornelius event before the Jerusalem Council, he uses καθαρίζω in the sense of moral blamelessness (15.9).

175. Apart from at 20.26, καθαρίζω/καθαρός appears in Acts only in connection with the stories of Cornelius and Crispus.

176. On the presence of other narrative gaps in Luke's account of Christian beginnings at Corinth, see Kurz, *Reading Luke–Acts: Dynamics of Biblical Narrative*, pp. 96-97.

Crispus believes in the Lord 'with all his household' (σὺν ὅλῳ τῷ οἴκῳ αὐτοῦ), signifying a household salvation event (10.2; 11.14; 16.15; 16.31-34). Moreover, many Corinthians, of which Crispus is the example *par excellence*,[177] hear (ἀκούω) the message of Paul, who formerly preached the word (λόγος, 18.5) in the synagogue but now keeps on speaking (λαλέω) in the house of Titius Justus (18.9). The result is that many 'were believing' (ἐπίστευον) and 'being baptized' (ἐβαπτίζοντο), adding to the nucleus of the community formed in the house of Titius Justus.[178]

In light of these rather standard elements of the household evangelizing pattern, the variation appearing at Acts 18.8 is nothing short of striking: in carrying out the pattern of the Seventy-two, Paul enters the house of a Gentile but converts a Jew! It is not Titius Justus, the owner of the house, who converts with all his household, but Crispus, the ruler of the synagogue.[179] As a synagogue president, Crispus was surely a man of great private means, 'for the cost of the upkeep, and occasionally even the building of a synagogue, could fall to them'.[180] His notable social distinction apparently earned him baptism at Paul's own hands (1 Cor. 1.14).[181] His conversion was strategic for the expanding mission at Corinth, making a great impression upon the gentile God-fearers and resulting in further conversions.[182]

The unlikelihood of an influential member of the synagogue converting in the house of a Gentile presents problems in the sequential

177. The conversion of such an influential member of the synagogue was no doubt highly significant, 'setting off a small wave of conversions' (Theissen, *The Social Setting of Pauline Christianity*, p. 73).

178. The presence of other believers in the house of Titius Justus is a new variation for Luke, although non-household believers may well be implied in the ἀδελφοί meeting in the house of Lydia (16.40).

179. One can reasonably assume that Titius Justus is already a believer because he offers his house for Paul's use (so Tannehill, *The Narrative Unity of Luke–Acts*, II, p. 222).

180. Malherbe, *Social Aspects of Early Christianity* (Philadelphia: Fortress Press, 2nd edn, 1983), p. 72. See also Theissen, *The Social Setting of Pauline Christianity*, pp. 73-75.

181. Judge, 'The Early Christians as a Scholastic Community: Part II', p. 130. That Paul also baptized Gaius (= Titius Justus?), a wealthy home owner, along with the household of Stephanas (1 Cor. 1.16), offers interesting insight into the strategy of Paul's baptismal practices.

182. Haenchen, *The Acts of the Apostles*, p. 535.

narrative of Acts 18.7-8. Krodel, for example, reconstructs the scene so that Crispus actually converts prior to Paul's entering the house of Titius Justus.[183] While this reconstruction reflects an attempt to determine the referential order of events, the poetic sequence of the narrative performs an important rhetorical function by making the house, not the synagogue, the place where the most highly esteemed member of the synagogue converts with his entire entourage.[184] The irony is further enhanced by the geographical note in 18.7c: the house where Crispus converts stands 'next door to the synagogue' (συνομοροῦσα τῇ συναγωγῇ)! That this detail appears at all is suggestive of its symbolic import in Acts. Luke's keen sense of irony is evident in the way he juxtaposes the two physical structures related to Judaism and Christianity.[185] If the writer of Acts reflects the struggle between church and synagogue in the aftermath of the temple's destruction of 70 CE, it is difficult to conceive of a better way to rub salt in the eyes of his Jewish opponents.[186]

The conversion of Crispus and the Corinthians in the house of Titius Justus creates a new people (λαός) of God composed of both Jews and Gentiles. While in the house, the Lord appears to Paul in a night vision and instructs him to keep speaking and not be silent (18.9), 'for I am with you, and no one will lay a hand on you in order to do you harm, for I have many people [λαός] in this city' (18.10). As in the story of Cornelius, a vision accompanies an accredited messenger's stay in a

183. Krodel, *Acts*, p. 344.

184. On the distinction between referential and poetic sequencing, see footnote 38 above.

185. Is it any accident that the composition of Acts dates to the time when the synagogue is beginning to identify itself architecturally (late first century)? Prior to 70 CE, συναγωγή primarily denoted a 'gathering' or 'assembly' of the Jews, a usage appearing in Acts (6.9; 9.2). Luke, however, almost always uses the term of a physical place of assembly (Lk. 4.15-16, 33; 6.6; 21.12; Acts 9.20; 13.5, 14; 17.1, 10, 17; 18.4, 19; 19.8), even showing knowledge of a special synagogue structure (τὴν συναγωγὴν αὐτὸς ᾠκοδόμησεν ἡμῖν, Lk. 7.5). Despite the fact that the earliest synagogue meetings took place in homes, Luke preserves the rhetorical contrast by reserving οἶκος/οἰκία terminology only for places of Christian worship and assembly.

186. On the likely post-70 date of Acts, see Werner G. Kümmel, *Introduction to the New Testament*, rev. edn. (trans. Howard C. Kee; Nashville: Abingdon Press, 1973), pp. 185-87. On the historical connection of Luke's community to post-70 conflict with the synagogue, see Esler, *Community and Gospel in Luke–Acts*, pp. 54-55.

house (10.17; 11.5; cf. 10.3); unlike the Cornelius incident, however, it occurs *after*, not before, the conversion of the household.[187] In the first case, the vision inaugurates the mission; in the second, it serves to sustain it.[188] The result is that many 'people' in Corinth experience salvation in the house of Titius Justus. While λαός usually refers exclusively to Israel in the Lukan writings, both here and in the story of Cornelius (15.14) it denotes the people of God, the church, composed of both Jew and Gentile.[189] 'What began earlier through Peter's conversion of Cornelius', observes Tannehill, 'is continuing through Paul's work in Corinth; the Lord's people is being gathered in a Gentile city'.[190]

c. *Paul Stays at Corinth, Teaching the Word of God.* In contrast to Paul's one-night stay in the house of the jailer, Paul's residence in the home of Titius Justus is unusually long in duration: 'And he stayed there a year and six months teaching the word of God among them' (18.11). The reference to 'a year and six months' is unusual, marking Paul's first extended stay in a city since his missionary work began in Acts 13. The verb translated 'he stayed' (ἐκάθισεν, literally, 'took his seat') draws attention to Paul's more settled frame of mind stemming from the assurance of the vision.[191] It also recalls the teaching posture of Jesus (Lk. 4.20; 5.3) as well as Paul (Acts 13.14; 16.13).

In emphasizing the unusual duration of Paul's stay in Corinth, the narrator passes over any express mention of the third element in the pattern of household evangelization, namely, the messenger's stay in the house

187. Tannehill notes that the reference to a large people 'is not a prediction of something new but an interpretation of what is already underway' (*The Narrative Unity of Luke–Acts*, II, p. 226).

188. In both cases, visions underscore the role of divine involvement in the household enterprise. Like Peter, Paul 'is under the direction of the Lord who called him and chose him to be his instrument...' (Krodel, *Acts*, p. 345).

189. See Nils Dahl, 'A People for His Name', *NTS* 4 (1958), pp. 319-27. Dahl contends that apart from Acts 15.14 and 18.10, λαός always signifies Israel (e.g., Lk. 2.32; Acts 4.10, 27; 13.17, 24; 26.17, 23). According to Jack T. Sanders, Luke is fully aware that at 18.10 'he is shifting the pre-Christian understanding of people of God as people of Israel to the Christian understanding of people of God as Christians' ('The Jewish People in Luke–Acts', in *Luke–Acts and the Jewish People*, p. 57).

190. Tannehill, *The Narrative Unity of Luke–Acts*, II, p. 225.

191. Williams, *Acts*, p. 317. Καθίσατε ('stay') at Lk. 24.49 suggests a settled frame of mind on the part of the early Jerusalem disciples.

for the purpose of table-fellowship (Lk. 10.7). This omission is yet a further example of a 'narrative gap' that is characteristic of Luke's account of Christian beginnings at Corinth. Since nothing in the text suggests that Paul changed his location subsequent to his withdrawal from the synagogue, the reader can only surmise that the house of Titius Justus remained the center of Paul's teaching activity in Corinth.[192] The reference to Paul's 'teaching the word of God' (διδάσκων τὸν λόγον τοῦ θεοῦ), the occasion of a new theme in Acts,[193] further allows the reader to envision Paul's continued table-fellowship practice with the newly established people of God since, as Tannehill notes, the combination of meal and instruction is a distinctive feature of Luke and Acts.[194]

Narrative Function

More than any other passage in Acts, the account of Christian beginnings at Corinth witnesses the emergence of a new religious community, complete with its own 'sacred' space. When Paul announces that he is 'going to the Gentiles' in the face of Jewish opposition, he promptly enters the house of a Gentile located 'next door to synagogue'. This action is at once practical and symbolic; as a practical act, it provides 'a convenient base when the breach with the Jews occurred';[195] as a symbolic act, it 'gives the Christian mission the appearance of being institutionally separate from Judaism'.[196] As the final story of household

192. Cf. Elliott, 'Temple versus Household in Luke–Acts: A Contrast in Social Institutions', in Jerome H. Neyrey (ed.), *The Social World of Luke–Acts: Models for Interpretation* (Peabody: Hendrickson, 1991), p. 226. Speaking of type-scenes generally, McMahan writes: 'The anticipated pattern has been so thoroughly reinforced that it can be predicted by the reader, who may even have to fill in gaps to complete the pattern' ('Meals as Type-Scenes in the Gospel of Luke', p. 58).

193. This note constitutes the first reference to Paul's teaching activity (διδάσκω) away from his home church in Antioch (Acts 15.35) and the first since his arrival in Europe. As such, it represents the beginning of Luke's focus on Paul the teacher (20.20; 21.21, 28; 28.31).

194. See Tannehill, *The Narrative Unity of Luke–Acts*, I, pp. 290-91. On this basis one might reasonably infer that instruction accompanied the meals in the homes of Cornelius, Lydia, and the jailer as well. See also Via, 'Women, the Discipleship of Service, and the Early Christian Ritual Meal in the Gospel of Luke', p. 51. Jerome H. Neyrey notes how food and bread often symbolize words and instruction in biblical thought ('Ceremonies in Luke–Acts: The Case of Meals and Table Fellowship', in *The Social World of Luke–Acts*, p. 366).

195. Judge, 'The Early Christians as a Scholastic Community: Part II', p. 129.

196. Charles H. Talbert, *Acts* (KPG; Atlanta: John Knox, 1984), pp. 79-80.

salvation, the conversion of Crispus brings to explicit fruition a theme that was subtly present in the stories of Cornelius and Lydia.

Each of the three elements of the household evangelizing pattern, richly varied by Luke, serves to highlight an aspect of this central function and theme. The first element emphasizes the utter rejection of the gospel by the synagogue. Paul enters the house of Titius Justus only after encountering the strong resistance and blasphemy of the Jews (ἀντιτασσομένων δὲ αὐτῶν καὶ βλασφημούντων, 18.6a). Unlike the previous instances of household conversion, opposition to the message accounts for the messenger's entry into the house.

Both the global and proximate contexts of the story contribute to this new development by depicting notable shifts in the geographical location of Paul's preaching due to Jewish opposition. While at Thessalonica, Paul transfers to the house of Jason when the Jews become jealous and foment public hatred against him (Acts 17.1-9); later, during the course of the third journey, Paul withdraws from the synagogue and moves to the school of Tyrannus when the Jews at Ephesus begin speaking evil of the Way (Acts 19.8-10). Both stories 'bracket' the story of Crispus, which contains the most explicit juxtaposition between two competing centers of religious life. Together, the three stories reveal a strong interest in the development of a new religious space for the burgeoning Christian movement. Even Paul's speech before the Areopagus at Athens contains a subtle geographical shift. By focusing attention away from Paul's preaching in the synagogue to the marketplace, the narrator anticipates Paul's movement toward the Gentiles that occurs in an explicit way in the house of Titius Justus.

The second element serves to further this theme but from an opposing angle. As in the story of Cornelius, the οἶκος that hears and receives the salvific message stands over against the synagogue that hears and rejects. In the story of Crispus, however, the person who converts is not the gentile owner of the house but the most esteemed member of the synagogue community.[197] Crispus and his household personally embody

Earlier on p. 79 Talbert remarks: 'That Christianity is institutionally separate from the synagogue is due to the rejection of the latter.' Talbert denies that such a separation is Luke's purpose, but Talbert's observation points to the presence of the symbol nevertheless.

197. If Cornelius and Lydia represent converts on the margins of Judaism, Crispus represents the very center of Judaism. His conversion lies in stark contrast to that of the jailer, who manifests no relation to Judaism whatsoever.

the transference of the people of God from the synagogue to the house. A note of triumphalism is perhaps detectable here in the conversion of a synagogue president (cf. Acts 6.7). That Crispus's conversion occurs *after*, not *before*, Paul enters the house of Titius Justus shows that the household mission has not rejected the Jews as such; they, too, can constitute the people of God alongside believing Gentiles.[198] Crispus's conversion prompts a new wave of gentile conversions, thereby adding to the Jew-Gentile composition of the church.

The third element of the pattern emphasizes the role of the house as the place of religious learning and instruction: Paul stays a year and a half at Corinth teaching the word of God in the house of Titius Justus (18.11). Instruction was a role traditionally assigned to the synagogue, as an inscription dating to the beginning of the first century CE well attests.[199] In the New Testament, 'διδάσκειν constantly figures as the main activity in the synagogues'.[200] Thus, at least in the founding of the church at Corinth, the house replaces the synagogue as the center of its religious life and learning. That the narrator mentions Paul's one and a half year ministry in Corinth is noteworthy in this context: the unusual duration seems to convey a sense of permanence to the arrangement.[201] The next time Paul stays in a city for an extended period of time, the narrator again focuses on Paul's role as teacher and the house as the place of religious instruction (cf. Acts 20.20, 31).[202]

While the narrator omits any express mention of Paul's eating and drinking in the house of Titius Justus (cf. Lk. 10.7), it is clear that Paul's

198. In subsequent cities Paul will continue his practice of going to the synagogue first (Acts 18.19; 19.8).

199. It describes the synagogue as a place built for 'the reading of the Law and the teaching [διδαχήν] of the commandments' (in Schürer, *The History of the Jewish People in the Age of Jesus Christ*, p. 425).

200. Schürer, *The History of the Jewish People in the Age of Jesus Christ*, p. 425. He notes such passages as Mt. 4.23; Mk 1.21; 6.2; Lk. 4.15,31; 6.6; 13.10; Jn 6.59; 18.20.

201. If δημοσίᾳ ('in public') at Acts 18.28 is a reference to the synagogue, then Apollos takes up preaching there. There is no note here, however, that the Christians of Corinth are continuing to meet in the synagogue. In light of 18.6, such an event appears doubtful.

202. Paul's teaching 'in public' (δημοσίᾳ) at Ephesus (20.20), insofar as it relates to the synagogue, occurs *prior* to his break from it to go to the school of Tyrannus (19.8). So Bruce, *The Book of Acts* (ET), p. 389.

teaching included regular acts of table-fellowship with both Jews and Gentiles. That Paul enters the house 'clean' or 'unpolluted' means that he is free to live and eat with Gentiles in the same way that Peter was free to live and eat with Gentiles in Cornelius's house. The house once again becomes the scene of inclusive table-fellowship between members of the people of God. That the Gentiles converted at Corinth included pagans without any connection to Judaism, in addition to the more traditional God-fearers, reveals the extent of Paul's radical eating activity.[203] Thus, the charge made against Paul by the Jews in the proximate context of the Crispus story, that he teaches people to worship God contrary to the Jewish law (18.13), is not without warrant. The charge is, as Esler notes, 'perfectly accurate, at least as far as the grave offence of living and eating with Gentiles is concerned'.[204] The subsequent vision of the Lord instructing Paul to continue his ministry in the house of Titius Justus implies divine confirmation of Paul's table-fellowship practice.

Conclusion

The stories of Lydia, the Roman jailer, and Crispus represent rich variations of a theme that begins in the house of Cornelius, the first gentile convert in Acts. Each reflects, modifies, or expands the pattern of the household mission in light of the particular placement of each in the larger narrative of Acts. Despite these variations, the general contours of the pattern remain visible to the reader: proclamation, initiation of an entire household, and hospitality.[205]

The placement of these stories after the story of Cornelius is important to their theme of hospitality that becomes the concrete expression of household salvation. Esler, for example, observes: 'It is surely not without significance that all of these occasions occur after the Cornelius narrative *and* the account of the Council in Jerusalem finally approving the mission to the Gentiles in a form obviously related to the establishment

203. Tannehill notes that Paul's move to the house of Titius Justus reveals a shift 'to a mission in the city at large, where the population is predominantly Gentile' (*The Narrative Unity of Luke–Acts*, II, p. 222). I would add 'and pagan'.

204. Esler, *Community and Gospel in Luke–Acts*, p. 128.

205. Pervo observes this pattern of Lydia and the jailer; it applies to the Crispus episode as well (*Luke's Story of Paul*, p. 59).

of table-fellowship between Jews and Gentiles.'[206] It now remains to consider the cumulative effect these stories have on an interpretation of Acts.

206. Esler, *Community and Gospel in Luke–Acts*, p. 100, emphasis his. A key difference with Esler, of course, involves his interpretation of Acts 15. Chapter 4 of this book stressed the *tension* between the 'compromise' decision reached in Acts 15 and Peter's indiscriminate table-fellowship with the household of Cornelius approved in Acts 10.1–11.18.

Chapter 6

CONCLUSION

Scholarship has generally cast Luke in the role of historian, theologian, or, more recently, literary artist.[1] In light of the results of this study, one more category now presents itself to the reader: Luke the missiologist.[2] In a two-fold work where universal salvation provides the key thematic link,[3] household evangelism functions as an important *modus operandi* of the expanding community of Jesus. The way the household mission creates inclusive communities of faith that embody this universal gospel is an indication of Luke's talent as a missionary strategist.[4]

Actually, the household conversion stories in Acts involve all three attributes traditionally ascribed to Luke. Historically, the household mission really did exist, and thus Luke cannot be credited with a new or novel approach.[5] Theologically, the mission to houses is Luke's

1. See, for example, Mark Allan Powell, *What Are They Saying About Luke*? (New York: Paulist Press, 1989), pp. 5-15.

2. Among the various aims of Acts are 'the strategies that may be employed in order to get the gospel through to potential hearers from a variety of religious and cultural contexts' (Howard Clark Kee, *Good News to the Ends of the Earth: The Theology of Acts* [London: SCM Press, 1990], p. 106). The mission to households represents one such 'evangelistic method' in Acts (cf. Michael Green, *Evangelism in the Early Church* [Grand Rapids: Eerdmans, 1970], pp. 194-235).

3. According to Robert C. Tannehill, the theme of universal salvation 'stretches from the beginning of Luke to the end of Acts, holding the narrative together in spite of the departure of major characters' (*The Narrative Unity of Luke–Acts: A Literary Interpretation*, II [Minneapolis: Fortress Press, 1990], p. 7).

4. According to Robert J. Karris, Luke is writing for communities that are essentially missionary communities, that is, 'communities which send people on mission to Jews and Gentiles' ('Missionary Communities: A New Paradigm for the Study of Luke–Acts', *CBQ* 41 [1979], p. 96).

5. So Donald Wayne Riddle ('Early Christian Hospitality: A Factor in Gospel Transmission', *JBL* 57 [1938], p. 153), who terms the conversion of households 'a notable phenomenon of the early days' of the Christian movement (p. 152).

preferred setting for vouchsafing some of the most profound truths of the messianic faith, such as the unqualified acceptance of the Gentiles in the story of Cornelius. Literarily, the stories manifest certain verbal and thematic links, reflecting a pattern of household evangelizing activity. The last two attributes are particularly germane to this study: the literary pattern of converting households becomes a vehicle for Luke's theological vision of universal salvation.

The Summary of the Pattern in Luke and Acts

History, theology, and literary artistry, then, converge in Acts to produce a strategic pattern of missionary endeavor. Part One of this book establishes the pattern of household evangelizing by linking it both to the words and actions of Jesus in the Gospel of Luke. Chapter 2 develops the pattern proper by carefully observing the instructions of Jesus to the Seventy-two (Lk. 10.1-16), a fictional sending in Luke that symbolizes the universal mission in Acts. Among the instructions given in this discourse is the command to offer salvation to households (10.5-7), which contains the constituent elements of a household conversion story. The pattern anticipates the universal mission in Acts: in sending out the Seventy-two, Jesus directs his messengers to enter homes of economically established (gentile) householders, preach the message of salvific peace to the household, and stay in those homes for purposes of inclusive table-fellowship. This three-fold action constitutes the 'taxonomy' of household evangelism,[6] resulting in the formation of a Lukan type-scene.[7] The didactic nature of the discourse invests the pattern of household evangelizing with dominical authority on the pages of Acts.

Chapter 3 traces the source of this pattern to the household ministry of Jesus as Luke presents it. While Luke no doubt found general literary and thematic precedent in the Greek Old Testament with its numerous pictures of household salvation,[8] the particulars of the pattern are

6. I borrow the term from Walter Brueggemann who, interestingly, sees biblical evangelism generally unfolding in a series of three distinct scenes (*Biblical Perspectives on Evangelism: Living in a Three-Storied Universe* [Nashville: Abingdon Press, 1993], pp. 14-47).

7. On the qualified notion of type-scene employed in this study, see ch. 1, p. 17.

8. Luke's fondness for the Septuagint was noted earlier in this study. Among the examples of corporate salvation are Noah (Gen. 7.1), Abraham (Gen. 17), Rahab (Josh. 2.12-13, 18-19; 6.25), and David (2 Kgs 7.8-16). 'Household salvation' was basic to the economy of salvation in ancient Israel (Deut. 6.4-9; 14.26). What

distinctively Lukan. Indeed, the literary artistry of the Third Evangelist is nowhere more evident than in the way he constructs the household mission of the Seventy-two out of certain 'core' elements with which he fashions the household mission of Jesus! Not only does Jesus often enter and stay in houses for purposes of table-fellowship, but at a critical juncture of his ministry he converts Zacchaeus and his household (19.1-10), the only synoptic account of household salvation and one in which all three elements appear. The only other narrative of a household conversion in the New Testament (Jn 4.46-54) bears no relation to the concomitant motifs of entering and staying in a house; they are distinctively Lukan.[9] The convergence of these motifs in the symbolic sending of the Seventy-two links the household mission not only to the words of Jesus but to the actions of Jesus as well. If the words of Jesus provide messengers in Acts with the pattern of household evangelizing, his actions provide them with the prototype.

Part Two of this book focuses on the way in which the pattern of the Seventy-two receives expression in Acts, which contains four distinct scenes of household conversion. Chapter 4 devotes a separate treatment to the story of Cornelius (10.1–11.18), the first instance of household conversion and the most pregnant expression of the household missionary pattern. Its paradigmatic function in Acts is evident from the way it becomes the occasion for the conversion of the first Gentiles, with whom Peter is free to eat and drink in the house after bringing salvation to the household (10.1-48). The calling of Peter into account by the more law-observant Jewish believers in Jerusalem results in his re-telling of the story (11.1-18) and the first 'variation' of the pattern in Acts, one that leads strategically to the confirmation of his actions.

Chapter 5 takes up the remaining stories of Lydia (16.11-15), the Roman jailer (16.25-34), and Crispus (18.1-11), heads of households who convert after the manner of Cornelius. That these stories occur *after* the decisive events in Cornelius's house bears intentional placement by the narrator of Acts since each reflects, modifies, or expands the seminal

Tannehill observes of other Old Testament parallels in Luke–Acts may also apply here: 'The narrator is not copying any one of these stories, but various features of the set of stories may have influenced the narration, consciously or unconsciously' (*The Narrative Unity of Luke–Acts*, II, p. 126).

9. The Lukan character of these typical elements shines through even more clearly if this passage represents a variant tradition of Lk. 7.1-10, a view dating to the time of Irenaeus (*Against Heresies* 2.22.3).

events associated with the first account of household conversion. By reiterating the key themes of household solidarity and inclusive table-fellowship, these stories contribute to the repetitive character of the household missionary pattern.

The Function of the Pattern in Acts

As demonstrated throughout the course of this study, each story of household conversion has its own special function to perform in light of its global and proximate context in Acts. What, however, is the overall function of these stories when considered cumulatively? How does the pattern of household evangelizing contribute to the story-line of Acts?

First, the household mission *inaugurates and expands the gentile mission in Acts*. Unlike in Mark, for whom the house is primarily a place of instruction for the disciples of Jesus,[10] the house functions in Luke's second volume as a place of evangelism and growth.[11] The household conversion narratives mark a series of 'firsts' in bringing the gospel to the unreached peoples of the world: the first Gentile man (Cornelius), the first gentile woman (Lydia), the first pagan (the Roman jailer), and the first synagogue president (Crispus), whose conversion results in even greater numbers of Gentiles coming to faith, both God-fearers and pagans. Apart from Cornelius, each conversion occurs on Paul's inaugural journey to Europe, the mission's key geographical advance in Acts. Each produces believing gentile communities along the pathway to Rome.[12] The strong note of divine prompting and/or intervention further contributes to their ground-breaking character: inclusive mission requires the initiation and direction of the Lord of the house.[13]

10. See, for example, Ernest Best, *Following Jesus: Discipleship in the Gospel of Mark* (Sheffield: JSOT Press, 1981), pp. 226-29. Also Elizabeth Struthers Malbon, 'THOIKIA AYTOY: Mark 2.15 in Context', *NTS* 31 (1985), p. 287. Cf. also her *Narrative Space and Mythic Meaning in Mark* (San Francisco: Harper & Row, 1986).

11. Y.K. Chang notes how the homes of Cornelius, Lydia, and the jailer were used as personal 'soul-winning centers' ('The Evangelistic Emphases of the Acts of the Apostles' [ThD dissertation, Southwestern Baptist Theological Seminary, 1951], p. 180).

12. Conversion stories in general are stories about 'beginnings' (see Beverly Roberts Gaventa, *From Darkness to Light: Aspects of Conversion in the New Testament* [Philadelphia: Fortress Press, 1989], p. 125).

13. On this important observation more will be said below, pp. 201-202.

Second, the pattern of the household mission legitimates the Gentiles as equal members of the new salvific community by stressing their full acceptance at table with Jews. Philip Francis Esler calls attention to the four instances in Acts featuring table-fellowship between Jews and Gentiles (11.3; 16.14-15; 16.25-34; 18.7); in doing so, however, he inadvertently enumerates the four stories of household salvation.[14] That this remarkable table commensality appears only in scenes depicting the salvation of households suggests that the pattern is distinctly the means by which Jew–Gentile relations are legitimized on the pages of Acts.

The story of Cornelius, of course, is the decisive one for Luke: by its abrogation of dietary regulations, it effectively and forever removes the cultic distinction between Jews and Gentiles in the new household of faith. The concern of Peter's Jerusalem accusers is not his conversion of Gentiles *per se* but the fact of his having lived and eaten with them (11.3). In the story of Lydia, a Gentile who becomes a believer offers her hospitality to Paul, thereby extending the theme of table-fellowship and providing the first real insight into the nature of Paul's ministry among the Gentiles. The conversion of the jailer is notable for the way Paul and Silas eat unabashedly at the table of outright pagans, bringing the theme of table-fellowship in Acts to its most radical apex. The final story of household conversion concludes the theme of table-fellowship by recalling the paradigmatic story of Cornelius: in pronouncing himself 'clean' to enter and eat in the house of a Gentile, Paul recalls the experience of Peter that led him to the house of Cornelius in the first place. In Acts, full and equal participation in the new inclusive community receives concrete expression by means of shared hospitality—believing Jews and Gentiles living under the same roof and eating the same (eucharistic) food.

This strategic use of the household missionary pattern, however, creates a basic tension in the narrative of Acts, one that Luke does not fully resolve. The type of social relations envisioned between Jews and Gentiles in the mission to households does not entirely square with the solution reached at the Jerusalem Council (Acts 15) nor does it accord with Luke's attempt to portray Paul as one faithful to the laws and

14. With regard to the latter three instances, Esler notes that 'Luke specifically describes Paul as engaging in fellowship with Gentiles, of precisely the kind established between Peter and Cornelius' (*Community and Gospel in Luke–Acts: The Social and Political Motivations of Lucan Theology* [Cambridge: Cambridge University Press, 1987], pp. 99-100).

decrees of Judaism. Tension at these two points suggests that the household conversion stories offer a unique and certainly the most radical perspective on a problem that vexed the early church.[15]

Some scholars contend that the narrator of Acts is basically unaware of this tension.[16] Indications exist, however, to suggest that he was, in fact, aware of it and has taken measures to 'limit' the effects of the decrees, which historical circumstances may have dictated that he place in his narrative.[17] First, he presents the decrees of the Jerusalem Council as geographically limited in scope, being directed only to the gentile communities of Syro-Cilicia and southern Galatia, the 'daughter churches' of the church at Antioch. That the Council convenes after Paul's first missionary journey in Acts suggests that the Jewish church was just beginning to feel the radical implications of gentile conversion, including the troublesome issue of table-fellowship. This fact suggests that the decrees belong essentially to a period of transition occasioned by the first systematic attempt to convert Gentiles. When the gospel crosses the crucial geographical barrier of Europe, however, the mission 'matures', and the decrees cease to be a viable factor. Apart from Cornelius, all the episodes of household conversion occur on this inaugural journey, intimating that the mission to the 'end of the earth' is one essentially free from the restraints imposed by the church in Jerusalem.

Secondly, the Jerusalem decrees appear to be a working compromise in Acts to facilitate table-fellowship between gentile believers and more law-conscious Jews. The compromised nature of the decrees is particularly apparent in Acts 21, where they re-surface in connection with Paul's final mission to Jerusalem. When Paul arrives in Jerusalem, he

15. Frank Stagg observes how pervasive this problem is both in Acts and in Paul's letters ('Paul's Final Mission to Jerusalem', in Naymond H. Keathley [ed.], *With Steadfast Purpose: Essays on Acts in Honor of Henry Jackson Flanders, Jr*, [Waco: Baylor University, 1990], p. 263). Note the historical Paul's fierce rebuke of the apostle Peter in this regard (Gal. 2.11-14).

16. Joseph B. Tyson, for example, claims that 'Luke himself expresses no sense of conflict between Acts 10 and Acts 15' ('The Gentile Mission and the Authority of Scripture in Acts', *NTS* 33 [1987], p. 628).

17. Evidence for the historical observance of the decrees by the gentile church appears both inside (Rev. 2.14, 20) and outside (Justin, *Dialogue* 34.8; Minucius Felix, *Octavius* 30.6) the New Testament. The historical Paul, however, appears to be unaware of the decrees, as witnessed by his discussion of meats at Corinth (1 Cor. 8.1-13; 10.14-33).

informs James and the elders of the church of his success among the Gentiles (v. 19), which directly leads to James's concern for Paul's reputation among the myriads of Jews who are 'zealous for the law' (v. 20). The reference to these Jews, in fact, becomes the occasion for a restatement of the 'Jewish case' against Paul: 'you teach apostasy from Moses by telling all the Jews among the Gentiles not to circumcise their children nor to walk in the customs' (21.21; cf. 18.13; 21.28; 24.5-6).[18] To allay the concerns of these Jewish traditionalists, James proposes that Paul take a vow in the temple (vv. 22-24) and, more importantly, that he adhere to the decrees of the Jerusalem Council (v. 25).[19] While the Lukan Paul goes to great lengths in Acts to dismiss the Jewish case against him, particularly in his defense speeches (24.10-16; 25.8, 10-11; 26.1-5), Esler astutely observes the accuracy of the Jewish charge in one vital respect: 'Whatever Luke might say about Paul, he could not obscure the fact that he lived and ate with Gentiles, thereby endangering the separate existence of the Jewish ἔθνος and almost certainly renouncing the Levitical food laws.'[20] In this respect complete agreement exists between the Lukan and the historical Paul.[21] As Frank Stagg observes, the bitter issue over Paul in Jerusalem was not his preaching *per se* but his relationship to the Gentiles (Acts 22.21).[22] While James and the

18. On the 'Jewish case' against Paul in Acts, see Esler, *Community and Gospel in Luke–Acts*, p. 126. The reference here to the Jews τοὺς κατὰ τὰ ἔθνη is significant, giving the charge an explicitly diaspora context.

19. The restatement of the Jerusalem decrees to Paul at 21.25 is curious since, if Paul was present at the Council (15.2, 4, 12), why would he need to be informed of them again? Does their reappearance in this context suggest that some doubt exists in James's mind that Paul has lived in accordance with them?

20. Esler, *Community and Gospel in Luke–Acts*, p. 128. According to Esler, 'the existence of table-fellowship between Jews and Gentiles substantiates the Jewish claim that Paul has opposed Moses and the customs of the Jewish people' (p. 129). This astute observation raises the specter of Paul's being an 'unreliable narrator' in his defense speeches, an intriguing subject that lies beyond the scope of this study.

21. The complete acceptance of Gentiles in table-fellowship was non-negotiable for Paul (see Stagg, 'Paul's Final Mission to Jerusalem', p. 263). It lay at the heart of the 'truth of the gospel' (Gal. 2.11-14; cf. Rom. 14.20 and 1 Cor. 10.27-28). In light of Paul's table-fellowship practices in Acts, one must question, at least on this score, Philipp Vielhauer's assertion that Luke attempts to portray Paul as a Jewish Christian who is utterly loyal to the law' ('On the "Paulinism" of Acts', in L.E. Keek and J.L. Martyn [eds.], *Studies in Luke–Acts: Essays Presented in Honor of Paul Schubert* [Nashville: Abingdon Press, 1966], p. 38).

22. Stagg, 'Paul's Final Mission to Jerusalem', p. 268. The very word 'Gentiles',

others could presumably converse freely in Jerusalem, it was 'the gospel proclaimed as including uncircumcised Gentiles in both salvation *and table-fellowship* which aroused the fiercest opposition'.[23]

This theme of table-fellowship reveals a third and related function of the household missionary pattern: the mapping out of a new 'sacred' space for the inclusive people of God. That Acts reserves table commensality between Jews and Gentiles solely for scenes of household conversion contributes to the emerging sacred character of the house in contrast to the temple and/or synagogue. Only the household, notes John H. Elliott, 'is capable of embodying socially and ideologically the structures, values, and goals of an inclusive gospel of universal salvation'.[24] In the Lukan writings, the household appears as 'the most apposite sphere and symbol of social life' under the universal reign of God, whom the author presents as a generous and merciful father.[25] The conversion of the household thus entails the 'conversion' of household space, the place of inclusive word and sacrament.[26] As in the mission of the Seventy-two, there is the closest of relationships between the newly converted household and its house (ἐν αὐτῇ δὲ τῇ οἰκίᾳ, Lk. 10.7). While the 'sacralization' of the house is essentially a work in progress in Acts,[27] it

he notes (p. 270), is inflammatory in this section of Acts (22.21; 28.25, 28).

23. Stagg, 'Paul's Final Mission to Jerusalem', p. 267, emphasis mine. Stagg provides a helpful overview of the various motivations lying behind the persecutions of Christians in Acts: 'Sadducees, fearful of antagonizing the Romans; Pharisees, protective of Jewish traditions; Herodians, opportunists trying to please the Jews; and pagans with their economic concerns, as at Philippi and Ephesus.' He notes that the persecution of Paul was 'primarily Pharisaic and related to his Gentile mission' (p. 267 n. 5).

24. John H. Elliott, 'Temple versus Household in Luke–Acts: A Contrast in Social Institutions', in Jerome H. Neyrey (ed.), *The Social World of Luke–Acts: Models for Interpretation* (Peabody: Hendrickson Publishers, 1991), p. 213. Elliott's observation, which stems principally from a sociological reading of the text, now finds confirmation from a narratological point of view.

25. Elliott, 'Temple versus Household in Luke–Acts', p. 227 (see the passages listed on p. 228). Elliott stresses the strong metaphorical reality of the inclusive household: 'The church which grows through household conversions becomes at the same time a worldwide household of faith' (p. 229).

26. In this light the emphasis on economically established householders is readily intelligible in Acts since only their conversion would entail the use of a house for an upstart church.

27. It is important here to recall the particular criterion of sacralization employed in this study—the transformation of the house from private domestic space to the

increasingly identifies the house as the 'house church', the place of religious assembly.[28]

This transformation in household space is noticeably present in the story of Cornelius. Here space that is formerly 'polluted' or 'unclean' becomes, in the course of the story, the locus for the outpouring of the Holy Spirit and the place for the first inclusive act of eating and drinking with Gentiles. The dismantling of the Jewish purity system within its sphere means that Gentiles now share in the salvation of the house.[29] As the gospel moves from Jerusalem to Rome, from the center of Jewish life to the center of the gentile world, the house gradually replaces both temple and synagogue as the sphere of the new salvific community.[30]

The Pattern and the Narrative Unity of 'Luke–Acts'

The principal method of investigation proposed in this book—reading the household conversion narratives against the backdrop of the mission of the Seventy-two—impinges significantly on the question of the

'public' space of the church, the locus for the inclusive act of 'eating and drinking' (Lk. 10.7). Historically, of course, one cannot speak of the full sacralization of the house until much later (see the four-fold progression in Lloyd Michael White, 'Domus Ecclesiae—Domus Dei: Adaption and Development in the Setting for Early Christian Assembly' [PhD dissertation, Yale University, 1982]). Interestingly, White sees early traces of sacralization in the 'upper room' (1.13; 9.37, 39; 20.8) locale of the house church in Acts (p. 603).

28. Saul ravages 'the church' (τὴν ἐκκλησίαν) by entering 'house after house' (κατὰ τοὺς οἴκους, 8.3); prayers are offered for Peter's release 'by the church' (ὑπὸ τῆς ἐκκλησίας, 12.5) which has gathered in 'the house of Mary' (τὴν οἰκίαν τῆς Μαρίας, 12.12); Paul teaches 'the church of God' (τὴν ἐκκλησίαν τοῦ θεοῦ) at Ephesus (20.28; cf. v. 17) by going 'house to house' (κατ' οἴκους; 20.20). For other close correspondences of these terms in the New Testament, see Rom. 16.5; 1 Cor. 16.19; Col. 4.15; 1 Tim. 3.5,15; Phil. 2; 2 Jn 10 = 3 Jn 10. Rosalie Beck notices the critical role of the house church in Acts: 'The house church became the foundation of the early church, and it provided a place for preaching the gospel, for teaching doctrine, for worship, and for fellowship between believers' ('The Women of Acts: Foremothers of the Christian Church', in *With Steadfast Purpose*, p. 295).

29. In contrast, for example, with the temple: 'For all those outside the holy boundaries of Israel, the physical limits of the Holy Place and the social restrictions of its purity system effectively prohibited the access of all to sanctification, health, and salvation' (Elliott, 'Temple versus Household in Luke–Acts', p. 224). For Elliott, the synagogue 'represents the extension of temple authority and values' (p. 217).

30. Elliott, 'Temple versus Household in Luke–Acts', p. 238.

narrative unity between the Lukan writings, long considered a 'given' since the time of Henry J. Cadbury.[31] Recently, however, Mikeal C. Parsons and Richard I. Pervo have called into question this pervasive *opinio communis*, contending that authorial unity alone does not presuppose the theological, literary, generic, or canonical unity of the texts in question.[32] The program of household evangelizing presented in this study obviously assumes a literary relationship between Luke and Acts, but a relationship of what kind?

Similarities in content, language, and theme in the presentation of the household mission compel one to add yet another parallel to the narrative quilt of Luke and Acts, a feature for which Luke has long been noted.[33] While one must be careful to distinguish the nature of the parallels one discovers in the process of reading, the way in which the household missionary pattern accords with and accentuates certain critical themes in Acts suggests that it belongs properly to the composition of the author.[34] The ultimate criterion for all such literary parallels is

31. See his classic *The Making of Luke–Acts* (London: SPCK, 1927, reprint 1958). Cadbury is generally credited with the hyphenated expression 'Luke–Acts'.

32. See Mikeal C. Parsons and Richard I. Pervo, *Rethinking the Unity of the Lukan Writings* (Minneapolis: Fortress Press, 1993). See also Parsons's 'The Unity of the Lukan Writings: Rethinking the *Opinio Communis*', in *With Steadfast Purpose*, pp. 29-53. Authorial unity remains a 'given' in Lukan scholarship with exceptions (e.g., Albert C. Clark, *The Acts of the Apostles: A Critical Edition with Introduction and Notes on Selected Passages* [Oxford: Clarendon Press, 1933]; more recently, A.W. Argyle, 'The Greek of Luke and Acts', *NTS* 20 [1973–74], pp. 441-45).

33. On the history of parallelisms in Luke–Acts, see W. Ward Gasque, *A History of the Interpretation of the Acts of the Apostles* (Peabody: Hendrickson 1989), pp. 21-54. See also Susan Marie Praeder, 'Jesus–Paul, Peter–Paul, and Jesus–Peter Parallelisms in Luke–Acts: A History of Reader Response', in K.H. Richards (ed.), *SBLSP* (Chico, CA: Scholars Press, 1984), pp. 23-39. Charles H. Talbert calls the literary parallels between Luke and Acts 'the primary architectonic pattern in Luke–Acts' (*Literary Patterns, Theological Themes and the Genre of Luke–Acts* [Missoula: Scholars Press, 1974], p. 15).

34. Praeder distinguishes between 'parallel composition', involving textual similarities in content, language, literary form, sequence, structure, and/or theme, and 'parallel reading', involving 'selective reading, remembering and forgetting, looking backward and forward in the text and to other texts, and long and painstaking reading' ('Jesus–Paul, Peter–Paul, and Jesus–Peter Parallelisms', p. 38). The contrast, however, is too tightly drawn to be of real help to the reader. Even compositional parallels require a degree of 'parallel reading'.

whether they fit together and whether they perform a viable function in the text.[35] These considerations suggest that narrative unity exists at the level of both 'discourse' and 'story': the mission of the Seventy-two anticipates the full inclusion of the people of God in Acts, thus furthering Luke's theme of universal salvation.[36]

Yet the nature of this unity is by no means total or complete, as the protocol of Jesus itself reveals: 'and if a son of peace is there, your peace will rest on him; otherwise, it will return to you' (Lk. 10.6). Here the Lukan Jesus envisions the possible rejection of his household messengers; in the sending out of the Seventy-two with the gospel of peace, 'a less than unanimous receptivity is expected'.[37] The precise nature of this rejection is not entirely clear: is the 'son of peace' the owner of the house or an individual member within it? If the former, the entire household rejects the offer of salvation by virtue of the householder acting on its behalf; if the latter, division occurs within the household itself.[38] Unlike elsewhere in the New Testament,[39] neither scenario is

35. Praeder writes: 'Certain parallelisms in Luke–Acts make sense. They fit together, and they fit the concerns and themes of Luke–Acts. Sometimes textual similarities seem to make sense as parallelisms. They can be made to fit together and to fit the rest of Luke–Acts, and it seems necessary to take the risk of making sense of the text by calling them parallelisms' ('Jesus–Paul, Peter–Paul, and Jesus–Peter Parallelisms in Luke–Acts', p. 39).

36. 'Story' refers to 'what is told', including the actions and actors portrayed in the discourse; 'discourse' refers to 'how it is told', the medium of the story. For this classical distinction, see Seymour Chatman, *Story and Discourse: Narrative Structure in Fiction and Film* (Ithaca: Cornell University Press, 1978). He is followed by Robert W. Funk, *The Poetics of Biblical Narrative* (Sonoma: Polebridge Press, 1988), p. 2.

37. Riddle, 'Early Christian Hospitality', p. 153.

38. On the identification of the 'son of peace' with the householder, see R.C.H. Lenski, *The Interpretation of St Luke's Gospel* (Minneapolis: Augsburg, 1946), p. 571; David P. Moessner, *Lord of the Banquet: The Literary and Theological Significance of the Lukan Travel Narrative* (Minneapolis: Fortress Press, 1989), p. 136; Leon Morris, *The Gospel According to Luke: An Introduction and Commentary* (TNTC; Grand Rapids: Eerdmans, 1974), p. 182. For the 'son of peace' as an individual member of the household, see C.F. Evans, *Saint Luke* (TPINTC; London: SCM Press, 1990), p. 447. According to Burton L. Mack, division within families occurred at a critical juncture in the history of the Jesus movement (*The Lost Gospel: The Book of Q and Christian Origins* [San Francisco: Harper & Row, 1993], pp. 136-41).

39. Household solidarity in conversion was a two-edged sword. If entire households could be won to the faith, they could also be lost to the faith (cf. Tit. 1.11; cf.

even remotely considered in Acts, for which there is only 'idyllic household unity'.[40]

The divisive effect of the gospel on the household is a particularly strong theme in the Gospel of Luke. The offer of salvific 'peace' by the household messengers lies in stark contrast to the 'peace' offered by Jesus at Lk. 12.51: 'Do not think that I came to bring peace on the earth; no, I tell you, but rather division!' The household character of this division is clear from the verses immediately following: 'for from now on five members in one house(hold) [ἐν ἑνὶ οἴκῳ] will be divided, three against two, and two against three. They will be divided, father against son, and son against father; mother against daughter, and daughter against mother; mother-in-law against her daughter-in-law, and daughter-in-law against mother-in-law' (12.52-53). Comparison with Matthew reveals that Luke offers perhaps the strongest statement of the gospel's divisive effects on the family.[41]

At the same time, the house remains the special object of mission in Luke. Jesus himself appears as the proto-typical missionary to the house, which becomes the place for healing, teaching, and eating as well as the place for conflict and division. He sends his messengers to houses (9.1-6; 10.1-16), anticipating the role that the house will perform for the early Christian communities in Acts. In certain passages Luke even shows a special interest in the house as the symbolic sphere of salvation and healing.[42] Nevertheless, the family often appears in Luke as an obstacle

2 Tim. 3.6; see Abraham J. Malherbe, *Social Aspects of Early Christianity* [Philadelphia: Fortress Press, 2nd edn, 1983], p. 97 n. 14). It is also apparent that Christianity sometimes exerted a divisive influence on the family, particularly when it entered the home via a non-householder (Rom. 16.11b; 1 Cor. 7.12-16; Phil. 4.22; 1 Pet. 3.1; 2 Tim. 1.5 [cf. Acts 16.1]; Tit. 1.6). As the case of Philemon and Onesimus shows, the conversion of a head of house did not always insure the conversion of the entire household.

40. Carolyn Osiek, 'The Lukan *Oikos*: An Exercise in Symbolic Universe', Unpublished Seminar Paper, Social Facets Seminar, Spring, 1987, p. 1.

41. 'Division within the old family structure is an inherent effect of Jesus' call' (Osiek, 'The Lukan *Oikos*', p. 2). Only Luke expressly speaks of the 'division' of the family as such, including the strong division-saying at 12.52 (cf. Mt. 10.34-36). Luke's house(hold), according to I. Howard Marshall, includes a 'family of five': father, mother, daughter, son, and son's wife (*The Gospel of Luke: A Commentary on the Greek Text* [NIGC; Grand Rapids: Eerdmans, 1978], p. 549).

42. Notice how the house functions as the place for restoration (Lk. 15.6, 8, 25), justification (Lk. 18.9-14), and wholeness (Lk. 8.39). All these house motifs are distinctively Lukan.

to evangelism (Lk. 9.59-62; 14.20,26; 18.28-9) rather than the object of evangelism as in Acts. The effect of this tension is that the gospel should expect a mixed reception in the house, perhaps akin to the synagogue (Lk. 4.16-30; Acts 13.44-52; 14.1-2; 17.4-5; 19.9; 28.24).[43]

The narrative of Acts, however, fails to provide any examples of divided or rejecting households, despite the fact that the protocol of Luke 10.6 envisions such a possibility occurring. The desire to follow only the positive trajectory into Acts is surely significant, creating a symbolic universe that is not entirely consistent with that of the Gospel.[44] In this context 'symbolic universe' refers to the way the implied reader of Luke and Acts understands the structure and order of the world, involving demarcations in people, time, and space so as to make the world intelligible and to define a person's or group's relation to it.[45]

What literary purpose might account for this difference in symbolic worlds? The twin themes of inclusive salvation and divine prompting provide the decisive clues. The first calls attention to the way that stories of household conversion function to break with significant social and ethnic barriers. Cornelius, of course, comes immediately to mind since his conversion represents the decisive inauguration of the mission to the Gentiles. Yet, as ch. 5 of this book has shown, Lydia, the jailer, and Crispus each contributes in significant ways to the spread of the gentile mission. They are representative monuments of universal salvation marking the progress of the gospel to the 'end of the earth'.

The second points to the initial reluctance of the household messengers. It is a notable feature of the household mission in Acts that both Peter and Paul must receive divine prodding in some way before they

43. A mixed reaction in the house is presupposed by the very existence of Luke's Gospel. In noting how the first readers of the Gospel were members of households, David E. Aune observes that 'the Gospels were consciously designed both to reinforce the personal and social implications of belief in Jesus as Messiah and Son of God, and *persuade non-Christian members of Christians households* (some of which doubtless functioned as church centers) of the ultimate religious significance of Jesus' (*The New Testament in Its Literary Environment* [Philadelphia: Westminster Press, 1987], p. 60, emphasis mine).

44. In this regard Osiek notes the way that Acts corrects the symbolic universe of Luke ('The Lukan *Oikos*', p. 1).

45. See, for example, Jerome H. Neyrey, 'The Symbolic Universe of Luke–Acts: "They Turn the World Upside Down"', in *The Social World of Luke–Acts*, pp. 272-304.

can perform their task of household evangelism. Before Peter goes to the house of Cornelius he receives the vision of the sheet declaring all foods clean and hears explicit instructions from the Spirit. Before Paul and Silas encounter Lydia, they receive direct guidance by the Holy Spirit and the 'Spirit of Jesus' as well as hear the call of the man from Macedonia; that they enter and stay in the house at all is due to the urging of the 'faithful' Lydia, whose heart is opened by the risen Lord. The conversion of the jailer, also due to the Lord's European initiative, is made possible only by the occurrence of an earthquake, which prompts the jailer to ask: 'Sirs, what must I do to be saved?' At Corinth, Paul enters the house of Titius Justus after encountering the blasphemy and resistance of the Jews. He stays in the house for an extended period only as the result of a vision which quiets his fears. For seemingly insuperable barriers to be broken down, the Lord of the house must initiate the mission and direct its course, a theme noticeably present in the mission of the Seventy-two.[46]

These two factors, when considered together, lead to the all-important observation: *obedience to a radical vision of universal salvation leads to the gospel's unqualified success among households*. The very unpredictability of the household conversion stories stresses the need for the disciples' complete obedience when the moment of the Lord's guidance arrives. The commitment of the seventy-two messengers to an inclusive program of household evangelism[47] foreshadows the successful mission in Acts as messengers obey the directives of the Lord of the house.[48] Noting the emphatic role of divine intervention in the conversion of Cornelius, Ernst Haenchen criticizes the story for the way it mitigates faith and the role of human decision.[49] Yet, in making this

46. The three-fold sending theme in the mission of the Seventy-two (Lk. 10.1-3) underscores the role of Jesus/God as the initiator and director of the mission.

47. The response of the apostles to Jesus' question at Lk. 22.35 'indicates that during their missionary journey, in spite of their lack of possessions, they did *not* experience need, with the clear implication that they *were* accepted by the households and were supported by them' (Luke T. Johnson, *The Literary Function of Possessions in Luke–Acts* [Missoula: Scholars Press, 1977], p. 164). On the relation of this verse to the sending of the Seventy-two, see ch. 2 of this book, p. 39 n. 66.

48. I am indebted to Professor R. Alan Culpepper, who first suggested this line of interpretation to me.

49. Ernst Haenchen, *The Acts of the Apostles: A Commentary*, trans. Bernard Noble and Gerald Shinn (Philadelphia: Westminster Press, 1971), p. 362. For Haenchen, the divine incursions in the story prove that 'God, not man, is at work'.

observation, Haenchen overlooks the critical role human response plays in making possible the fulfillment of God's salvific desire.[50] The obedience of the household messengers culminates in the sharing of food with those previously regarded as unclean, the ultimate expression of universal salvation in Acts. The symbolic universe of first-century Judaism is transformed in the process of converting the household.[51]

This difference in symbolic worlds cautions one against adopting a too facile understanding of 'narrative unity' between Luke and Acts. Pointing out the pitfalls of such an assumption, Parsons tentatively identifies Acts as a 'sequel' to Luke, one that 'is distinct from Luke on the discourse level and which supplies additional material about the community of Jesus at the story level'.[52] Parsons's notion of 'sequel' has the advantage of recognizing a close literary relationship between Luke and Acts as well as accounting for differences between them. It does not preclude the kind of reading envisioned in this study, only the insistence that Luke and Acts form a single, continuous work.[53] While the household missionary pattern may argue for a greater degree of unity at the level of discourse than Parsons perhaps allows, the nature of this 'unity' is by no means total or complete. Indeed, the presence of discontinuity permits additional insight into the way a literary pattern functions on the pages of Acts.

Contributions of Study

In the broadest terms, the contributions of this study are three-fold. First, a study of the household conversion narratives opens up a new line of interpretative inquiry in Acts previously uncharted in Lukan scholarship. Apart from the story of Cornelius, Lukan scholars have focused minimal attention on the remaining accounts of Lydia, the jailer, and Crispus. When viewed against the backdrop of the mission of the Seventy-two

50. Tannehill, for example, observes that 'Peter will discover the meaning of his vision only if he follows the Spirit's prompting' (*The Narrative Unity of Luke–Acts*, II, p. 128). For Tannehill, the divine promptings in the story of Cornelius 'are incomplete in themselves. They require *human action* or reflection' (emphasis mine).

51. Of Jesus and his followers, Neyrey writes: 'Luke does not present them as lawless or mapless people. They do not advocate chaos in place of cosmos. On the contrary, Luke portrayed Jesus drawing new maps and reforming old ones, not destroying the system' ('The Symbolic Universe of Luke–Acts', p. 299).

52. Parsons, 'The Unity of the Lukan Writings', pp. 44-45.

53. Parsons, 'The Unity of the Lukan Writings', p. 39.

and the paradigmatic story of Cornelius, however, these figures suddenly ascend in importance. Their conversion stories take on new meaning as important variations of a key Lukan soteriological principle: salvation of both Jew and Gentile concretized through table-fellowship.

A careful scrutiny of the meaning and function of the household conversion narratives compels one to pursue neglected themes in the text of Acts, particularly the critical role of table-fellowship. The recent study of Esler sounds the indictment: 'An almost universal failure to appreciate the centrality of this phenomenon...is one of the most outstanding deficiencies in Lucan scholarship.'[54] Doing so, however, immediately raises the question of the relation of Acts 15 to Acts 10.1–11.18, both of which propose solutions to the problem of social discourse with Gentiles that stand in some tension with each other.[55] That both receive the endorsement of the Jerusalem church only clouds the picture on the pages of Acts! Paying close attention to table-fellowship practice in Acts raises the further question of Paul's relation to Judaism: is he entirely truthful when he claims that he believes everything in accordance with the Law (24.14), that he has committed no offense against it (25.8), and that he has maintained a good conscience before God and all the people (24.16)? Or does some basis exist for the Jewish charge that he disregards the Law of Moses and leads the people astray? This study can make only a provisional survey of the tensions raised by the household conversion stories in Acts; but recognizing *that* they exist is an important first step toward a better understanding of Luke's story of the early church.

A second contribution is that, while household conversion has been perceived primarily in doctrinal or social terms, this study establishes a basis for understanding the phenomenon from a distinctly literary point of view. By recognizing the verbal and thematic connections between the household mission of the Seventy-two and the subsequent stories of household conversion, one is able to trace the development of a critically important theme as it undergoes degrees of repetition and variation on the pages of Acts. Reading the household conversion narratives thus

54. Esler, *Community and Gospel in Luke–Acts*, p. 71. Esler's study is a step in the right direction.

55. I say 'tension' rather than 'contradiction' because both models ultimately allow for table-fellowship between Jews and Gentiles in the church. The question is the nature and character of this fellowship. As long as Jewish Christians decide the 'menu', gentile Christians remain in an inferior position.

becomes an exercise in biblical interpretation, opening up new vistas of insight into Luke's literary and theological aims. As a result of this study, one is now in a position, perhaps for the first time, to appreciate the *literary* function of these stories in both their proximate and global contexts of Acts.

Third, the method developed in this study not only recognizes, but assigns a literary function to, both the 'unity' and 'disunity' of the household mission at the level of discourse. Unlike prior treatments of Lukan literary patterns that seemingly rest on facile assumptions regarding the unity of the Lukan writings,[56] this study is careful to observe a more finely nuanced notion of narrative unity, one that accounts for the verbal and thematic parallels between Luke and Acts but recognizes a key point of difference. The failure of Acts to follow the negative trajectory envisioned at Lk. 10.6 results in a wholly positive outcome for the household mission in Acts, creating a symbolic universe that is quite different in some respects from that of Luke. In this way both the continuity and discontinuity of the Lukan writings contribute to their all-encompassing theme of universal salvation.

56. See, for example, the critiques of Parsons ('The Unity of the Lukan Writings', pp. 38-41) and Praeder ('Jesus–Paul, Peter–Paul, and Jesus–Peter Parallelisms in Luke–Acts', pp. 23-39).

BIBLIOGRAPHY

Aland, K., *Did the Early Church Baptize Infants?* (trans. G.R. Beasley-Murray; Philadelphia: Westminster Press, 1963).

Alter, R., *The Art of Biblical Narrative* (New York: Basic Books, 1981).

Anderson, J.C., 'Double and Triple Stories, the Implied Reader, and Redundancy in Matthew', *Semeia* 31 (1985), pp. 71-89.

Argyle, A.W., 'The Greek of Luke and Acts', *NTS* 20 (1973–74), pp. 441-45.

Arndt, W.F., *The Gospel according to St Luke* (St Louis: Concordia Publishing House, 1956).

Aune, D.E., *The New Testament in its Literary Environment* (Philadelphia: Westminster Press, 1987).

Balch, D.L., *Let Wives Be Submissive: The Domestic Code in 1 Peter* (Chico, CA: Scholars Press, 1981).

Balz, H., 'φοβέω', in *TDNT*, IX, pp. 189-219.

Banks, R., *Paul's Idea of Community: The Early House Churches in their Historical Setting* (Grand Rapids: Eerdmans, 1980).

Bauer, W., *A Greek–English Lexicon of the New Testament and Other Early Christian Literature* (trans., adapted, rev. and aug. W.F. Arndt and F.W. Gingrich; Chicago: University of Chicago Press, 2nd edn, 1979).

Beare, F.W., 'The Mission of the Disciples and the Mission Charge: Matthew 10 and Parallels', *JBL* 89 (1970), pp. 1-13.

Beasley-Murray, G.R., *Baptism in the New Testament* (Grand Rapids: Eerdmans, 1962).

Beebe, H.K., 'Ancient Palestinian Dwellings', *BA* 31 (1968), pp. 38-58.

Behm, J., 'κλάω', in *TDNT*, III, pp. 726-43.

Best, E., *Following Jesus: Discipleship in the Gospel of Mark* (Sheffield: JSOT Press, 1981).

Betz, H.D., 'The Origin and Nature of Christian Faith According to the Emmaus Legend', *Int* 23 (1969), pp. 32-46.

Black, R.A., 'The Conversion Stories in the Acts of the Apostles: A Study of Their Forms and Functions' (PhD dissertation, Emory University, 1985).

Blass, F. and A. DeBrunner, *A Greek Grammar of the New Testament and Other Early Christian Literature* (trans. and rev. Robert W. Funk; Chicago: University of Chicago Press, 1961).

Booth, W.C., *The Rhetoric of Fiction* (Chicago: University of Chicago Press, 2nd edn, 1983).

Bratcher, R.G., *A Translator's Guide to the Gospel of Luke* (New York: United Bible Societies, 1982).

Brawley, R.L., *Luke–Acts and the Jews: Conflict, Apology, and Conciliation* (Atlanta: Scholars Press, 1987).

Bruce, F.F., *The Acts of the Apostles: The Greek Text with Introduction and Commentary* (Grand Rapids: Eerdmans, 3rd edn, 1990).
—*The Book of Acts* (NICNT; Grand Rapids: Eerdmans, rev. edn, 1988).
Brueggemann, W., *Biblical Perspectives on Evangelism: Living in a Three-Storied Universe* (Nashville: Abingdon Press, 1993).
Bryan, C., 'A Further Look at Acts 16.1-3', *JBL* 107 (1988), pp. 292-94.
Bultmann, R., *The History of the Synoptic Tradition* (trans. John Marsh; New York: Harper & Row, 1963).
Cadbury, H.J., 'Lexical Notes on Luke–Acts: Luke's Interest in Lodging', *JBL* 45 (1926), pp. 305-22.
—*The Making of Luke–Acts* (London: SPCK, 1927).
Caird, G.B., *Saint Luke* (Philadelphia: Westminster Press, 1963).
Carpenter, R.H., 'Stylistic Redundancy and Function in Discourse', *Language and Style* 3 (1970), pp. 62-68.
Chang, Y.K., 'The Evangelistic Emphases of the Acts of the Apostles' (ThD dissertation, Southwestern Baptist Theological Seminary, 1951).
Chatman, S., *Story and Discourse: Narrative Structure in Fiction and Film* (Ithaca: Cornell University Press, 1978).
Cherry, R.S., 'Acts 16.14f.', *ExpTim* 75 (1964), p. 114.
Clark, A.C., *The Acts of the Apostles: A Critical Edition with Introduction and Notes on Selected Passages* (Oxford: Clarendon Press, 1933).
Cohen, C.L., 'Two Biblical Models of Conversion: An Example of Puritan Hermeneutics', *CH* 58 (1989), pp. 182-91.
Cohen, S.J.D., 'Was Timothy Jewish? Patristic Exegesis, Rabbinic Law, and Matrilineal Descent', *JBL* 105 (1986), pp. 251-68.
Conn, H.M., 'Lucan Perspectives and the City', *Missiology* 13 (1985), pp. 409-428.
Conzelmann, H., *Acts of the Apostles* (trans. James Limburg, A. Thomas Kraabel and Donald H. Juel; Hermeneia; Philadelphia: Fortress Press, 1987).
Cosgrove, C.H., 'The Divine ΔΕΙ in Luke–Acts: Investigations into the Lukan Understanding of God's Providence', *NovT* 26 (1984), pp. 168-90.
Craddock, F.B., *Luke* (IBC; Louisville: John Knox, 1990).
Crampsey, J.A., 'The Conversion of Cornelius (Acts 10.1–11.18): Societal Apologetic and Ecclesial Tension' (PhD dissertation, Vanderbilt University, 1982).
Crockett, L.C., 'Luke 4.25-27 and Jewish–Gentile Relations in Luke–Acts', *JBL* 88 (1969), pp. 177-83.
Crossan, J.D., *The Historical Jesus: The Life of a Mediterranean Jewish Peasant* (San Francisco: Harper & Row, 1992).
Cullmann, O., *Baptism in the New Testament* (trans. J.K.S. Reid; Chicago: Alec R. Allenson, 1950).
Culpepper, R.A., *Anatomy of the Fourth Gospel: A Study in Literary Design* (Philadelphia: Fortress Press, 1983).
—*The Gospel of Luke* (NIB; Nashville: Abingdon Press, forthcoming).
—'Redundancy and the Implied Reader in Matthew: A Response to Janice Capel Anderson and Fred W. Burnett', (Unpublished Seminar Response Paper; SBL Literary Aspects of the Gospels and Acts, 1983).
Dahl, N.A., 'A People for his Name', *NTS* 4 (1958), pp. 319-27.
Dana, H.E. and J.R. Mantey, *A Manual Grammar of the of the Greek New Testament* (New York: Macmillan, 1955).

Danker, F.W., *Jesus and the New Age: A Commentary on St Luke's Gospel* (Philadelphia: Fortress Press, 1988).

—'The υἱός Phrases in the New Testament', *NTS* 7 (1960–61), p. 94.

Darr, J.A., *On Character Building: The Reader and the Rhetoric of Characterization in Luke–Acts* (Louisville: Westminster Press/John Knox, 1992).

Delling, G., 'Zur Taufe von "Häusern" in Urchristentum', *NovT* 7 (1964–65), pp. 285-311.

Dibelius, M., *Studies in the Acts of the Apostles* (ed. Heinrich Greeven; trans. Mary Ling; New York: Charles Scribner's Sons, 1956).

Dillon, R.J., *From Eyewitnesses to Ministers of the Word: Tradition and Composition in Luke 24* (AnBib; Rome: Biblical Institute Press, 1978).

Dodd, C.H., *The Apostolic Preaching and its Developments* ([repr.] Grand Rapids: Baker, 1980).

Drury, J., *The Gospel of Luke* (New York: Macmillan, 1973).

Durken, D. (ed.), *Sin, Salvation, and the Spirit* (Collegeville: Liturgical Press, 1979).

Edwards, O.C., Jr, *Luke's Story of Jesus* (Philadelphia: Fortress Press, 1981).

Egelkraut, H.L., *Jesus' Mission to Jerusalem: A Redaction Critical Study of the Travel Narrative in the Gospel of Luke, Lk. 9.51–19.48* (Frankfurt: Peter Lang, 1976).

Eliade, M., *The Sacred and the Profane: The Nature of Religion* (trans. Willard R. Task; New York: Harcourt, Brace & Co., 1959).

Elliger, W., *Paulus in Greichenland* (Stuttgart: Verlag Katholisches Bibelwerk, 1978).

Elliott, J.H., *A Home for the Homeless: A Social-Scientific Criticism of 1 Peter, its Situation and Strategy, with a New Introduction* (Minneapolis: Fortress Press, 1990).

—'Household and Meals vs. Temple Purity Replication Patterns in Luke–Acts', *BTB* 21 (1991), pp. 102-108.

Ellis, E.E., The Gospel of Luke (NCBC; Grand Rapids: Eerdmans, 1966).

Esler, P.F., *Community and Gospel in Luke–Acts: The Social and Political Motivations of Lucan Theology* (Cambridge: Cambridge University Press, 1987).

—'Glossolalia and the Admission of Gentiles into the Early Christian Community', *BTB* 22 (1992), pp. 136-42.

Evans, C.F., *Saint Luke* (TPINTC; London: SCM Press, 1990).

Evans, C.A., *Luke* (NIBC; Peabody: Hendrickson,1990).

Ferguson, E., *Backgrounds of Early Christianity* (Grand Rapids: Eerdmans, 2nd edn, 1987, 1993).

Filson, F.V., 'The Significance of the Early House Churches', *JBL* 58 (1939), pp. 105-112.

Fish, S.E., *Is there a Text in This Class? The Authority of Interpretive Communities* (Cambridge: Harvard University Press, 1978).

—'Literature in the Reader: Affective Stylistics', *New Literary History* 2 (1972), pp. 123-62.

Fitzmyer, J.A., *The Gospel according to Luke I–IX, X–XXIV* (AB; New York: Doubleday, 1985).

Flender, H., *St Luke: Theologian of Redemptive History* (trans. Reginald H. and Ilse Fuller; Philadelphia: Fortress Press, 1967).

Fowler, R.M., *Let the Reader Understand: Reader-Response and the Gospel of Mark* (Minneapolis: Fortress Press, 1991).

—'Who is "The Reader" in Reader Response Criticism?', *Semeia* 31 (1985), pp. 5-23.

Funk, R.W., *The Poetics of Biblical Narrative* (Sonoma: Polebridge Press, 1988).
Garrett, S.R., *The Demise of the Devil: Magic and the Demonic in Luke's Writings* (Minneapolis: Fortress Press, 1989).
Gasque, W.W., *A History of the Interpretation of the Acts of the Apostles* (Peabody, MA: Hendrickson, 1989).
Gaventa, B.R., *From Darkness to Light: Aspects of Conversion in the New Testament* (Philadelphia: Fortress Press, 1986).
—'Toward a Theology of Acts: Reading and Rereading', *Int* 42 (1988), pp. 146-57.
Genette, G., *Narrative Discourse: An Essay in Method* (trans. J. Lewin; Ithaca: Cornell University Press, 1980).
Giles, K.N., 'The Church in the Gospel of Luke', *SJT* 34 (1981), pp. 97-146.
Goetzmann, J., 'house', in *NIDNTT*, II, pp. 247-56.
Goodspeed, E.J., 'Gaius Titius Justus', *JBL* 69 (1950), pp. 382-83.
Gowler, D.B., *Host, Guest, Enemy, and Friend: Portraits of the Pharisees in Luke and Acts* (Emory Studies in Early Christianity; New York: Peter Lang, 1991).
Green, M., *Evangelism in the Early Church* (Grand Rapids: Eerdmans, 1970).
Haenchen, E., *The Acts of the Apostles* (trans. Bernard Noble and Gerald Shinn; Philadelphia: Westminster Press, 1971).
Hahn, F., *Mission in the New Testament* (trans. Frank Clarke; Naperville: Allenson, 1965).
Hamm, D., 'Luke 19.8 Once Again: Does Zacchaeus Defend or Resolve?', *JBL* 107 (1988), pp. 431-37.
Harnack, A., *The Expansion of Christianity in the First Three Centuries* (trans. James Moffatt, II; New York: Putnam's Sons, 1905).
Haslam, J.A.G., 'The Centurion at Capernaum: Luke 7.1-10', *ExpTim* 96 (1985), pp. 109-10.
Hays, R.B., *Echoes of Scripture in the Letters of Paul* (New Haven: Yale University Press, 1989).
Heine, S., *Women and Early Christianity: Are the Feminist Scholars Right?* (trans. John Bowden; London: SCM Press, 1987).
Hengel, M., *Property and Riches in the Early Church: Aspects of a Social History of Early Christianity* (trans. John Bowden; Philadelphia: Fortress Press, 1974).
Hodges, Z., 'The Centurion's Faith in Matthew and Luke', *BSac* 121 (1964), pp. 321-32.
Hoffmann, P., 'Lk. 10,5-11 in der Instruktionsrede der Logienquelle' (EKKNT, 3; Neukirchen–Vluyn: Neukirchener Verlag, 1971), pp. 37-53.
House, C., 'Defilement by Association: Some Insights from the Usage of ΚΟΙΝΟΣ/ΚΟΙΝΟΩ in Acts 10 and 11', *AUSS* 21 (1983), pp. 143-53.
Iser, W., *The Act of Reading: A Theory of Aesthetic Response* (Baltimore: The Johns Hopkins University Press, 1978).
—*The Implied Reader: Patterns of Communication in Prose Fiction from Bunyan to Beckett* (Baltimore: The Johns Hopkins University Press, 1974).
Jellicoe, S., 'St Luke and the Seventy[-two]', *NTS* 6 (1959–60), pp. 319-21.
Jeremias, J., *The Eucharistic Words of Jesus* (trans. Norman Perrin; London: SCM Press, 1966).
—*Infant Baptism in the First Four Centuries* (trans. David Cairns; Philadelphia: Westminster Press, 1960).

—*The Origins of Infant Baptism: A Further Reply to Kurt Aland* (trans. Dorothea M. Barto; Naperville: Allenson, 1963).

Jervell, J., and W.A. Meeks (eds.), *God's Christ and his People: Studies in Honor of Nils Alstrup Dahl* (Oslo: Universitetsforlaget, 1977).

Jervell, J., *Luke and the People of God: A New Look on Luke–Acts* (Minneapolis: Augsburg, 1972).

—*The Unknown Paul: Essays on Luke–Acts and Early Christian History* (Minneapolis: Augsburg, 1984).

Johnson, L.T., *The Acts of the Apostles* (Collegeville: Liturgical Press, 1992).

—*Decision-Making in the Church: A Biblical Model* (Philadelphia: Fortress Press, 1983).

—*The Literary Function of Possessions in Luke-Acts* (Missoula: Scholars Press, 1977).

—'On Finding the Lukan Community: A Cautious Cautionary Essay', in P.J. Achtemeier (ed.), *SBLSP* (Missoula: Scholars Press, 1979), pp. 87-100.

—*Sharing Possessions: Mandate and Symbol of Faith* (Philadelphia: Fortress Press, 1981).

Judge, E.A., 'The Early Christians as a Scholastic Community: Part II', *JRH* 1 (1960–61), pp. 125-37.

—*The Social Pattern of the Christian Groups in the First Century: Some Prolegomena to the Study of New Testament Ideas of Social Obligation* (London: Tyndale, 1960).

Just, A.A., Jr, *The Ongoing Feast: Table Fellowship and Eschatology at Emmaus* (Collegeville: The Liturgical Press, 1993).

Karris, R.J., *Luke: Artist and Theologian* (New York: Paulist Press, 1985).

—'Luke 24.13-35', *Int* 41 (1987), pp. 57-61.

—'Missionary Communities: A New Paradigm for the Study of Luke–Acts', *CBQ* 41 (1979), pp. 80-97.

Keathley, N.H. (ed.), *With Steadfast Purpose: Essays on Acts in Honor of Henry Jackson Flanders, Jr* (Waco: Baylor University, 1990).

Keck, L.E., and J.L.Martyn (eds.), *Studies in Luke–Acts: Essays Presented in Honor of Paul Schubert* (Nashville: Abingdon Press, 1966).

Kee, H.C., *Good News to the End of the Earth: The Theology of Acts* (London: SCM Press, 1990).

Kennedy, D., 'Roman Army', in *ABD*, V, pp. 789-98.

Kingsbury, J.D., *Conflict in Luke: Jesus, Authorities, Disciples* (Minneapolis: Fortress Press, 1991).

—*Matthew as Story* (Philadelphia: Fortress Press, 2nd edn, 1988).

—'Reflections on "The Reader" of Matthew's Gospel', *NTS* 34 (1988), pp. 442-60.

Koester, H., 'τόπος', in *TDNT*, VIII, pp. 187-208.

Krodel, G.A., *Acts* (ACNT; Minneapolis: Augsburg, 1986).

Kümmel, W.G., *Introduction to the New Testament* (trans. Howard C. Kee; Nashville: Abingdon Press, rev. edn, 1973).

Kurz, W.S., 'Narrative Approaches to Luke–Acts', *Bib* 68 (1987), pp. 195-220.

—*Reading Luke–Acts: Dynamics of Biblical Narrative* (Louisville: Westminster Press/John Knox, 1993).

Lake, K., and H.J. Cadbury, *The Beginnings of Christianity*, IV. *The Acts of the Apostles* (Grand Rapids: Baker; reprint, 1979).

Lenski, R.C.H., *The Interpretation of St.Luke's Gospel* (Minneapolis: Augsburg, 1946).

Liddell, H.D. *et al.*, *A Greek–English Lexicon* (Oxford: Clarendon Press, 1968).
Loewe, W.P., 'Towards an Interpretation of Lk. 19.1-10', *CBQ* 36 (1974), pp. 321-31.
Lohfink, G., '"Meinen Namen zu tragen..." (Apg 9,15)', *BZ* 10 (1966), pp. 108-115.
Macgregor, G.H.C., *The Acts of the Apostles* (*IB*; Nashville: Abingdon Press, 1954).
Mack, B.L., *The Lost Gospel: The Book of Q and Christian Origins* (San Francisco: Harper & Row, 1993).
Malbon, E.S., *Narrative Space and Mythic Meaning in Mark* (San Francisco: Harper & Row, 1986).
—'TH OIKIA AYTOY: Mark 2.15 in Context', *NTS* 31 (1985), pp. 282-92.
Malherbe, A.J., *Paul and the Thessalonians: The Philosophic Tradition of Pastoral Care* (Philadelphia: Fortress Press, 1987).
—*Social Aspects of Early Christianity* (Philadelphia: Fortress Press, 2nd edn, 1983).
Malina, B.J., *The New Testament World: Insights from Cultural Anthropology* (Atlanta: John Knox Press, 1981).
—and Richard L. Rohrbaugh, *Social-Science Commentary on the Synoptic Gospels* (Minneapolis: Fortress Press, 1992).
Malinowski, F.X., 'The Brave Women of Philippi', *BTB* 15 (1985), pp. 60-64.
Maloney, L.M., *'All that God had Done with Them': The Narration of the Works of God in the Early Christian Community as Described in the Acts of the Apostles* (New York: Peter Lang, 1991).
Manson, T.W., *The Sayings of Jesus* (London: SCM Press, 1949).
Marshall, I.H., *The Acts of the Apostles: An Introduction and Commentary* (TNTC; Grand Rapids: Eerdmans, 1980).
—*The Gospel of Luke: A Commentary on the Greek Text* (NIGC; Grand Rapids: Eerdmans, 1978.
—*Luke: Historian and Theologian* (Exeter: Paternoster Press, 1970).
Martin, C.J., 'A Chamberlain's Journey and the Challenge of Interpretation for Liberation', *Semeia* 47 (1989), pp. 105-135.
Mathews, J.B., 'Hospitality and the New Testament Church: An Historical and Exegetical Study' (ThD dissertation, Princeton Theological Seminary, 1964).
McKay, A.G., *Houses, Villas, and Palaces in the Roman World* (Ithaca: Cornell University Press, 1975).
McMahan, C.T., 'Meals as Type-Scenes in the Gospel of Luke' (PhD dissertation, The Southern Baptist Theological Seminary, 1987).
Meeks, W.A., *The First Urban Christians: The Social World of the Apostle Paul* (New Haven: Yale University Press, 1983).
Metzger, B.M., 'Seventy or Seventy-two Disciples?', *NTS* 5 (1958–59), pp. 299-306.
—*A Textual Commentary on the Greek New Testament* (New York: United Bible Societies, corrected edn, 1975).
Michel, O., 'οἶκος, οἰκία', in *TDNT*, V, pp. 119-34.
Mills, W. (ed.), *Mercer Commentary on the Bible* (Macon, GA: Mercer University Press, 1995).
Mitchell, A.C., 'Zacchaeus Revisited: Luke 19.8 as a Defense', *Bib* 71 (1990), pp. 153-76.
Moessner, D.P., *Lord of the Banquet: The Literary and Theological Significance of the Lukan Travel Narrative* (Minneapolis: Fortress Press, 1989).
Morris, L., *The Gospel according to Luke: An Introduction and Commentary* (TNTC; Grand Rapids: Eerdmans, 1974).

Moule, C.F.D., *An Idiom Book of New Testament Greek* (Cambridge: Cambridge University Press, 1963).

Moxnes, H., *The Economy of the Kingdom: Social Conflict and Economic Relations in Luke's Gospel* (Philadelphia: Fortress Press, 1988).

Munck, J., *The Acts of the Apostles: Introduction, Translation and Notes* (revised by William F. Albright and C.S. Mann; New York: Doubleday, 1967).

Navonne, J., 'The Lucan Banquet Community', *The Bible Today* 51 (1970), pp. 155-61.

—*Themes of St Luke* (Rome: Gregorian University Press, 1978).

Neyrey, J.H., *Paul in Other Words: A Cultural Reading of his Letters* (Louisville: Westminster Press/John Knox, 1990).

Neyrey, J.H. (ed.), *The Social World of Luke–Acts: Models for Interpretation* (Peabody: Hendrickson, 1991).

Nicoll, W.R. (ed.), *The Expositor's Greek Testament*, II (New York: Hodder & Stoughton, n.d.).

Nolland, J., *Luke 1–9.20* (WBC; Dallas: Word Books, 1989).

Oakman, D.E., 'The Ancient Economy in the Bible' (unpublished paper, Westar Meeting, October, 1989).

Osiek, C., 'The Lukan *Oikos*: An Exercise in Symbolic Universe' (unpublished seminar paper, Social Facets Seminar, 1987).

O'Toole, R.F., 'The Literary Form of Luke 19.1-10', *JBL* 110 (1991), pp. 107-116.

—*The Unity of Luke's Theology: An Analysis of Luke–Acts* (Wilmington: Michael Glazier, 1984).

Parsons, M.C., and J.B. Tyson (eds.), *Cadbury, Knox, and Talbert: American Contributions to the Study of Acts* (Atlanta: Scholars Press, 1992).

—'Christian Origins and Narrative Openings: The Sense of a Beginning in Acts 1–5', *RevExp* 87 (1990), pp. 403-422.

Parsons, M.C., and R.I. Pervo, *Rethinking the Unity of the Lukan Writings* (Minneapolis: Fortress Press, 1993).

Pervo, R.I., *Luke's Story of Paul* (Minneapolis: Fortress Press, 1990).

Petersen, N.R., *Rediscovering Paul: Philemon and the Sociology of Paul's Narrative World* (Philadelphia: Fortress Press, 1985).

Polhill, J.B., *Acts* (NAC; Nashville: Broadman Press, 1992).

Powell, M.A., *What Are they Saying about Luke*? (New York: Paulist Press, 1989).

—*What is Narrative Criticism*? (Minneapolis: Fortress Press, 1990).

—*What Are they Saying about Acts* (New York: Paulist Press, 1991).

Praeder, S.M., 'Jesus–Paul, Peter–Paul, and Jesus–Peter Parallelisms in Luke–Acts: A History of Reader-Response', in K.H. Richards (ed.), *SBLSP* (Chico, CA: Scholars Press, 1984), pp. 23-39.

Rhoads, D., and D. Michie, *Mark as Story: An Introduction to the Narrative of a Gospel* (Philadelphia: Fortress Press, 1982).

Rice, G.E., 'Luke 4.31-44: Release for the Captives', *AUSS* 20 (1982), pp. 23-28.

Richard, E. (ed.), *New Views on Luke and Acts* (Collegeville: Michael Glazier/The Liturgical Press, 1990).

Riddle, D.W., 'Early Christian Hospitality: A Factor in the Gospel Transmission', *JBL* 57 (1938), pp. 141-54.

Robertson, A.T., *A Grammar of the Greek New Testament in the Light of Historical Research* (New York: C. H. Doran, 1914).

Robertson, A.T., and W. Hersey Davis, *A New Short Grammar of the Greek Testament* (Grand Rapids: Baker, 1977).
Robinson, B.P., 'The Place of the Emmaus Story in Luke–Acts', *NTS* 30 (1984), pp. 481-95.
Rohrbaugh, R.L., 'The City in the Second Testament', *BTB* 21 (1991), pp. 67-75.
Ryan, R., 'Lydia, A Dealer in Purple Goods', *The Bible Today* 22 (1984), pp. 285-89.
Sanders, J.T., *The Jews in Luke–Acts* (Philadelphia: Fortress Press, 1987).
Schmitz, O., and G. Stählin, 'παρακαλέω, παράκλησις', in *TDNT*, V, pp. 773-99.
Schürer, E., *The History of the Jewish People in the Age of Jesus Christ (175 bc–ad 135)* (2 vols.; rev. Geza Vermes, Fergus Millar, and Matthew Black; Edinburgh: T. & T. Clark, 1979).
Schwartz, D.R., 'The Accusation and the Accusers at Philippi', *Bib* 65 (1984), pp. 357-63.
Schweizer, E., *The Good News according to Luke* (trans. David E. Green; Atlanta: John Knox, 1984).
Scott, J.J., 'The Cornelius Incident in the Light of its Jewish Setting', *JETS* 3 (1991), pp. 475-84.
Scott, J.W., 'Dynamic Equivalence and Some Theological Problems in the NIV', *WTJ* 48 (1986), pp. 351-61.
Seifrid, M.A., 'Jesus and the Law in Acts', *JSNT* 30 (1987), pp. 39-57.
Sellers, O.R., 'house', in *IDB*, II, p. 657.
Smalley, S.S., 'Spirit, Kingdom and Prayer in Luke–Acts', *NovT* 15 (1973), pp. 59-71.
Smith, D.E., 'Table Fellowship as a Literary Motif in the Gospel of Luke', *JBL* 106 (1987), pp. 613-38.
Sonne, I., 'Synagogue', in *IDB*, IV, pp. 476-91.
Stagg, F., *The Book of Acts: The Early Struggle for an Unhindered Gospel* (Nashville: Broadman Press, 1955).
Stählin, G., 'ξένος', in *TDNT*, V, pp. 1-36.
—*Studies in Luke's Gospel* (Nashville: Convention Press, 1967).
Stauffer, E., 'Zur Kindertaufe in der Urkirche', *Deutsches Pfarrerblatt* 49 (1949), pp. 152-54.
Stein, R.H., *Luke* (NAC; Nashville: Broadman Press, 1992).
Stewart, R.A., 'Shekinah', in *NBD*, pp. 1101-1102.
Stott, J.R.W., *The Spirit, the Church, and the World* (Downers Grove: Intervarsity Press, 1990).
Talbert, C.H., *Acts* (KPG; Atlanta: John Knox, 1984.
—*Literary Patterns, Theological Themes, and the Genre of Luke–Acts* (Missoula: Scholars Press, 1974).
Talbert, C.H. (ed.), *Perspectives on Luke–Acts* (Edinburgh: T. & T. Clark, 1978).
—*Reading Luke: A Literary and Theological Commentary on the Third Gospel* (New York: Crossroad, 1982).
Tannehill, R.C., 'The Composition of Acts 3–5: Narrative Development and Echo Effect', in K.H. Richard (ed.), *SBLSP* (Chico, CA: Scholars Press, 1984), pp. 217-40.
—'"Cornelius" and "Tabitha" Encounter Luke's Jesus', *Int* 48 (1994), pp. 347-55.
—*The Narrative Unity of Luke–Acts: A Literary Interpretation* (2 vols.; Minneapolis: Fortress Press, 1986, 1990).

Tanner, W.E., *Jews, Jesus and Women in the Apostolic Age* (Mesquite: Ide House, 1984).

Theissen, G., *The Social Setting of Pauline Christianity: Essays on Corinth* (ed. and trans. John H. Schutz; Philadelphia: Fortress Press, 1982).

Thomas, W.D., 'The Place of Women in the Church at Philippi', *ExpTim* 83 (1971–72), pp. 117-20.

Tiede, D.L., 'Acts 11.1-18', *Int* 42 (1988), pp. 175-80.

—*Luke* (ACNT; Minneapolis: Augsburg, 1988).

Turner, N., *A Grammar of New Testament Greek*. IV. *Style* (Edinburgh: T. & T. Clark, 1976).

Tyson, J.B., 'The Gentile Mission and the Authority of Scripture in Acts', *NTS* 33 (1987), pp. 619-31.

—*Images of Judaism in Luke–Acts* (Columbia: University of South Carolina Press, 1992).

—'The Jewish Public in Luke–Acts', *NTS* 30 (1984), pp. 574-83.

Tyson, J.B. (ed.), *Luke–Acts and the Jewish People: Eight Critical Perspectives* (Minneapolis: Augsburg, 1988).

—'The Problem of Food in Acts: A Study of Literary Patterns with Particular Reference to Acts 6.1-7', in P.J. Achtemeier (ed.), *SBLSP* (Missoula: Scholars Press, 1979), pp. 69-83.

Verner, D.C., *The Household of God: The Social World of the Pastoral Epistles* (Chico, CA: Scholars Press, 1983).

Via, E.J., 'Women, the Discipleship of Service, and the Early Christian Ritual Meal in the Gospel of Luke', *Saint Luke Journal of Theology* 29 (1985), pp. 37-60.

Vorster, W.S., 'The Reader in the Text: Narrative Material', *Semeia* 48 (1989), pp. 21-39.

Watson, N.M., 'Was Zacchaeus Really Reforming?', *ExpTim* 77 (1965–66), pp. 282-84.

Weigandt, P., 'Zur sogenannten "Oikosformel"', *NovT* 6 (1963), pp. 49-74.

Weinert, F.D., 'Luke, Stephen, and the Temple in Luke–Acts', *BTB* 17 (1987), pp. 88-90.

—'The Meaning of the Temple in Luke–Acts', *BTB* 11 (1981), pp. 85-89.

White, A.N., *Roman Society and Roman Law in the New Testament* (Grand Rapids: Baker, 1978; reprint).

White, L.M., 'Domus Ecclesiae—Domus Dei: Adaption and Development in the Setting for Early Christian Assembly' (PhD dissertation, Yale University Press, 1983).

White, R.C., 'Vindication for Zacchaeus?', *ExpTim* 91 (1979–80), p. 21.

Wilcox, M., 'The God-Fearers in Acts—A Reconsideration', *JSNT* 13 (1981), pp. 102-122.

—*The Semitisms of Acts* (Oxford: Clarendon Press, 1965).

Williams, D.J., *Acts* (NIBC; Peabody: Hendrickson, 1985, 1990).

Wilson, S.G., *The Gentiles and the Gentile Mission in Luke–Acts* (Cambridge: Cambridge University Press, 1973).

Wuellner, W., 'Is there an Encoded Reader Fallacy?', *Semeia* 48 (1989), pp. 41-54.

Indexes

Index of References

Old Testament

NEW TESTAMENT

INDEX OF AUTHORS